In *Responding to Youth Crime in Canada*, Anthony Doob and Carla Cesaroni address the subject of youth crime in the context of the Youth Criminal Justice Act, which came into force on 1 April 2003. The authors describe what is currently known about youth crime in Canada, and discuss the operation of the youth justice system in response to the changes in the law that are taking place.

The study suggests that the youth justice system has a relatively modest impact on youth crime. In order to respond intelligently to youth crime and to evaluate the response of the state, the authors argue that we need, first, to have a realistic picture of youth crime in Canada, and second, a clear understanding of the manner in which the youth justice system currently operates. The authors recommend that, instead of relying on the youth justice system to solve the problem of youth crime, we look to the youth justice system to respond appropriately to the realities of what constitutes youth crime and look elsewhere for approaches to address the level of youth crime in our society.

ANTHONY N. DOOB is a professor in the Centre of Criminology at the University of Toronto.

CARLA CESARONI is a doctoral candidate in the Centre of Criminology at the University of Toronto.

ANTHONY N. DOOB AND CARLA CESARONI

Responding to Youth Crime in Canada

UNIVERSITY OF TORONTO PRESS
Toronto Buffalo London

© University of Toronto Press Incorporated 2004
Toronto Buffalo London
Printed in Canada

ISBN 0-8020-8856-2 (cloth)
ISBN 0-8020-8624-1 (paper)

Printed on acid-free paper

National Library of Canada Cataloguing in Publication

Doob, Anthony N., 1943–
    Responding to youth crime in Canada / Anthony N. Doob, Carla Cesaroni.

    Includes bibliographical references and index.
    ISBN 0-8020-8856-2 (bound).   ISBN 0-8020-8624-1 (pbk.)

    1. Juvenile justice, administration of – Canada.   2. Juvenile delinquency –
    Canada.   I. Cesaroni, Carla   II. Title.

    HV9108.D657 2004   364.36′ 0971   C2003-904837-3

University of Toronto Press acknowledges the financial assistance to its
publishing program of the Canada Council for the Arts and the Ontario
Arts Council.

University of Toronto Press acknowledges the financial support for its
publishing activities of the Government of Canada through the Book
Publishing Industry Development Program (BPIDP).

In memory of
Magdalena Gryc,
a woman who was destined to make a difference,
and to her family and friends
who know that she already had.

Contents

Preface

This book attempts to summarize what is known about the manner in which the youth justice system responds to youth crime in Canada. It builds on – and sometimes borrows directly from – an earlier book (Doob, Marinos, & Varma, 1995).[1] We are fortunate that an enormous amount of research has been carried out in Canada on youth crime and the youth justice system in the eight years since that earlier book was written. Hence, it is appropriate to look, again, at what is known about our youth justice system.

The 1995 book was written in the context of amendments that had been introduced into the Young Offenders Act and two national reviews of the youth justice system that were soon to begin: one by the House of Commons Standing Committee on Justice and Legal Affairs (1997) and one by the Federal–Provincial–Territorial Task Force on Youth Justice (1996). Since that time, Parliament decided that we are to have a new youth (criminal) justice law – the Youth Criminal Justice Act – which came into force on 1 April 2003. The time, then, is ideal to look at where we have been, and to think about where we might be going on youth justice matters.

We rely, largely though not exclusively, on published information about youth crime and youth justice. The focus, obviously, will be on Canadian information. We will however, refer to material from else-

---

1 In addition to using material taken from Doob, Marinos, & Varma (1995), this book also benefited from – and uses material taken directly from – Criminological Highlights, an information service produced by the Centre of Criminology, and various other chapters, reports, and articles that one or both of us have authored or co-authored in recent years.

where when it appears to us to be relevant and, in particular, when no adequate Canadian data exist. In addition, we will be presenting information (e.g., from data available from the Canadian Centre for Justice Statistics) derived from material about the youth justice system. Much of the data we present are, in a technical sense, publicly available. However, we have often abstracted and combined information in a manner which will be new even to many who work in the area.

This book describes what is known about Canadian youth crime, and the operation of the youth justice system in the context of the changes in the law that are taking place. Its underlying premise is that in order to respond intelligently – and to evaluate the response of the state – to youth crime, two sets of information must be understood. First, we must try to understand what 'youth crime' looks like in Canada. If a system has been created to respond to a phenomenon, we should have a clear idea of what this phenomenon looks like and how it is changing. Second, in order to understand – and evaluate – the changes that are being made in youth justice legislation in Canada, a clear understanding of the manner in which the youth justice system currently operates is necessary. Furthermore, it is necessary to know something about the identified effects of the youth justice system on youths. A theme running throughout the book is that the youth justice system has a relatively modest impact on youth crime. Unlike those who look to the youth justice system to solve the problem of youth crime, we suggest that we should look to the youth justice system to respond appropriately to the realities of what constitutes youth crime and look elsewhere to address how one might affect the level of youth crime in our society.

In the past twenty years in Canada, an enormous amount of research has been carried out in addressing the issues described in the previous paragraph. We decided that providing adequate answers to two questions – 'What does youth crime look like?' and 'How do we, as a society, respond to youth crime?' – were coherent tasks that could be combined in one book. The book is, however, limited by the research findings that are available. Thus certain topics (e.g., the impact of race on police decisions to charge, or the effects of race or class on ordinary sentencing decisions) that are, unfortunately, inadequately researched in Canada, are not given much attention. At the same time, we decided that a book that included a discussion of theories of involvement in crime, or theories that attempt to explain the state's responses to crime, were beyond the scope of this book. Other books look at the justice system through the lens of criminological theory or in a more historical–theoretical context. We felt that what was needed was an examination of the operation of the youth justice system in the context of the laws that govern it. Hence, we were not trying to write a book on juvenile delinquency per se, nor were we trying to examine in detail the development of youth justice legislation. Finally, although we include a fair amount of discussion of the current law governing young offenders – the Youth Criminal Justice Act – we would suggest that those who would like a thoughtful and detailed analysis of this legislation should turn to Nicholas Bala's (2003) excellent book entitled *Youth Criminal Justice Law*.

Given that we are now in a new era of youth justice, we thought it useful to review, in very brief form in Chapter 1, the shifts that have taken place over the past century in the way in which we conceived of, and have dealt with, young people who apparently have broken laws. We will then discuss, in chapter 2, the reasons that have been given for having a separate youth justice system. With these two chapters as a background, we will, in Chapter 3, try to get a picture of what 'youth crime' looks like, and in Chapter 4 we will look at changes that have taken place in youth crime in Canada. Chapter 5 will examine who these 'youths' are who commit crimes, and Chapter 6 will investigate society's response to offending, with a special focus on the decision to bring youths into the formal justice system. In Chapters 8 and 9 we will look at the way in which the youth justice system processes youths. Chapter 10 examines the impact of the most intrusive sentence in the youth system – custody. Finally, Chapter 11 will look at the 'quick fixes' that plague youth justice reform and contrast them with approaches that appear either to address youth crime or to respond to youthful offending.

The preparation of this book was supported directly by funding from the Department of Justice, Canada. We thank the department and, in particular, Dick Barnhorst and Catherine Latimer, not only for their support, but for their patience. The interpretation of findings and implicit and explicit opinions are our own and do not necessarily reflect the views of the Department of Justice, Canada, or of any of the other organizations that have contributed directly or indirectly to this project.

Much of the data reported here derive from work supported by the Social Sciences and Humanities Research Council of Canada (SSHRC). We have each benefited enormously from SSHRC funding – funds made available to A.N.D. from the SSHRC research grants program, and to C.C. through SSHRC's graduate fellowship program. A careful reading of the footnotes of many of the papers referred to in this book would demonstrate the importance of SSHRC to Canadian criminology directly through its support of research and indirectly through its support of the *Canadian Journal of Criminology*.

The book also draws directly on material prepared in connection with Criminological Highlights, an information service produced by the Centre of Criminology, University of Toronto, and supported in part by the Department of Justice, Canada, and the Correctional Service of Canada. We wish also to thank those who financially support it as well as the 'Highlights' group of graduate students and faculty at the Centre of Criminology. The University of Toronto's Centre of Criminology, and its Information Service and Library, provided the home and support without which this project could not have happened. In particular, we would like to thank Andrea Shier, of the Criminology Information Service and Library, who helped us identify and locate many of the papers, books, and reports that we used in this book. Finally, we would like to recognize the help we received from the late Magdalena Gryc. As with everything that she did, she showed enormous care and intelligence combined with a quiet but wonderful sense of humour. We regret not being able to thank her adequately. We owe a lot to others. Thank you.

Anthony N. Doob
Carla Cesaroni
Toronto
April 2003

RESPONDING TO YOUTH CRIME IN CANADA

CHAPTER ONE

Introduction: Youth Crime and Youth Justice

A cartoon in the 27 May 1996 Toronto *Sun* illustrated an important mis-understanding of Canada's youth justice system. The editorial cartoon showed two children looking into a store window which featured a 'Little murderer's tool kit: Free copy of the Young Offenders Act inside.' The message was clear. Youth crime – in this case murder – is caused largely by the law that governs the way in which we, as a society, respond to youth crime. This is one of the persistent myths surrounding the youth justice system.

In 1890, the Annual Report of the Chief Constable of the City of Toronto noted that 'vagrant bands parading the streets at night have given the police a good deal of trouble, composed as they are, of rowdy youths belonging to no responsible Society or organization' (p. 48, cited in Doob, Marinos, & Varma, 1995). It is not clear whether the Chief Constable of the day would have been happier if the youths had been part of an 'organization' that we might now label as a gang. Like police today, he did note that he saw himself fighting an uphill battle since, as he put it, 'boys are ubiquitous' and the constables are 'not omnipresent.'

When one looks at another country at another time, the same type of imagery is used. More than sixty years ago, the English publication *Picture Post* (28 January 1939, p. 38) noted that 'the great increase in juvenile crime is certainly one of the most horrible features of our time.' The editors of the *Picture Post* criticize one public figure who 'is credited with the desire to keep all people under 21 out of prison. Suffice it to say that in the ranks of those who employ young criminals there is rejoicing and exceeding joy.'

When one of us was skiing (some years ago), a stranger on a ski lift in Ontario, in talking about the relative merits of skiing in upstate New

York, suggested that 'Skiing [in the United States] is different. The kids don't run into the back of you or cut across you on the hills the way they do here. The reason is that down there you're allowed to beat your kids. And down there they don't have the Young Offenders Act the way we do here. That's why the young people are so much better behaved in the U.S. than they are here.'

Separating 'Youth Crime' from 'Youth Justice'

Each of these stories illustrates what we see as one of the most important challenges for youth justice in Canada: to differentiate 'youth justice' issues from 'youth crime' problems. We will be suggesting, throughout this book, that youth justice and youth crime are separate phenomena, each of which is important. Each needs to be understood and addressed properly. But for the most part, one does not address the problem of 'youth crime' by way of the youth justice system. We could, in fact, differentiate among three phenomena:

- Youth crime, as it exists in our community
- The youth justice system, and how it responds to those youths who are apprehended for offending
- The causes of youth crime.

This book concentrates on the first two of these phenomena more than on the third. The reason is simple: there appears to be more misunderstanding about the first two than about the third.

Many Canadians clearly do understand that the level of youth crime in our communities is not affected greatly by the type of youth justice system we have. When people are asked about the causes of youth crime, many do not look to the youth justice system as being a major determinate of the level of crime. In 1997, a representative sample of residents of Ontario was asked to indicate what they saw as the most effective way of controlling crime (Doob, Sprott, Marinos, & Varma, 1998). They were given five choices (see Table 1.1). Some of these choices focused on 'criminal justice' approaches, some focused on social issues. A substantial number of respondents looked outside of the justice system for the most effective way to reduce crime. Twenty-four per cent thought that 'increasing social programs' was the most effective way, and an additional 19 per cent saw reducing unemployment as the best approach to addressing the levels of youth crime in their community.

Table 1.1 Views of the best way to control youth crime as a function of respondents' assessment of sentencing

	View of youth court sentences		
Best way to control crime	Too severe or about right (%)	Not severe enough (%)	All respondents (%)
Reduce unemployment	25	16	19
Increase social programs	41	22	24
Increase the use of punishments other than prison	19	23	22
Make sentences harsher	10	28	25
Increase the number of police	5	11	10
Total	100	100	100

Source: Doob et al., 1998.

But views of how to approach the reduction of youth crime were related (in a statistically significant way)[1] to views of the system itself. About 86 per cent of respondents in this survey thought that youth court sentences were not severe enough. Those who believed that youth court sentences are not harsh enough were much more likely to look to criminal justice control measures as solutions to youth crime.

Only 10 per cent of those who thought that youth court sentences were too severe or about right thought that the best way to control crime was through harsher sentences. In contrast, 28 per cent of those who thought that sentences were not harsh enough saw 'toughening sentencing' as the best way to control youth crime.

Concern about crime generally, and youth crime in particular, is completely understandable. However, as we will discuss more fully in later chapters, views that simple 'criminal justice' changes will solve the problems of youth crime are almost certainly wrong. What we see in Table 1.1 is the finding that those who believe that the youth justice system is not harsh enough are considerably more likely to believe that the

---

1 Generally speaking we will not refer to the 'statistical significance' of differences involving samples. Instead, we will use the convention that only when a difference *is* significant will we refer to it as being a real difference.

justice system controls crime. On the other hand, clearly many people understand that crime generally and youth crime in particular are largely a product of the society in which children develop. In Chapter 11 we will discuss some of the approaches to addressing youth crime that appear to make sense. These, as we will see, are largely approaches that lie outside of the youth justice system.

'Youth crime' is such a consistently controversial topic for two basic reasons. The first is fairly straightforward, but worth remembering. As we will see, adolescents do lots of things – including offending – that adults do not like. This book is not about the sociology of adolescents, but as one expert on this part of the life cycle noted, 'no other social group receives as much negative attention as the young; they are viewed variously as troubling and troubled, a constant source of fear and worry' (Tanner 1996, p. 1). One does not need to be a sociologist to know that their elders view adolescents with a certain amount of fear, distrust, and lack of understanding. The second problem is that there is not complete consensus on how we should think about offending by youths.

Understanding Youthful Offending

There are various approaches to understanding youthful offending. These approaches translate, to some extent, into different models of what a youth justice system should look like. Looking at each of these models on its own, in isolation from others, creates something of a caricature of youthful offending. Nevertheless, it is useful as a way of looking at differences.

In the first place, one can look at offending as a symptom of some kind of underlying problem. This problem could be biological or psychological, or it could be social (e.g., a symptom of inadequacy in child rearing or the impact of poverty). Second, one can see youthful offending as a symptom of an inadequate crime control system (e.g., inadequate numbers of police, inadequate severity of punishments, or inadequate forms of social control in the community). Third, one could look at youthful offending as being a natural consequence of growing up (see, e.g., Moffitt, 1993).

These different 'models' of understanding youthful offending are not simply part of an academic exercise. They suggest quite different approaches for responding to youthful offending. The first model would suggest a focus on the characteristics of individual offenders. If 'offending' is a symptom of a problem, then official responses should focus on the problem, not the symptom. This assumes, of course, that one's goal is 'fixing' the problem. It further assumes that courts, or those responding to youthful offending, both know how to intervene effectively and have adequate available resources.

If, on the other hand, youth crime is seen as the result of an inadequate justice system – the view implicit in the cartoon we described at the beginning of this chapter – then the focus of society would be largely on the youth justice system as a 'crime control' system. The underlying justification of a youth justice system would be to stop youth crime. The specific focus would be on the tools available within that system to address this goal.

Finally, a model that is based on the assumption that youthful offending is, to a large extent, a 'natural' consequence of growing up would have a quite different orientation. Such a system might focus more on responding in a measured way to offending rather than on the traditional utilitarian purposes. If part of what we see as being 'just' in our society is that inappropriate behaviour has consequences, the focus of youth justice would be on ensuring not only that there are consequences, but that these consequences are seen as being appropriate.

Various explanations for youth crime have been offered over the years. Often they are implicit in what is being said. One prominent member of Parliament, for example, in a talk a few years ago to a Canadian victims group described youth crime in the following words: 'According to Statistics Canada, the number of youths under the age of 18 who were charged with violent crime nationwide more than doubled from 1986 to 1991, reaching nearly 19,000. Of these, in 1991, 20% involved female youth. This represents a marked increase over a decade previously. By 1990, five years after the Young Offenders Act came into effect, violent crimes by young offenders had increased 30%' (Kilgour, 1994).

Aside from the difficulties of knowing whether 'youths ... charged with violent crimes' is a good proxy for youthful offending, and aside from being confused by the statement that the number of youths charged with violence 'doubled' but 'violent crimes by young offenders had increased 30%,' there is an important implicit message. Violent crime is described as going up in the first five years after the Young Offenders Act came into effect. The Young Offenders Act, it would seem, was implicated in this increase.

In choosing what kind of justice system we want, it makes sense to look at both what our goals are and whether the most effective way of accomplishing these goals is through the youth justice process. Some of the material covered in this book (see Chapter 11) will focus on the ability of the youth justice system to achieve the goals that are sometimes attributed to it. As we will see, the goals of the youth justice system have changed over the past century. Many of the concerns expressed by people about the system come from unrealistic expectations about what it can accomplish.

Explanations for Youth Crime: Is Anything New?

Many of the explanations offered for youth crime over the years sound as if they could have been said just yesterday or could appear, with slightly different wording, in tomorrow's newspaper. Two psychologists writing in 1928 for the most prestigious American academic journal in the field of personality, abnormal, and social psychology, noted that 'not only have the concepts of sin, wickedness, piety, and righteousness completely lost meaning for the modern young person, but the authority upon which the right and wrong standard is based – the authority of church, home, school, and state – is fast waning' (Anderson & Dvorak, 1928). The words may differ, but the thoughts expressed here are much the same as those offered today by many commentators on youth crime.

   Each generation, it seems, manages to rediscover youth crime while simultaneously forgetting about the nature of its own youth. Much like our parents, grandparents, and great-grandparents, we tend to look to the criminal justice system rather than to other state institutions for the answers to youth crime. The 1939 *Picture Post* article referred to earlier suggested how to reform adolescents in the 1930s – those who are now in their eighties and quite possibly expressing concern about 'kids today.' The 1939 commentators suggested that, 'We have the task of giving something which is a deterrent and also reforming.' But even at that time, concern was being expressed about the overuse of incarceration. They went on to suggest that 'perhaps a stiff whopping and a kindly admonition not to do it again have more English healthiness about it [*sic*] than [prison].'

The Public's View of Youth Justice

It would be easy to suggest that the public is tired of hearing about serious crimes committed by youths and wants a tough system, or perhaps it wants to treat youthful offenders the same as adults. The slogans 'Adult time for adult crime' and 'Do the crime, do the time' imply that people want young offenders treated the same as adult offenders. A survey of Ontario residents in 1997 (Doob, et al., 1998; Sprott, 1998) found that most people (64 per cent of respondents) indicated that they were opposed to having a separate justice system for youth. One might infer from this that people would, then, want the justice system to treat youths in the same manner as it does adults. This is not the case. First, almost nobody wants youths to be sent to the same prisons as adults. Even among those who are opposed to having a separate youth justice system, 83 per cent believe that youths should serve time in prisons that are separate from those for adults.

If they reject the ideas of having a separate justice system for youth, people still differentiate between the ways in which they want their justice system to deal with youths and adults. Using 1997 Ontario survey data, Varma (2000) looked at the importance that people placed on five different purposes of sentences. Some respondents were asked to indicate how important they thought each factor was in the sentencing of adults; the others were asked to indicate how important they thought each factor was in the sentencing of youths. Each of these groups can be broken down according to the respondents' views on whether there should be a separate youth justice system. The findings are shown in Table 1.2.

There are two important findings in Table 1.2. The first is that people differentiate, in their views of what is important at sentencing, between the factors that are important for youths and what is important for adults. 'Separating offenders from society' is a more important consideration in the sentencing of adults than it is in the sentencing of youths. 'Assisting in the rehabilitation of offenders' is seen as being more important in the sentencing of youths than it is in the sentencing of adults.

The second finding, which follows from this first one, is most critical in understanding the apparent opposition to having a youth justice system. Even those people who say that they oppose a youth justice system seem to think that rehabilitation is a more important consideration for the sentencing of youths than it is for adults and that incapacitation should be less important for sentencing of youths than for adults.

Another finding that suggests that one should be cautious in interpreting 'opposition' to a separate youth justice system comes from a

Table 1.2   Importance of factors at sentencing for adults and youth for those who favour and those who oppose a separate youth justice system

Purpose	Respondents who favour having a separate youth justice system		Respondents who oppose having a separate youth justice system	
	Importance for sentencing youths	Importance for sentencing adults	Importance for sentencing youths	Importance for sentencing adults
Expressing the community's disapproval of the crime	7.9	7.1	7.6	7.4
Deterring the offender and other persons from committing offences	8.1	8.1	8.3	8.2
Separating offenders from society	5.7	6.2	6.5	7.4
Assisting in the rehabilitation of offenders	8.3	7.8	8.1	7.8
Compensating victims or the community	7.3	7.2	7.9	7.9

Source: Varma, 2000.
Note: Respondents answered on a scale where 1 = Not at all important, and 10 = Very important.

Table 1.3   Percentage of respondents recommending prison for 'young offender' and 'adult offender' for each of four offence–offender combinations

	Young offender	Adult offender
Break and enter, first offence	23	40
Assault with minor injuries, first offence	20	31
Break and enter, second offence	48	74
Assault with minor injuries, second offence	48	69

Source: Canadian Centre for Justice Statistics, 2000.

national survey carried out by Statistics Canada, Canadian Centre for Justice Statistics (CCJS, 2000). In this survey, people were asked whether they thought a case should result in imprisonment. The case was described in one of two ways:

1 Breaking into a house when the owners are on vacation and taking goods worth $400
2 An assault in which the victim received minor injuries but did not require medical attention.

The offender was described as being either a first-time offender or as someone who had been found guilty of a similar offence once before. People were asked about an adult offender and a young offender. Respondents were asked, in all cases, to choose between a prison and a non-prison sentence. The percentage of people who recommended prison for the adult and young offender for each of the four offence–offender combinations is shown in Table 1.3.

What we see, then, is that although the majority of Canadians may say they would like to have no distinctions made between youthful and adult offenders, when it comes down to specific decisions about individual cases, they do, in fact, make very real distinctions. Thus, it terms of the details of how to respond to youth versus adult crime, many want (1) less harsh sentences for youths, (2) different principles applied, and (3) youths not to serve their sentences in the same way as adults.

'Adult time for adult crime' apparently does not look as attractive as it sounds when one considers it carefully with respect to specific cases (Sprott, 1998). Nevertheless, it is politically attractive slogan. It is not surprising, therefore, that politicians frequently appeal to that aspect of public opinion. As the Youth Criminal Justice Act (YCJA) was going

Table 1.4   Preference for spending money on building more
prisons versus on alternatives, for adults and youth (%)

Offender being considered	Prefer bulding more prisons	Prefer alternatives to prison	Total
Adult	35	65	100
Youth	22	78	100

Source: Doob et al., 1998.

through the legislative process, the Government of Ontario (2001) recommended amendments that would result, as they put it, in 'adult
time for adult crime.' The reason behind these proposals was that 'the
federal government's proposals for young offender legislation have
failed to protect the public and hold offenders accountable' (ibid.). We
will examine whether it would be possible to 'protect' society from
youth through changes in the youth justice system in Chapter 11.

Freiberg (2001) suggests that people's views of crime are affectively
driven. He argues that the affective components of crime have to be
addressed, but that raw punishment need not be the only adequate
response to crime. Public opinion research in a number of countries
(Doob & Roberts, 1988; Roberts, 1992; Cullen, Fischer, & Applegate,
2000; Doob, 2000) suggests that, although an adequate response to
wrongdoing may, as Freiberg suggests, be necessary, the support for
simple punitiveness is rather soft. As can be seen by comparing the
proportions of respondents preferring prison for the adult and young
offender in Table 1.3, Canadians are more reluctant to imprison a
youth than an adult. A shift towards 'punitive segregation' of offenders, then, may occur in large part because people are not provided with
an attractive alternative that meets their emotional response to crime.

If people really believed that harsher sentences should be imposed
on youthful offenders, they should be enthusiastic about building more
prisons. However, they are not – especially not for youth. In an Ontario
survey (Doob et al., 1998), respondents were told that prisons were full
and then asked whether they would prefer money be spent on finding
more alternatives to prison or building more prisons. Half of the sample were asked to choose between spending money on prisons versus
alternatives for adults, the other half were given the choice with respect
to youth. As shown in Table 1.4, the public preferred spending money
on alternatives for both adult and youthful offenders, but this preference was considerably stronger in the case of youth.

Table 1.5   Preference for prisons versus alternatives for those who think that youth court sentences are not severe enough vs those who think that sentences are all right or too severe (%)

View of youth sentences	Prefer more prisons	Prefer alternatives to prison	Total
Too lenient	25	75	100
About right / too severe	9	91	100

Source: Doob et al., 1998.

Clearly, people not only do not want to build more prisons, but in particular, they do not want to build more prisons for youth. The majority of respondents (86 per cent) thought that sentencing of youths was too lenient. But even for these respondents, the idea of spending more money on prisons is not very attractive (see Table 1.5). People may believe that sentences for youth are too lenient, but three-quarters of them would prefer money to be spent on alternatives to prison rather than on building more prisons for youths.

Those who believe that youth sentences are too lenient are, obviously, much more likely to prefer investing in prisons. However, the majority even of this group would prefer investing money in alternatives to prison.

When respondents in this same survey were asked to choose between building more prisons and investing in prevention, the vast majority (86 per cent when asked with respect to adults, and 89 per cent when asked about youth) preferred investing in prevention. Once again, residents of Canada's largest province and one which, at the time of the survey, had recently elected a very conservative government, were not enthusiastic about prison construction when given a choice of investing in prevention. Even those who thought that sentences (adult or youth) were too lenient were much more likely to prefer prevention to prisons.

Models of Youth Crime: The Juvenile Delinquents Act

The way in which we respond to youth crime – our youth justice system – has changed substantially over the past century. The three legislative models that we have experienced in Canada illustrate various perspectives on how society can respond to youth crime. Until 1908

Canada had no separate youth justice system: youths suspected of having committed an offence were legally treated as adults. Among other things, this meant that they were legally subject to being hanged if found guilty of a capital offence. Yet, this does not mean that youths and adults were treated in the same manner. Administrative decisions (e.g., to try to keep youths in separate facilities) and judicial decisions (e.g., to treat youths more leniently at sentencing) could obviously differ for the two groups.

Parliament, in 1908, changed all that. Under the federal government's jurisdiction over the criminal law, the federal government created a separate criminal law to deal with youths – the Juvenile Delinquents Act (JDA). This act governed the manner in which youths, age 7 years to adulthood were handled if they were suspected of having committed an offence. 'Adulthood' was determined by provincial preference and varied between age 16 (e.g., for Ontario youths) to 18 (e.g., for Quebec youths). The law clearly represented a social welfare approach to criminal law. This assertion can be supported by looking at statements contained in the act relating to its overall philosophy and by looking at the rules governing how youth were treated.

The welfare orientation was clearly captured in Section 38 of the JDA which indicated how youths were to be handled: 'The care and custody and discipline of a juvenile delinquent shall approximate as nearly as may be that which should be given by his parents, and that as far as practicable every juvenile delinquent shall be treated, not as a criminal, but as a misdirected and misguided child, and one needing aid, encouragement, help, and assistance.' Similarly, the act required, at Section 3(2), that 'where a child is adjudged to have committed a delinquency he shall be dealt with, not as an offender, but as one in a condition of delinquency and therefore requiring help and guidance and proper supervision.'

It made sense to treat offences as symptoms of underlying problems rather than as matters in their own right. Thus, a delinquency was defined as the violation of a federal law (e.g., offences under the Criminal Code), a provincial law (e.g., a driving offence), or a municipal by-law 'or sexual immorality or any similar form of vice' (Section 2(1)). With very few exceptions, then, youths who rode a bicycle in a park where bicycle riding was prohibited, who exhibited sexual behaviour that was not approved of, or who killed someone, were all, under the JDA, delinquents and were to be treated in the same manner: Their specific offences were symptoms of the reasons they had been misbehaving. What they needed was 'help and guidance and proper supervision' (Section 3(2)).

Under such a theory it made sense to have sentences be indeterminate. Thus, in theory, a court could maintain jurisdiction over a 7-year-old until he or she was 21 years old. A youth sent to 'training school' (the equivalent of what is now referred to as 'secure custody') was turned over to the training school officials, who could release the youth when they saw it as appropriate to do so. The effect of this was that a training school official had the power to release back into the community a youth who had committed a very serious violent offence, even if that release took place the day after the youth arrived in the facility. Alternatively, the training school officials could hold a youthful shoplifter for years if it was deemed to be in the best interest of the youth to do so.

The law was quite clear: the goal was to help the youth. Given this welfare orientation, it made sense to treat each case individually and allow as much flexibility in decision making as possible. Some youths, however, were not seen as appropriate candidates for this type of treatment. The JDA, like the laws that replaced it, allowed almost any youth age 14 years or older, who was charged with almost any non-trivial offence, to be 'transferred' to adult court and, thereafter, to be treated as an adult. As we will show in Chapter 8, few youths received this treatment. If a youth were to be transferred under the JDA (or its successor, the Young Offenders Act), the youth would be treated for almost all purposes as if he or she were an adult.

The general welfare orientation of the court in dealing with a youthful offender, however, was certainly more important in understanding youth justice in the first half of the twentieth century than were transfers of youths to adult court. Such transfers have always been rare in Canada, in large part because the Parliament of Canada has always left the decision on transfers to the youth court judge.

The welfare orientation is not, of course, unique to Canada. For almost a century (i.e., until the last twenty years or so of the twentieth century), most states in the United States had juvenile delinquency laws based largely on welfare principles. However, as concern about youth crime grew in the latter part of the past century, almost every state legislature 'toughened' its laws in various ways. The most notable ways were to move more and more cases away from the welfare-oriented youth courts to the criminal courts (see Feld, 1999; Snyder & Sickmund, 1999). This move was accomplished in two ways: (1) by giving the prosecutor the power to place certain types of cases directly into adult court or (2) by laws which deemed certain youths who were charged with certain offences to be adults. In addition, some jurisdictions allowed youths who remained in youth court to be given adult sentences or 'mixed' youth and adult sentences (e.g., a youth sentence followed by a possible adult sentence to be imposed when the youth attained a specified age). The U.S. jurisdictions maintained, as well, the traditional power of the youth court judge, on application from the prosecutor, to determine that a particular case was more appropriately dealt with in adult court. The eroding of the jurisdiction of the youth court in the United States can be seen not only as a 'toughening' of the manner in which youths are dealt with, but also as a dramatic shift away from the idea that the youth court's role is to hand down rehabilitative decisions.

In Europe, although most countries have a blended welfare–justice approach, there has been increasing pressure for an orientation to stricter punishment (Walgrave & Mehlbye, 1998; Tonry & Doob, 2003).

The welfare orientation of Canada's youth court does not necessarily mean that youth court decisions have been lenient. In a survey of Canadian youth court judges in early 2001, 30 per cent of the respondents indicated that, in half or more of the cases where youths were detained prior to trial, 'the detention [was imposed] only because the young person had no adequate place to stay, or for some other child welfare reason' (Doob, 2001, p. 15). These same judges were also asked to indicate how often certain factors were relevant in their decisions to impose a custodial sentence on youths who appeared before them. Thirty-seven per cent of judges indicated that in half or more of the cases in which they had imposed custody, the poor home or living conditions of the youth were relevant in determining that custody was the appropriate sentence. Treatment goals may be benevolent from the perspective of the judge, but from the perspective of the young person, treatment may mean custody – normally considered to be the most serious disposition in the youth justice system. As we will see in Chapter 10, custody, regardless of judicial intention, is rarely a neutral event in the life of a youth.

Advent of the Young Offenders Act

In 1961, the Department of Justice, Canada, started a process of examination of the Juvenile Delinquents Act that would, in the end, take twenty-three years to complete. A departmental committee was established in that year to examine various aspects of Canada's youth justice law. That committee reported in 1965. Between that date and 1982, various steps were taken:

- A bill was introduced and allowed to die.
- A committee was struck, its report released and debated but not acted upon.
- Two sets of legislative proposals were released (one by each major party).

Finally, in 1982, the government introduced the Young Offenders Act as a bill to replace the JDA. After receiving all-party approval in the House of Commons, the YOA became law in April 1984. A year later, a uniform maximum age of its jurisdiction (18 years) came into effect. From 1984–5 until the replacement of the YOA by the Youth Criminal Justice Act in 2003, the YOA governed the manner in which youth justice was structured in Canada.

A number of changes in youth justice laws accompanied the advent of the YOA. Many of them can be traced to changes that had occurred across North America in the way in which offending by youth was seen. From both the political left and the right, concerns about the 'welfare' or 'treatment' orientation of the JDA made the transfer to a more 'offence'-oriented act relatively painless. The left was concerned about the unbridled amount of discretion that judges had in imposing their will on youths who had apparently done very minor offences. The right was concerned that court decisions to imprison youth could be negated by administrative decisions (e.g., on the length of the term of custody).

The YOA still focused a considerable amount of attention on the youth, as opposed to the offence. However, this attention was much more clearly formulated under criminal law principles. Some of the act's important provisions illustrate this point:

- Only federal offences (e.g., the Criminal Code, Controlled Drugs and Substances Act) come under the jurisdiction of the act.
- All dispositions are definite in length, although they can be modified by judicial actions.
- Maximum sentence lengths are provided.
- Appeal procedures are congruent with those available for adult offenders.

- Certain protections (e.g., the right to a lawyer, special provisions governing the taking of statements) are part of the law.

Attacking Youth Crime Legislation

The YOA was a target even before it became law. Some provinces, such as Ontario, were disappointed that they had not prevailed in certain areas (e.g., the decision to move the maximum age of a youth to the eighteenth birthday). Concern was raised immediately about those youths under age 12 who committed offences. Many members of the public, it would appear, believe that because youths age 11 and under are not subject to *criminal* law, they are not subject to *any* law. This, of course, is not the case: those under age 12 can be apprehended under provincial child welfare laws for acts which otherwise would be deemed to be criminal.

This type of public misperception can perhaps best be illustrated by the media coverage which surrounded the 1996 trial of several youths charged with the sexual assault of a teenaged girl. The media at the time focused on the fact that the 11-year-old 'ringleader' was 'by far the worst offender' and 'knew he was too young to be charged' (Unland, 1996). Statements from the arresting officers seemed to confirm two things: (1) that the youth 'got away with it' and (2) that this was due, in part, to faulty legislation. The arresting officer suggested that 'it's a shame that the main player in this got away with it ... If they can bump 16- or 17-year-olds to adult court, we should be able to charge those under 12 who commit serious crimes' (Krivel, 1996, p. A3). Media coverage at the time underplayed the fact that the youth was taken into custody by the Children's Aid Society for psychiatric testing and remained in care for a substantial period of time.

The first set of amendments to the Young Offenders Act came into effect in November 1986. Probably the single most important amendment was one that facilitated the laying of charges for failure to comply with a disposition. Prior to that time, a youth who, for example, breached a probation order would typically have that order reviewed, and perhaps modified. It would not normally have resulted in a new charge being laid. As we will see, within ten years, this one offence would account for approximately one out of eight cases that were brought to the youth court and, as noted in Chapter 9, almost a quarter of the cases that would end up with custodial sentences.

During the late 1980s, concern about serious violent youth crime led to another two major changes to the YOA that came into effect in 1992. First, the test for transfer to adult court was changed such that 'protection of the public' was given greater prominence. Second, the maximum sentence for murder in youth court was changed from three-years in custody to five years less a day, where a maximum of three of those years were to be served in custody and a maximum of two years less a day were to be spent under supervision in the community. (The reason for the maximum sentence being one day less than five years is that this avoided the requirement, under the Canadian Charter of Rights and Freedoms of giving a youth the option of a jury trial in youth court. Anyone in jeopardy of receiving a sentence of five years or more has a right to a jury trial under Section 11(f) of the Charter.)

At the same time that the maximum sentence in youth court for murder was increased, the mandatory sentence for a youth transferred to adult court was relaxed. Up until 1992, if a youth were to be transferred to adult court for murder, the standard adult parole ineligibility periods would apply. Thus, for example, a 15-year-old sentenced for first degree murder would be first eligible for parole twenty-five years later at age 40. The 1992 amendments reduced this parole ineligibility period dramatically as shown in Table 1.6.

In 1993 the Liberals came into power at the federal level on an election platform that included changing the Young Offenders Act yet again. Among these amendments (described in Table 1.6) parole ineligibility periods were changed, and, for 16 to 17-year-olds, were made 'tougher.' Within youth court, sentences for murder were also changed, yet again – this time to a maximum of seven years (second degree murder) or ten years (first degree murder). Procedurally, the extension of a maximum sentence in youth court to five years or more was important because this meant that a youth *in youth court* had to have access to a jury trial. For the first time, then, youths could choose to face a jury in youth court.

In addition, a new way of dealing with serious cases was devised. For a 16- to 17-year-old facing charges, including any of four very serious violent offences (first or second degree murder, manslaughter, or aggravated sexual assault), the youth would 'presumptively' be transferred to adult court. A presumption does not mean that it will actually happen. The hearing for 'presumptive transfers' still takes place in youth court, and the test of whether the youth should be transferred is the same. The burden of proof, however, where there is a 'presumptive' transfer, switches to the youth. The youth must then demonstrate

Table 1.6 Penalties for youth convicted of murder, 1984 to present

Period	Maximum sentence in youth court	Sentence in adult court, age 14–15 at time of offence	Sentence in adult court, age 16–17 at time of offence
1984–92	3 years	Mandatory life, no parole 25 years (1st degree) (2nd degree)	Mandatory life, no parole 25 years (1st degree), 10–25 years
1992–6	3 years' custody + 2 years less a day 'conditional supervision in the community'	Mandatory life, no parole eligibility for 5–10 years	
1996–2003	6 years' custody + 4 years conditional supervision in the community (1st degree) and 4 + 3 years (2nd degree)	Mandatory life, no parole eligibility for 5–7 years	Mandatory life, no parole eligibility for 10 years (1st degree) or 7 years (2nd degree)
2003 onwards	6 years' custody + 4 years conditional supervision in the community (1st degree) and 4 + 3 years (2nd degree)	Mandatory life, no parole eligibility for 5–7 years	Mandatory life, no parole eligibility for 10 years (1st degree) or 7 years (2nd degree)

Source: Young Offenders Act and amendments thereto; Youth Criminal Justice Act (2003).

that it is not in the public interest for the case to be moved to adult court.

Does Tough Mean Tough?

There were, from the beginning, reasons to believe that the 1992 amendments would not have much impact. In the first place, the decision makers were still the same youth court judges. For the most part, youth court judges appeared, from their decisions, to have a fair amount of confidence in the youth court process. As described in more detail in Chapter 8, typically fewer than 100 youths were transferred each year into adult court. Although the creation of a 'presumptive transfer' might appear to make it easier to transfer a youth into adult court, the test remained the same. In addition, as we will see later in Chapter 8, the 1992 amendments themselves had not had a discernible impact on transfer decisions.

Eight Years of Review

On 2 June 1994, then (federal) Minister of Justice Allan Rock wrote to the chair of the House of Commons Standing Committee on Justice and Legal Affairs indicating that he was, that day, not only introducing the amendments we have just discussed, but also requesting that the House of Commons committee begin a 'broader review' of the Young Offenders Act (Standing Committee on Justice and Legal Affairs, 1997). Minister Rock noted that 'the Act is highly controversial, and questions have been raised about whether it remains the best model of juvenile justice for Canada in the current age' (ibid., p. 78). The proposed review was to be broad in its approach looking at such matters as transfers, statements, sentencing, and alternatives to legislative responses to juvenile crime.

Although the minister had requested that the review be completed by 1 February 1995, the Commons committee, in fact, did not report until April 1997. In addition, because the provinces were not an official part of the House of Commons review process, a parallel federal–provincial–territorial review was initiated. The task force carrying out that review began its work in January 1995. Its report was released in August 1996. Thus, by April 1997, the government had two reports on youth justice to respond to. It had made a commitment in 1994 to respond to the perceived need for major changes in youth justice.

Clearly, however, the process was taking more time than had been forecast.

Introduction of the Youth Criminal Justice Act

In May 1998, more than a year after the House of Commons report had been released and after an election and a change in ministers, the new Minister of Justice, Anne McClellan, released a report entitled *A Strategy for the Renewal of Youth Justice* (Department of Justice, 1998). McClellan's strategy included two separate components: (1) replacing the Young Offenders Act with a new piece of legislation and (2) focusing on prevention outside of the youth justice system by linking it with 'other federal government initiatives aimed at children and youth.' Not surprisingly, however, it was the replacement of the YOA that received the most attention.

The bill to replace the YOA was first introduced into Parliament in March 1999. Clearly, the intent of the launch of the new bill was to convince Canadians that they were about to get a much tougher piece of legislation than the Young Offenders Act. Canadians appear to believe that their legislation requires judges to be lenient. In a 1997 survey of Ontario residents (Doob et al., 1998), for example, people were asked what they thought the maximum penalty was, in youth court, for breaking and entering a dwelling and for a minor assault. In fact, the maximum penalties available under the YOA are three years in custody for the break and enter, and two years in custody for the minor assault. Many Ontario residents were unable to provide an estimate (21 per cent in the case of the break and enter, and 24 per cent in the case of the minor assault). Of those who did provide an estimate, 54 per cent thought that the maximum sentence available under the YOA for the break and enter was a year or less in custody, and 84 per cent thought that the maximum sentence available for the minor assault was one year or less in custody. This suggests that when Canadians want 'longer' sentences in their legislation for youthful offenders, they may mean 'longer than they think are available' rather than 'longer than the sentence that is contained in the legislation.'

The press release announcing the introduction of the Youth Criminal Justice Act (YCJA) into the House of Commons on 11 March 1999 contains a description of a bill that is hardly recognizable to anyone who reads the actual bill as it was introduced. What it appears to reflect, more than anything else, is a concern that the new legislation would be seen as being too lenient. There were thirteen 'bullet points' contained in the press release (Department of Justice, 1999). Many of these appeared to be designed to give the impression that the bill was 'tough' and would increase the punitiveness of the system. These bullet points included the following:

- Allow an adult sentence for any youth 14 years old or more who is convicted of an offence punishable by more than two years in jail, if the Crown applies and the court finds it appropriate in the circumstances
- Expand the offences for which a young person convicted of an offence would be presumed to receive an adult sentence to include a new category of serious violent offences
- Allow the Crown greater discretion in seeking adult sentences and publication of offenders' names
- Create a special sentence for serious violent offenders who suffer from mental illness
- Give the courts more discretion to receive as evidence voluntary statements by youth to police
- Permit tougher penalties for adults who wilfully fail to comply with an undertaking made to the court to properly supervise youth who have been denied bail and placed in their care

It is hard to avoid the conclusion that the intent of most of the first eleven points that were listed was to paint the new act as punitive law. Ordinary readers of the press release probably would not have known, in reference to the first point, for example, that the harshness was more in perception than reality. Under the Young Offenders Act (and in the Juvenile Delinquents Act before it) youths 14 and over could be transferred to adult court, and given adult sentences, for a slightly larger number of offences. Although some might interpret this as being substantially new, it was not. What did change, in the area of 'adult sentences' was important, but obscured by this bullet point. Under the Youth Criminal Justice Act, youths would no longer be transferred to adult court before they were found guilty. Instead, they would remain in youth court and could, if appropriate, be sentenced as adults.

Another example of this press release being best thought of as a sheep in wolf's clothing is the last point listed here. Under the YOA and the YCJA, a youth who would otherwise be detained in custody awaiting trial can be placed in the care of a responsible person (under Section 31 of the YCJA). The responsible person must undertake in writing to be responsible for getting the young person to court and to comply with any conditions that the judge imposes. It is an offence if the responsible person 'willfully fails to comply with ... an undertaking' under this section. It would appear, from available statistics, that almost nobody (at most two or three people a year) is ever charged with this offence. Raising the penalty for an offence that never is prosecuted does not appear very important. This point was also, occasionally, interpreted as meaning that parents were to be made criminally responsible for the wrongdoing of their children, a principle that would have contradicted directly the intent of the law to hold *youths* accountable for their actions.

What is important about the first eleven bullet points is that they precede the following:

- Allow for and encourage the use of a full range of community-based sentences and effective alternatives to the justice system for youth who commit non-violent offences.[2]

The twelfth point is interesting because it contains in it two large parts of the act. The YCJA creates a presumption that dealing with matters outside of the formal justice system ('extrajudicial measures') is appropriate for many cases. It states that extrajudicial measures 'should be used if they are adequate to hold a young person accountable.' It even makes it clear that they can be used repeatedly and for youths who have previously been taken to court (Section 4). Clearly, extrajudicial measures have the potential of reducing dramatically the number of youths dealt with under the formal youth justice system.

The sentencing provisions of the YCJA are also both complex and completely different from the sentencing provisions under the YOA. They differ on two important dimensions:

1 The YCJA provisions provide a coherent overall 'theory' of sentencing, in contrast to the YOA provisions which allowed much more judicial variability in the approach to sentencing.
2 The YCJA provisions are much more directive than the YOA provisions. Where the YOA allowed judicial flexibility, the YCJA requires the judge to follow certain rules.

---

2 The final point was that the act would 'recognize the principles of the United Nations Convention on the Rights of the Child.'

Clearly, these two parts of the YCJA are very important. They deal with two aspects of the youth justice system – who gets into it and how those found guilty are sentenced – that are of critical importance to the public, victims, young offenders, and those interested in youth justice. One can speculate that in March 1999 the minister of justice was not comfortable in highlighting these aspects of her bill.

The YCJA had a rocky legislative history. Among other things, its life was placed in suspension during the 2000 election, and it was, therefore, reintroduced in Parliament in February 2001. Perhaps because Minister McClellan's bill had upset many people and groups, including the Government of Quebec, by being seen as being too 'tough,' the YCJA that was reintroduced in 2001 was described in quite different terms from the way in which the almost identical bill had been introduced almost two years earlier. The press release accompanying the bill in 2001 stated:

> The new Act is built on the values Canadians want in their youth justice system. They want a system that prevents crime by addressing the circumstances underlying a young person's offending behaviour, that rehabilitates young people ... Canadians know that this is the most effective way to achieve the long-term protection of society ... the Act reflects a balanced approach to youth justice that aims to instill values such as accountability, responsibility and respect. The Act includes more effective, targeted measures to deal with both serious, violent offences and the vast majority of youth offences which are less serious. (Department of Justice, 2001)

In the background material released in February 2001, the first substantive area described was sentencing, where the first bullet point stated that community-based sentences would be encouraged. The next two bullet points mentioned adult sentences and the presumption of adult sentences for certain offences. Essentially, the same bill as had been introduced two years earlier was being dressed up in somewhat different clothes.

The Youth Criminal Justice Act

The YCJA came into force on 1 April 2003. It is difficult to describe, in a few words, the essential elements of the YCJA. Because we will be discussing various aspects of it throughout this book, we will give here a very brief overview of some of the more important parts. Clearly, however, this description should be seen as a way of 'orienting' the reader to the new law rather than being a definitive description.

General Principles

The YCJA describes the youth justice system as trying to prevent crime by addressing the circumstances underlying a youth's offending, focusing on rehabilitating offenders, and 'ensuring that a young person is subject to meaningful consequences for his or her offence.' These intentions, it is stated, are there 'in order to promote the long-term protection of the public.' What is important in this is that the 'protection of the public' has become the 'long term protection of the public,' and is to be seen, in effect, as the *result* of having a sensible justice system rather than a goal in and of itself.

Extrajudicial Measures

There are a set of principles that clearly are meant to encourage police officers and others to consider dealing with youthful offending outside of the formal youth justice system. They are 'presumed to be adequate' for many young persons. In addition, and contrary to much current practice, it is made clear that they can be used for those who have been handled this way before, as well as for those who previously had gone to court. A long list of possible approaches (e.g., warnings, formal cautioning etc) are available. Police are instructed that they 'shall, before starting judicial proceedings ... consider whether it would be sufficient ... to [use extrajudicial measures in a case]' (Section 6(1), emphasis added).

Pretrial Detention

Various attempts are made to limit the use of pretrial detention of youths. The judicial officer running a bail hearing must enquire as to whether a 'responsible person' might be available for a youth who, otherwise, would be sent to custody. Detention shall not 'be used as a substitute for appropriate child protection, mental health or other social measures' (Section 29(1)). And, when considering whether a youth should be detained because of the possibility of future offending or interference with the administration of justice, a judicial official shall presume that detention is not necessary if the youth would, if found guilty, not be eligible for a custodial sentence (Section 29(2)).

Sentencing Principles

The focus of sentencing is on holding youths accountable for their behaviour. The principles endorse a belief that holding youths accountable with just and rehabilitative sanctions will *contribute* to the *long-term* protection of society. The words 'deterrence' and 'incapacitation' do not appear in this legislation. The key sentencing principles are easy to identify, namely:

- The sentence must be proportionate to the seriousness of the offence and the degree of responsibility of the young person for that offence (Section 38(2)(c)).
- Subject to [the proportionality principle] the sentence must be the least restrictive sentence capable of achieving the principle [of holding youths accountable through the imposition of just sanctions that have meaningful and rehabilitative consequences] (Section 38(2)(d)(i)).
- Subject to [the proportionality principle] the sentence must be the one that is most likely to rehabilitate the young person and reintegrate him or her into society (Section 38(2)(d)(i)).

The YCJA also creates a set of hurdles for the use of custody. Under Section 39 of the YCJA, it is made clear that custody can only be given if the youth has met one of three quite explicit criteria or 'in exceptional cases where the young person has committed an indictable offence, the aggravating circumstances of the offence are such that the imposition of a non-custodial sentence would be inconsistent with the purpose and principles [of sentencing]. The YOA, in contrast, had relatively weaker restrictions on custody. For example, it stated that 'a young person who commits an offence that does not involve serious personal injury should be held accountable to the victim and to society through non-custodial dispositions *whenever appropriate*; and that custody should be imposed when all available alternatives to custody *that are reasonable* in the circumstances have been *considered'* (Sections 24(1.1)(b) and (c), emphasis added).

Adult Sentences
Under the YOA and the JDA before it, a 14-year-old charged with any offence other than the most trivial could be 'transferred' to adult court and thereafter dealt with for almost all purposes as if he or she were an adult. Thus, for example, before guilt had been determined, a youth could have his or her name published in the newspaper even though the YOA normally prohibited such publication. Traditionally, one of the arguments in favour of 'transfer' provisions is that they allow for longer (adult) sentences for those few cases where the maximum sen-

tences allowable under the youth justice legislation would be inappropriate. The *YCJA* takes this principle and enshrines it directly into the legislation by keeping the youth in youth court and, in those cases where the normal youth sentence was of insufficient length, allowing the judge to impose an adult (length) sentence.

New Dispositions

The YCJA lists a number of new sanctions that are available to the judge at sentencing. These include such provisions as an attendance order (where a youth would be required to attend a non-residential program) and a 'deferred custody and supervision order' which, like the 'conditional sentence' available for an adult, would allow a judge to order a sentence of up to six months that would be served in the community as long as the youth remained on good behaviour and followed the conditions imposed on him or her.

Probably the most important change in the dispositions, however, relates to the 'custody and supervision order.' Under the YOA, in 1994–5, only 51 per cent of the custodial orders were followed by probation orders. Put differently, in 49 per cent of the cases when youths were placed in custody, they were released 'cold' into the community, with no conditions and no support from the justice system. The custody and supervision order in the YCJA requires that a youth serve two-thirds of the sentence in custody and one-third supervised in the community. The conditions of the supervision are to be set on release (rather than by the court, as would be the case in a probation order). The importance of the supervision is highlighted by the fact that, when a youth is placed in custody, there is a requirement that the province or territory 'shall, without delay, designate a youth worker to work with the young person to plan for his or her reintegration into the community, including the preparation and implementation of a reintegration plan' (Section 90).

Obviously, the provisions of the YCJA that we have described in this chapter describe only a very small part of the full 157 sections of the act. Other parts of the YCJA will be described as they become relevant to the discussion in the later chapters.

Conclusion

The laws that govern the way in which we handle youth crime have been the subject of debate and legislative change for many decades.

We are not, however, the only country that has experienced rather dramatic change in recent years. Youth justice laws in most states in the United States have changed dramatically in the past twenty years, as have the laws in some other countries (e.g., England and New Zealand). The laws have various quite different purposes attributed to them and, therefore, respond to youthful offending in quite different ways.

CHAPTER TWO

Why Have a Separate Youth Justice System?

Setting Age Limits

In a wide range of different domains, our society accepts the idea that young people are not to be treated the same as those who are beyond some arbitrarily set age. Among these arbitrarily fixed limits are the ages at which a person can:

- legally purchase and possess alcohol
- purchase cigarettes
- legally drive an automobile
- enter into binding contracts
- legally leave school
- purchase and possess a firearm
- drive a personal watercraft
- consent to sexual activity
- collect welfare, completely independent of his or her parents
- work in certain industries
- apply for certain Canadian Armed Forces programs

Two important factors should be kept in mind when going through this list. First, there is little debate about whether there should be some age limits involved in each of these areas. Second, the age that a society sets for these activities varies over time and location and, to some extent, is arbitrary. Why is it, for example, that in Niagara Falls, Ontario, a 19-year-old may purchase and possess alcohol, but in Niagara Falls, New York, this would not be allowed until the youth was 21 years old? Few would suggest that there are developmental differences that would justify this difference or that the cultures are that different that it makes sense for there to be this variability. On the other hand, there would be few who would argue that there should not be *some* limit on a how young a person can be to work in a factory or consent to sexual activity.

Reasons for Having a Separate Justice System for Youth

Within this context, then, it is not surprising that most countries have different laws for youths who offend from the laws designed for adults who offend. As various people have pointed out, there are two broad reasons for separate youth justice policies: 'diminished responsibility due to immaturity and special efforts designed to give young offenders room to reform in the course of adolescent years' (Zimring, 2000, p. 277).

Those countries whose *adult criminal laws* govern the manner in which youths who offend are treated (e.g., Denmark; see Kyvsgaard, 2003), typically have different laws or practices governing the sentencing of youthful offenders. Not surprisingly, in Denmark, as in other places where the distinction between adults and youths is more blurred than it is in Canada, youths are generally treated less harshly than are adult offenders. The reason for this, as Zimring (2000, p. 283) points out, is that

> [diminished responsibility] is not merely a doctrine of juvenile justice but a principle of penal proportionality. The nature of adolescent immaturity would raise the same issues we now confront in juvenile justice even if all young offenders were tried in [adult] criminal courts. In other words, even if there were no separate youth policy to consult in making decisions about younger offenders and even if there were no juvenile court, the just punishment of young offenders would still be a distinctive moral and legal problem. So, changes in the jurisdictional boundaries of juvenile and criminal courts do not remove the necessity of determining variations in [a] moral desert.

Drawing the Line between Adulthood and Youth

The question, then, is where one draws the line between the adult and youth justice system and how that line is drawn. When one looks across western countries, it is clear that there is no consensus on the optimum age at which a young person should no longer be considered to be a youth for the purpose of criminal justice. Even in the United States, there is variation across states. For example, in New York and North Carolina, the dividing line is the sixteenth birthday, whereas in Alabama and Minnesota it is the eighteenth birthday (Snyder & Sickmund, 1999). Even in Canada, it is relatively recent (1985) that the federal Government established a uniform maximum age of 18. As we pointed out in Chapter 1, under the Juvenile Delinquents Act, the uniform age varied from 16 to 18 in different provinces with one province (Alberta) having, for some time, a different dividing line for males (16) than females (18).

Although it may seem intuitively obvious to many people that youths should generally be treated differently for their criminal acts, this is not necessarily the case. In 2001, after the Youth Criminal Justice Act had been passed by the House of Commons, but before it had gone to the Senate, the Ontario government recommended that for very serious cases, a youth age 16 or 17 should automatically be tried and sentenced as an adult, and for a substantial number of other cases, a youth age 14 or older should presumptively be sentenced as an adult, under adult sentencing principles (ibid.). Although the Ontario government would have extended the presumption in favour of adult sentences for youths, the Youth Criminal Justice Act, itself, creates 'presumptive adult sentences' for youths age 14 or older who have been found guilty of any of the four most serious offences or who have been found guilty of a pattern of serious violent offences in the past.

This approach – treating youths as adults if they commit a serious crime – appears to fly in the face of our approach to youths in other areas: 'Failing to regard persons under the age of eighteen as anything other than significantly less mature than adults who meet the full adult standard for punishment contradicts the laws regarding the age of majority [everywhere] in every area of nonpenal law' (Zimring, 2000, p. 286).

The reasons for treating youths differently from adults include other empirical issues which relate more directly to the justice system:

- Youths may not fully understand, appreciate, or consider the consequences of their actions as carefully as adults do.
- Youths may not fully understand court procedures and, therefore, need special protections.
- The justice system itself is stigmatizing and, therefore, special protections are needed in order to minimize these impacts.

- Youths who offend are likely to be in need of special services and, therefore, a special 'treatment oriented' court is necessary to address the youth's needs.

From these four general empirical assumptions, one might expect to find the following differences between the youth court and the adult court.

- To minimize the negative impact of contact with the criminal justice system, different principles need to be used in deciding which cases should be brought into the formal system.
- Procedures for handling youths in the formal justice system should be different.
- Sentencing provisions for youth, because they are more malleable than adults, should emphasize different principles from those used for adults.

These 'justice' assumptions cannot, however, be understood without looking – at least briefly – at some of the conclusions that have been drawn about adolescence.

Adolescence

It has been argued (Steinberg & Schwartz, 2000) that developmentally, adolescence (age 12–17) can be considered to be a 'special' period in a person's life. To the extent it is different from childhood and adulthood, it makes sense for society to treat youths who offend differently from adults. Steinberg and Schwartz argue that adolescence can be characterized as follows:

- There are 'rapid and dramatic changes in physical, intellectual, emotional, and social capabilities ... Other than infancy, there is probably no period of human development characterized by more rapid or pervasive transformations in individual competencies' (ibid., p. 23).
- There are a multitude of influences on the youth – family, peers, schools – that have large impacts.
- It is a 'formative period during which many developmental trajectories become firmly established and increasingly difficulty to alter' (ibid.).

• Finally, there is tremendous variability within and across individuals such that two youths of the same age may be at very different stages of their development, and the changes that take place within an individual may be rapid and somewhat unpredictable.

It would appear that throughout adolescence, youths are becoming more mature on such dimensions as the ability to have perspective in what they are doing, control their impulses, and see that they, themselves, are responsible for what happens in their lives. These are general characteristics and are not tied to specific types of anti-social behaviours.

Part of the public's ambivalent feelings regarding adolescents, and fears over youth crime generally and youth violence in particular, may stem from the incorrect belief that 'adolescence is the age at which innocent, mild-mannered boys become strong, uncontrolled and aggressive predators' (Tremblay et al., 1996, p.127).

Youths' Understanding of the Consequences of Their Actions

One of the mistakes people sometimes make is to assume that the reason we have a separate justice system for youths is that there is a belief that youths do not understand that certain acts are morally wrong. This does not seem to be the case. Very young children are likely to be able to understand that certain acts are wrong. Few would suggest that ordinary 11- or 17-year-olds do not understand, almost as well as adults understand, that either taking something from a store without paying for it, or stabbing someone, is not morally acceptable. Understanding that something is 'wrong,' however, may be only part of the issue. Similarly, it appears that youths understand – or at least can articulate – that certain criminal behaviours involve risks. Hence this, too, does not differentiate younger from older youths.

Recent research suggests that the developmental changes that are important in understanding the differences between adolescents and adults with respect to criminal behaviour have more to do with much more subtle changes taking place during this period. Cauffman and Steinberg (2000), for example, examined the way in which developmental changes through adolescence (into adulthood) are related to antisocial judgments. Using a sample of 810 adolescents in Grades 8, 10, and 12 from the same school district, respondents were given tests that measured the following:

- responsibility (e.g., respondent's agreement with questions such as 'luck decides most things that happen to me')
- perspective (e.g., 'I often do things that don't pay off right away but will help in the long run' or 'Before I do something, I think about how it will affect the people around me')
- temperance (e.g., 'I do things without giving them enough thought' or 'I lose my temper and "let people have it" when I'm angry')
- 'psychosocial maturity' (a combination of the above scales)
- antisocial decision-making (hypothetical situations were described in which participants had to indicate how they would behave – an antisocial choice and a socially acceptable choice were given).

The results show that as psychosocial maturity increases, decision-making becomes less antisocial. Age is related to psychosocial maturity – older youths are more mature than younger ones. (From other data, it appears likely that psychosocial maturity does not increase significantly after approximately age 19.) However, age does not add to the predictability of the degree of antisocial attitudes above and beyond psychosocial maturity. In fact, within each age group, the more mature the youth, the less likely that he or she reported antisocial decisions.

More generally, psychologists have concluded that

adolescents and young adults generally take more risks with health and safety than do other adults ... Adolescents, perhaps because they have less knowledge and experience, are less aware of risk than are adults ... Adolescents seem to be less averse to risk than are adults, tending to focus less on protection against losses and more on opportunities for gains in making choices.' (Scott, 2000, pp. 304–5)

Compared to adults, young people may be less future-oriented, less risk-averse, more impulsive, and more susceptible to the influence of others, and these differences may result in age differences in judgment. (Steinberg & Schwartz, 2000, p. 26)

Youths' Understanding of Court Procedures

The Charter of Rights and Freedoms as well as youth justice legislation provide various 'rights' to youths who come in contact with the justice system. Canadian legislation gives special rights to youths on the assumption that there is a need for special protection of youths.

For example, in the Young Offenders Act and the YCJA, a young person has a legislated right to counsel (Section 25(1) of the YCJA) and if the young person is not represented by counsel in court, the court must advise the youth of the right and give the youth a reasonable opportunity to get counsel. Furthermore, if the youth is refused legal aid, the court can order that counsel be provided to the youth. Where the court believes that the interests of the youth and the youth's parents are in conflict, the court can ensure that the youth is represented by counsel independent of his or her parents. Notice of the right to counsel must be included in various documents related to the youth's participation in the justice process (Section 25(9) of the YCJA).

The Young Offenders Act and the YCJA also outline special provisions for the admissibility of a statement by a youth requiring that a detailed set of procedures be followed. As Anand and Robb (2002) point out, before the enactment of the YOA, there was common law support for special protections for youths being questioned by the police. The principles in common law were fairly clear before 1984 and became even more clear after 1984. These legislated procedures are specific to youth and include a requirement that the various warnings regarding the statement be 'in language appropriate to his age and understanding' (YOA, Section 56(2)(b); YCJA, 146(2)(b)). These special provisions were controversial, in part because 'technical' mistakes on the part of the police could invalidate a statement made by the youth. In May 1998, when the Minister of Justice announced her intention to replace the Young Offenders Act with a new act, she described this provision as 'overly prescriptive' (Department of Justice, 1998). The Youth Criminal Justice Act indicates that if the procedures whereby a youth waived rights not to make a statement were 'not made in accordance [with the legislated provisions] owing to a technical irregularity, the youth justice court may determine that the waiver is valid if it is satisfied that the young person was informed of his or her rights, and voluntarily waived them' (Section 146(5)) and if the court is 'satisfied that the admission of the statement would not bring into disrepute the principle that young persons are entitled to enhanced procedural protection to ensure that they are treated fairly and their rights are protected' (Section 146(6)). As Bala (2003) points out, however, what constitutes a 'technical irregularity' is not defined by the YCJA.

The law makes it clear that youths need special protections. What is the empirical evidence for this? Bala (2003) cites a children's legal aid organization which pointed out that 'Many youth have a vague recollection of being told their rights but do not truly understand what their rights entail' (p. 211).

The problem appears to be that young persons often understand, in a literal sense, what they are doing. Delinquent youths do not understand what a 'right' is. In particular, they do not see it as an entitlement; rather they see it as something that they are allowed to do, or they see it as conditional on other behaviour (Feld, 2000, p. 149). Thus, they often do not understand the consequences of their decisions. Compared with adults, youths were less likely to understand the meaning of the warning that police give against self-incrimination (Grisso cited in Feld, 2000, p. 112). For example, in one study it was found that 'Youths interpreted the warning that 'anything can and will be used against you in a court of law' to mean that 'any disrespectful words directed toward police would be reported to the police' (Novak, cited in Feld, 2000, p. 114)

Addressing the cognitive abilities of youths who are under stress at the time of arrest does not appear to be easy. One American researcher noted that 'changing the format of the 'Miranda' warning does not appreciably alter a youths understanding of it' (Zaremba, 1994). The best predictor of whether a youth understands the impact of the waiving of rights turns out to be the intelligence of the young person. Other factors (such as sex, age, socioeconomic factors, race) were related to understanding, but intelligence was, clearly, the most important single predictor. One serious problem identified by Zaremba was that youths, like adults, did not fully understand the role of defence counsel in criminal proceedings. Given that many parents did not fully understand the meaning of various warnings, Zaremba was not enthusiastic about allowing the parents of a young accused to be responsible for waiving a young person's rights.

Since many of the rights that youths have under the law are exercised most effectively through defence counsel, it is important to look at youths' understanding of the right to retain and instruct counsel. Abramovitch, Higgins-Biss, and Biss (1993) looked at youths' understanding of the decision to waive this right, finding that only a few young people had a full appreciation of the consequences of waiving their right to a lawyer. Thus, although young people understood *what* they were doing, they did not understand, for example, that if they were to waive their right to a lawyer, they could then be questioned fully by the police without having another person present. Interestingly enough, the level of understanding of the full implications of waiving the right to counsel did not vary much within the age range covered by the Young Offenders Act.

In understanding the right to silence, however, it appeared that older youth were significantly more likely to understand their right not to make a statement. About three-quarters of the youngest people questioned in the study (Grade 6, students, which would place them just below the minimum youth justice age of 12) indicated that, if asked, they would make a statement to the police. This dropped to about half of the young people who were in the other grades (Grades 8, 10, and 13; roughly age 13, 15, and 18): 'It seems likely that many if not most juveniles who are asked by the police to waive their rights do not have sufficient understanding to be competent to waive them' (Abramovitch et al., 1993: p. 319).

The complexity of children's understanding of their legal rights is demonstrated when answers to some specific questions are examined. Children at all ages, but particularly older children, understood the general concept of the confidentiality of information given to lawyers. Over two-thirds of the children who participated in one study (Peterson-Badali & Abramovitch, 1992) indicated that a lawyer cannot tell others what a client tells them. But when asked whether information could be divulged to specifically named people, even the oldest children (those in Grade 9, roughly 15 years old) thought that lawyers would have to communicate what they had been told. When asked general questions, most Grade 9 children indicated that lawyers had to maintain confidentiality. Nevertheless, 56 per cent of these same children thought the lawyer would have to tell the child's parents, 44 per cent thought the judge had a right to communications from the young person to the lawyer, and 25 per cent thought the lawyer would have to tell the police. These answers were somewhat more likely to be 'correct' for older than for younger children. As Peterson-Badali and Abramovitch (1992, p. 143) note,

> Children's understanding of the roles and functions of legal personnel (particularly defence counsel) is central to their capacity to instruct counsel. Two aspects of the legal system are deemed critical in this respect: the notion of defence counsel as advocate for the client, and the principle of lawyer-client confidentiality. Without understanding that defence counsel's express duty is to carry out the client's wishes, and that any information given in the context of the lawyer-client relationship is strictly private, an individual would be operating at a marked disadvantage within the adversarial context of criminal procedure.

Youths' relationships with counsel were not the only problem that they faced: 'Virtually all the misconceptions expressed by subjects ... related to the concept of presumption of innocence; many of the [young people] had difficulty understanding and recalling that an accused is presumed innocent unless the prosecution can prove otherwise' (ibid., p. 157).

It seems that young people do have an understanding of some aspects of the criminal process – the decision to plead guilty being one of them. Peterson-Badali and Abramovitch (1993) gave case vignettes to young people in Grades 5, 7, and 9. The vignettes portrayed people of the same age and gender as the person being interviewed. The young person was described as having committed the offence but the evidence against the accused person was described as either strong or weak. They were asked to indicate how they would plead. One standard against which these pleas could be evaluated was what lawyers, experienced in representing young offenders, thought was reasonable.

The results were quite straightforward. First, young people at all grade levels were much more likely to indicate that they would plead guilty if the evidence against them were strong rather than weak. The older youths, however, gave more weight to the strength of the evidence than did the younger children. Older youths, then, were more likely to be making pleas which lawyers saw as reasonable. Since most of the participants indicated that they would plead guilty when the evidence against them was strong, this effect is really the result of the decisions made in cases where the evidence was weak. Older children under these conditions were more likely to do what the lawyers thought was reasonable. Unfortunately, as the researchers themselves point out, we do not know how those with experience in the youth justice system would differ from 'ordinary young people' in most of these findings.

Generally speaking, however, it appears that understanding of the trial process increases dramatically between childhood (age 7) and early adolescence (age 13) (Peterson-Badali & Abramovitch, 1992; Peterson-Badali, Abramovitch, and Duda, cited in Grisso, 2000). 'For youths who are under fourteen years old, the balance of evidence ... suggests that as a group they are at greater risk than most adults for deficits in abilities associated with adjudicative competence' (Grisso, 2000, p. 163).

Looking at this research as a whole, it is clear that we cannot assume that young people have sufficient knowledge of the legal system and the criminal law provisions that govern proceedings in the youth justice system to fully and freely participate in criminal proceedings against them.

Although it is undoubtedly true that many adult accused do not fully understand their rights (see, e.g., Ericson & Baranek, 1982), these problems appear to be especially serious with youths and become even more serious when one examines the understanding of children below the age of criminal responsibility in Canada (age 12). If a proceeding is inherently criminal in its orientation, and the assumption is that the accused youth is an active participant in the process looking after his or her best interest, the data, then, support the conclusion that laws related to youthful offending need to provide special protections. These special protections for the most part are encapsulated in procedural protections for young people in conflict with the law. But they are also linked to larger theoretical principles regarding the young person's future potential and rehabilitation.

Avoiding the Stigmatization of Youthful Offenders

One of the most controversial parts of the Canadian youth justice system is its legislated attempt to reduce the stigmatization of youth who have offended. This is done most notably by the provisions that limit dramatically the amount of public disclosure of young offenders' identities. Although youth courts are open to the public, with rare exceptions youths cannot be named or otherwise identified publicly. Partly this is based on the theory that efforts should be made to allow a youth to 'outgrow' adolescent misbehaviour. In Chapter 4, we review the data that suggest that substantial numbers of youth do things that could be considered to be criminal. Moffitt (1993) and others have suggested that much of this offending is carried out by those whom she describes as 'adolescent limited' offenders – those who begin committing offences during early adolescence and, for the most part, stop as they approach adulthood. For these, it appears likely that the justice system can do little that is good, but can have negative effects. One of the advantages of having a separate justice system for young offenders, therefore, is that procedures can be set up to limit the contact of minor offenders with the system, and to limit the negative impact for those who do penetrate the formal youth court system.

Zimring (2000, pp. 283–4) suggests that there are at least three important implications of the fact that much youthful offending is transitory in nature:

1 Given that much offending is best thought of as a normal phenomenon, we should focus our attention on policies that address issues
   related to youth generally, not just on youthful offending.
2 If the cure for adolescent limited offending is simply growing up,
   there is no need for major interventions in the youth's life.
3 Given the transitory nature of most youthful offending, policies
   should avoid 'treatments' that carry with them significant life risks.
   Negative effects of being brought into the justice system is likely to
   be one such 'risk.'

These premises have been part of Canada's youth justice legislation
for some time. The Young Offenders Act, for example, contained a
principle that 'Where it is not inconsistent with the protection of society, taking no measures or taking measures other than judicial proceedings under this Act should be considered for young persons who have
committed offences' (Section 4 (1)(d)). The provisions to reduce the
unnecessary use of the formal youth justice system are much stronger
in the Youth Criminal Justice Act. Part I, of the Youth Criminal Justice
Act (Extrajudicial Measures) lays out an elaborate system for keeping
much of what is probably 'adolescent limited' offending out of the formal system. For example, extrajudicial measures (non-court methods of
holding the youth 'accountable') are 'presumed to be adequate' to hold
a first time non-violent offender accountable for his or her behaviour
(Section 4(c)). Furthermore, extrajudicial measures 'should be used' if
they are an adequate method of holding the youth accountable even if
the youth has previously offended or has previously been brought to
court (Section 4(d)).

Does Criminal Justice Processing of a Young Person Affect the Likelihood of Future Offending?

Interestingly, there are two opposing theories about the impact of
criminal justice processing on young people. Without going into much
detail, it is traditionally argued from the perspective of individual
deterrence that the more severe the processing of young people, the
less likely it is that the young person will commit further delinquencies. The opposing perspective – labelling theory – suggests that the
effect of criminal justice processing, particularly on a young person, is
that a young person's self-concept changes to be consistent with the
label. In this case, then, processing leads a youth to 'be' a young

offender. Being labelled as an offender makes behaviour that is consistent with that label more likely.

In other words, we have opposing theories. The first suggests that the more criminal justice processing that a youth experiences (or the harsher the treatment the youth receives), the less future delinquency that youth will exhibit. The other suggests that treatment as a criminal amplifies tendencies on the part of the young person to commit offences. In the current context, one of the traditional purposes of a youth justice system is to reduce the formal (criminal) processing of a youth and, where possible, treat the youth outside of the formal system.

There is quite a bit of research on the impact of criminal justice processing and, although the theories are in opposition to one another, the findings are quite consistent. Criminal justice processing (e.g., charging, taking the young person to court) does not reduce the likelihood of re-offending. The research on this question began some time ago and has been carried out in a number of different countries. Because 'criminal justice processing' can mean so many things, it is worthwhile to look carefully at some of these studies.

The first question that can be asked is whether being apprehended stops youths from committing offences. This is one of the most basic forms of criminal justice processing. As will be discussed in Chapter 4, most young people commit offences and most of these offenders do not get caught. In one American study (Klemke, 1978), for example, 1,189 high school students were asked about shoplifting. It turned out that 63 per cent admitted to shoplifting at some time in their lives; 29 per cent of these young people admitted that they had shoplifted during the previous school year. A surprisingly high proportion of the young people – 25 per cent of the shoplifters – admitted to having been apprehended by the store at least once, though this accounted for only a small proportion of the amount of shoplifting they had done. Seventeen per cent admitted to being caught by their parents. There was a very small effect on future shoplifting for females (but not for males). Those females who were apprehended either by their parents or the store were *more* likely to shoplift in the future. This and other similar studies should not be taken as evidence that being apprehended is automatically criminogenic. But the studies do suggest that there is no individual deterrence impact of being caught that serves to reduce future offending.

In England, this question was addressed in a longitudinal study of a group of London boys who have been followed and interviewed at specific points in their lives since the early 1960s. By following the same group from early childhood into adulthood, it is possible to examine the effects of different experiences that these boys have on the likelihood that they would offend. Because of the wealth of information that exists on this sample of boys, the researchers were able to examine not only the experiences that these boys had with the formal youth and adult justice systems, but they were able to examine their confidential self-reports of what offences they had committed that did not land them in the hands of the police. The researchers (Farrington, 1977; Farrington, Osborn, & West, 1978) compared two groups, those who had been apprehended for offending, and similar boys who reported committing the same number of offences, but who had not been apprehended. The result were clear: those who had been apprehended by the police were *more* likely to offend than were those who had not been apprehended. Prior to being apprehended, the two groups were equal in both their rate of offending and their views of the police. After apprehension, the boys developed significantly more hostile attitudes towards the police than were evident in the youths who had not been apprehended. The effect of apprehension on offending persisted from the mid-adolescent years (ages 14–18) through the age of 21.

Canadian research has looked at the effect on future offending of taking a youth to court. Since many youths who are apprehended by the police are dealt with informally, it is possible to compare the impact of the police decision to charge on the likelihood of future contact with the police for offending. Kijewski (1983) matched (on a variety of relevant dimensions such as age, offence, record of offending) those youths who were apprehended by the police and taken to court with a very similar group of youths. This second group had been apprehended by the police but had been dealt with informally. Typically this meant that the young person would be taken home and there would be a discussion including the police officer, the youth, and one or more parents about how to stop the offending. The results were quite straightforward: There was no difference in subsequent police recorded offending between those who were charged and sent to court and those who were cautioned by the police and released without any charges being laid. Although the youth court experience (in this case, a court convened under the Juvenile Delinquents Act) was not stigmatizing, it also did not act as an individual deterrent.

Another way in which youths are often exposed to the youth justice system is by way of the 'short sharp shock.' It is sometimes suggested that one can reduce future offending by an individual young person by subjecting them to short-lived, unpleasant, punishment. The theory seems to be that a short but intensive punishment will act as an individual deterrent but will not be long enough for the youth to be labeled as an offender. In Canada in 1999–2000, 34 per cent of the secure and open custody sentences that were handed down to those found guilty were for less than one month (CCJS, 2001, Table 6). In a survey of Canadian youth court judges (Doob, 2001) 63 per cent of the judges indicated that the belief that 'the youth would be deterred from offending in the future by a 'short sharp shock' was very or somewhat important in their decision to use custodial sentences of sixty days or less.

In the nineteenth century, whipping was recommended as an even shorter, and perhaps sharper, shock (Cox, 1870, p. 32). The data are not as encouraging as either those who would like to bring back the lash or those who advocate short terms of imprisonment would suggest. There is some suggestion from the existing data that for different kinds of young offenders the impact of criminal justice processing could either increase or decrease subsequent offending.

In one study carried out some time ago (Klein, 1974), it appeared that detaining young people in the police station after apprehension (one version of the 'short sharp shock') had quite different effects on first offenders as opposed to young people who had been previously apprehended. For first offenders, taking the young person into police custody appeared to *increase* the likelihood of subsequent offending; for young people who had been in trouble with the police before, there was some evidence that holding the young person in custody reduced subsequent delinquency. Caution is necessary in generalizing any particular complex finding such as this one. Probably the safest conclusion one can draw from such a study is that whatever the effects of criminal justice processing are, they are not invariably good or neutral.

Nevertheless, the data appear to be reasonably consistent on the effects of criminal justice processing for young people who have not had much contact with the youth justice system: contact with the system often *increases* the likelihood of subsequent offending. In an Australian study, Kraus (1978) examined more directly the use of short custodial remands as 'short sharp shocks.' He took a group of first offenders, all of whom subsequently received sentences of probation. One group had been given a 'short sharp shock' of being remanded in custody for a short time prior to trial; the others had been released prior to their court appearances. The groups were the same in terms of their age as well as the type and number of their charges. The researchers monitored their court records for the two years after the one group had received its 'shock.' The data were clear: recidivism rates were dramatically higher for those who had received the 'shock' of being remanded in custody (64 per cent) than they were for those who had been sent home (37 per cent).

Processing by the justice system can be harmful to youths, particularly those who have, up to that point in their lives, kept clear of the justice system. It would appear that Franklin Zimring's (2000) admonition not to take risks with 'treatments' that can have harmful impacts on youth who otherwise would 'grow out of' their offending has some empirical justification.

Need for Treatment

The 'needs' of young people who offend has always been an important part of the argument for a separate youth justice system. Although much of adolescent offending is probably best described as 'adolescent limited' and will disappear with age, some of those who offend are likely to be what has been described as 'life course persistent' offenders (Moffitt, 1993). The causes of serious, violent, 'life course persistent' offending are complex and have been traced to a combination of early biological factors (e.g., related to low birth weight) combined with low socioeconomic status (Tibbetts & Piquero, 1999). There is no doubt, however, that those who are heavily involved in the youth justice system (e.g., those likely to be in custody for long periods of time and who, therefore, are likely to be the subjects of studies of 'delinquents') have various identifiable deficits.

Studies have shown that the prevalence of certain disorders appears to be much higher within 'delinquent samples' than among 'community samples' of adolescents. For example, in community samples it is estimated that at least one of a list of nine disorders was present in approximately 20 per cent of the adolescents. For those who were adjudicated as delinquents, the equivalent proportion was about 80 per cent. However, there is a range, depending on the diagnostic criteria and the samples that are used. Thus, for example, in the community samples the rate of youths identified as having a mood disorder has been estimated as being as low as 2 per cent and as high as 8 per cent. For delinquent samples, the estimates vary from 19 per cent to 78 per cent. Though the size of the differences between the two sets of samples varies, the direction does not: delinquent groups tend to have a much higher proportion of youths who show some kind of disorder (Kazdin, 2000, p. 39).

Young people with disorders who exhibit troublesome behaviour may be referred to a psychiatric or mental health professional in the community, or they may end up in front of a youth court judge who believes their treatment needs are best served with a stay in custody. The probability of either of these two outcomes is likely related to the resources they have available to them in their homes and in their community – the same resources, or lack of resources that will have an impact on both their disorder and their delinquent behaviour.

The combination of the prevalence of symptoms or social problems (e.g., homelessness) in seriously delinquent youths as well as the assumption of malleability has, historically, been a justification for state intervention. When this occurs, of course, the distinction between needy youths and delinquent youths becomes blurred. That blurring, as we pointed out in Chapter 1, was contained in Canada's first delinquency law, the Juvenile Delinquents Act.

And, of course, if the justification for intervention in a youth's life was to serve his needs, then all of the protections inherent in *criminal law* become irrelevant. As Zimring (2000, pp. 275–6) put it:

> If [delinquency hearings are thought not to be punitive], there is no need to find any minimum standard of accountability or ability to assist a defense counsel. No minimum age or level of capacity is necessary for a juvenile to take dependency jurisdiction or to investigate neglect. If the sole aim of delinquency jurisdiction were the assistance and the best interests of the minor, then kids of any age and capacity would be eligible for such help, no matter the level of their comprehension.

Historical Ambivalence Concerning the Purpose of a Separate Justice System for Youth

Although the Juvenile Delinquents Act was the first comprehensive delinquency legislation in this country, there had been earlier attempts to separate youths from adults. Trépanier (1999, p. 307) notes that in 1843 there was a resolution in the legislative assembly 'to draw the vagrant juvenile portion of the population from their bad influences, and to provide a receptacle for the punishment and reformation of those who come under the eye of the police as guilty of petty crimes.' Similarly, Quebec in 1869, and Ontario five years later, began the process of separating delinquent from neglected children, though Trépanier suggests that this distinction was not very clear cut. In any case, however, by the end of the nineteenth century 'the view was ... widely shared that children were to be treated differently and separately from adults' (ibid., p. 308).

It was believed that professional interventions could reform wayward youths. Such interventions need not involve taking children from their homes. Children's Aid societies, in the 1890s, developed programs designed to help children while leaving them with their families.

As we pointed out in Chapter 1, Canada's first delinquency legislation, though technically 'criminal,' had a definite welfare orientation. As one of the people influential in its design suggested: 'Children should never be treated or spoken of as criminals, but should be studied and dealt with in exactly the same way that a sick or defective child is handled. Wherever there is an offence there is a cause behind it and our children's court and probation system should be able to reach that cause and by some means or other remove it for the safety and protection of the children in the home' (quoted by Leon, 1977, p. 86).

Interestingly enough, however, the special protections that were associated with youthfulness (e.g., trials separate from other accused persons and without publicity) were not always fully accepted. As is the case now, there were suggestions in the late nineteenth century that these provisions should not apply to youth who had apparently committed very serious crimes (ibid., p. 89). When the Juvenile Delinquents Act was being debated, a number of police officials circulated a report that, with different language, sounds quite similar to the Ontario government's criticisms, in 2001, of the Youth Criminal Justice Act and its support for its correctionally unsuccessful boot camp (see Chapter 11). This 1907 report suggested that the supporters of the welfare approach

> work upon the sympathies of philanthropic men and women for the purpose of introducing a jelly-fish and abortive system of law enforcement, whereby the judge or magistrate is expected to come down to the level of the incorrigible street arab and assume an attitude absolutely repulsive to British Subjects. The idea seems to be that by profuse use of slang phraseology he should place himself in a position to kiss and coddle a class of perverts and delinquents who require the most rigid disciplinary and cor-

rective methods to ensure the possibility of their reformation. I would go further to affirm from extensive and practical experience that this kissing and coddling, if indiscriminately applied, even to the best class of children, would have a disastrous effect, both physically, mentally, morally and spiritually. (quoted by Leon, 1977, p. 96)

Notwithstanding these criticisms, the criminal law was modified for youths such that youths, from 1908 onwards could, for their own good, be put under the control of the state for indefinite periods of time (until the youth was 21 years old). Criminal law was, however, only the mechanism for accomplishing a 'child saving' goal.

The important 'new' focus of the Juvenile Delinquents Act was not, however, its power to remove the child from his or her home for an indefinite period for even the most trivial of offences. It was, instead, the focus on probation. Trépanier (1999, p. 310) suggests that in the late nineteenth century probation had been viewed 'as nothing more than what was already being done by children's aid societies for neglected and dependent children.'

The indeterminacy of the dispositions and the rejection of notions of proportionality made sense within the welfare model that was incorporated into the Juvenile Delinquents Act.

The judge's function would be to establish whether the child convicted of an offence considered symptomatic of his needs was actually in need of assistance, and how in particular the factors deemed to be at the root of his delinquent behaviour could be neutralized. This was a protective model, where the fatherly and kindly judge was not one against whom the child had to protect himself. The normal guarantees offered by the due process of law appeared irrelevant. Since the emphasis was on the child's needs and on the benevolent attitude of those taking charge of him, there no longer seemed to be a need to safeguard all his procedural rights. (ibid., p. 314)

In the United States, this orientation was effectively challenged in the 1960s by two cases: *Kent v United States* in 1966 and *In re Gault* in 1967. The words of the United States Supreme Court were clear: 'The child receives the worst of both worlds. He gets neither the protections accorded to adults nor the solicitous care and regenerative treatment postulated for children' (*Kent v United States* cited in Feld, 2000, p. 105).

The 1967 case of *In re Gault* (cited in Steinberg & Schwartz, 2000,

p. 13), though it was an American case, reflected concerns that existed in Canada at the time. There is no question that it influenced the replacement of Juvenile Delinquents Act with the Young Offenders Act. A 15-year-old boy, Gerald Gault, was found to have been making calls to his next door neighbour 'of the irritatingly offensive, adolescent, sex variety.' He was given no notice of the charges he was facing. He had no access to a lawyer. The neighbour who was 'victimized' by him was not required to appear in court to give evidence and be cross-examined by Gault. The only evidence in the case was testimony by the arresting officer. Gault found himself committed to the Arizona State Industrial School for up to six years. The United States Supreme Court found this to be inappropriate and ruled that children are persons and could not be deprived of liberty without due process of law.

As bizarre as Gault's original 'trial' may seem today, it is, of course, completely consistent with the view of juvenile courts at the beginning of the twentieth century. An American judge, writing in the 1909 *Harvard Law Review*, put it: 'The problem for determination by the judge is not Has this boy or girl committed a specific wrong, but What is he, how has he become what he is, and what had best be done in his interest and in the interest of the state to save him from a downward career. It is apparent at once that the ordinary legal evidence in a criminal court is not the sort of evidence to be heard in such a proceeding' (Judge Mack, cited in Steinberg, 2000, p. 12).

Welfare Orientation in the Twenty-First Century

Writing in 2000, Zimring notes that 'as a matter of constitutional law, then, we have known for a generation [since *In re Gault*] that those who administer juvenile court delinquency dockets are in the business of punishing adolescent law violators' (Zimring, 2000, p. 276).

Nevertheless, it does not appear that all Canadian judges are completely content with such a characterization. Thirty-seven per cent of Canadian youth court judges (Doob, 2001, p. 39) indicated that in at least half of the cases where they imposed custody, one of the factors that led to that decision was that 'the youth's home (and/or parents) or living conditions were such that there was a need to get him or her into a more stable environment.' Twenty-five per cent of judges indicated that in half or more of the cases where they placed a young offender in custody, a contributing reason for the decision was that 'The youth was in need of a program that was only available in custody.' The welfare orientation of judges varied enormously in all regions of Canada, although it was highest in the Atlantic provinces, Quebec, and the Territories, and lowest in Ontario.

Detention before trial, although largely governed by traditional criminal law purposes (e.g., the likelihood that the youth would show up for trial or would commit another offence) was, in the case of youths, also influenced by welfare considerations. Canadian judges were asked to 'think about the cases where a youth has been detained prior to his or her trial. For how many of these youth was the detention necessary *only* because the young person had no adequate place to stay, or for some other child welfare reason?' Thirty per cent of Canadian judges (ibid., p. 16) indicated that welfare reasons were the basis of the detention order for half or more of the youths they detained.

We noted in Chapter 1 that a majority (64 per cent) of Ontario residents, in a 1997 poll, indicated that they did not want there to be a separate justice system for youth. Sprott (1998) looked carefully at these data and concluded that opposition to a separate justice system was, however, only skin-deep. When they looked at specific types of policies and cases, people appeared to believe that young offenders should, indeed, be dealt with differently from adults.

Conclusion

We began this chapter by noting that society sets various arbitrary ages at which a youth becomes an adult. For purposes of criminal justice, the distinction between being a youth and an adult has been justified in various ways. Most importantly, however, youths have been seen as having diminished responsibility for their actions. This is consistent with a good bit of literature that says that even though youths may understand that their acts are 'wrong,' they do not reason and consider consequences in the same way as adults. Put simply, we do not consider 15-year-olds old enough to be punished in the same way we punish adults, and we also assume that they are not old enough to be able to make their own decisions on the purchase of alcohol or cigarettes. In addition, given the nature of youths, youthful offending, and the justice systems, it appears to be sensible to have a justice system that reflects the differences between youthful and adult offending.

Special 'treatment' of youth, however, has been a double-edged sword. On the one hand, it has meant that the state has traditionally put more emphasis on the 'needs' of the young offender than it does on the needs of the adult offender. This emphasis reflects the reality of serious young offenders: they have dramatically more 'needs' than do youths in the general population. On the other hand, more 'treatment' has, at times, been operationalized as simply more punishment, often without consideration of due process rights. This conflict – between due process and punishment on the one hand, and treatment on the other – is consistent with a century-long tension between these two sets of concepts in the youth justice system. In the late twentieth century, we found Canadian judges giving custodial sentences and holding youths in pretrial detention for welfare reasons. These decisions may be consistent with past legislation, but the sentencing decisions appear to be inconsistent with the Young Offenders Act (under which these decisions were made), and the sentencing and the pretrial detention decisions would both have been inconsistent with the Youth Criminal Justice Act. The Young Offenders Act has a provision that 'an order of custody shall not be used as a substitute for appropriate child protection, health and other social measures' (Section 24(1.1)(a)). The Youth Criminal Justice Act has a similar provision (Section 39(5)). In addition, the Youth Criminal Justice Act prohibits pretrial detention for welfare purposes (Section 29(1)). Interestingly, the Youth Criminal Justice Act allows a youth court judge, 'at any stage of the proceedings ... [to] refer the young person to a child welfare agency for assessment to determine whether the young person is in need of child welfare services.' This provision would appear to be a legislative attempt to separate youth justice (criminal) matters from welfare concerns.

In law, then, Canada's youth justice system has moved away from a 'child welfare' approach towards a more 'accountability-based' or criminal law system. It has, however, largely maintained its separation from the adult justice system for reasons that were as appropriate a century ago as they are now. In a similar fashion, it has maintained the division between the criminal law (for those at least 12 years old) and child welfare law (for those under 12 years old). The issues surrounding the setting of the lower boundary age of criminal responsibility will be discussed in Chapter 3.

CHAPTER THREE

The Youth Justice System and Very Young Children

Setting the Minimum Age of Criminal Responsibility

The issue of the minimum age of criminal responsibility has been a political concern for quite some time. It should be recalled that under the Juvenile Delinquents Act children as young as age 7 could be charged for a criminal offence. This was changed, in 1984, to a minimum age of 12. At present, in Canada, before his or her twelfth birthday, a youth cannot be charged criminally, no matter how serious the offence might be. The Youth Criminal Justice Act does not alter this fact.

As youths age, they are more likely to meet the various criteria that are relevant to holding them criminally responsible. Nevertheless, one cannot ignore the fact that young people mature at different rates. If the purpose of a minimum age is to establish a time when young people understand that an act is wrong and that there are consequences for those who act in such a way, a single age will not be adequate for all cases. Young people's understanding of the criminal process will develop at different rates; there is no single age when we can be certain that a youth can fully participate in the process. As children get older, they become more likely to meet the criteria that might be used to establish an age of criminal responsibility. And as they get older, we may be more likely to want them to suffer the full (long-term) consequences of being dealt with under the criminal law.

At the same time, there is obviously no single point in development when a child first becomes capable of committing serious offences. Very young children can commit very serious offences, knowing that these acts are wrong and, at some level, knowing that they will be punished if caught. That acts which could be considered to be criminal are committed by the very young does not mean that the criminal law is the most effective way of dealing with these problems. Nor does it mean that the state has no interest in dealing with misbehaviour of the very young. The issue being addressed here is what limits should be put on the use of the *criminal law*. We assume that the state has an interest in maintaining its ability to intervene in the lives of young children for other reasons.

These two points illustrate an important fact to keep in mind: the age of criminal responsibility is a political decision more than an empirical one. Many jurisdictions in the United States (e.g., Minnesota, Mississippi, Pennsylvania, and Vermont) have 10 as the age of criminal responsibility. In North Carolina, a 6-year-old can be brought to juvenile court and in New York a 7-year-old is eligible to be classified as a juvenile delinquent (Snyder & Sickmund, 1999). Some European countries have older ages. In Germany, for example, there is no criminal culpability for youths under the age of 14 (Albrecht, 2003).

The problem facing those trying to set an appropriate age is one of balancing various important values. It must be remembered that the criminal law, in this case the Young Offenders Act or the Youth Criminal Justice Act, is not the only tool society has to control the misbehaviour of children. Young people who commit harmful acts can be controlled under various provincial child welfare laws without resorting to the criminal law. The test as to whether they need to be brought under state control is, of course, different from the criteria one might use in determining whether the criminal law should be invoked. The issue, then, is not one of when young people should be liable to social control from the state. Rather it is when they should be subject to the criminal law.

A substantial number of young children do things that could be considered offences. However, the measured rates depend, to a large extent, on the specificity of the questions asked. The larger the number of questions that are asked (and the more specific these questions are), the more likely it is that a youth will report offending. In a national survey of 10- and 11-year-old children in 1994/5 and again in 1996/7 (Sprott, Doob, & Jenkins, 2001, table 5), 17 to 18 per cent admitted to at least some property offending. The rate of violent offending was between 33 and 38 per cent. Committing violent or property offences is not a rare event.

Although there is *some* level of consistency across time in offending, it should not be assumed that youths who are relatively troublesome at

Table 3.1   Relationship between level of self-reported aggressive
behaviour at age 10–11 and level of self-reported aggressive behaviour
at age 12–13 (%)

Aggressive behaviour at 10–11	Aggressive behaviour at 12–13			
	None	Some	A lot	Total (n)
None	82	12	5	100 (1,006)
Some	55	28	17	100 (386)
A lot	45	31	24	100 (233)

Source: Sprott et al., 2001.

Table 3.2   Relationship between level of self-reported delinquent acts
involving property at age 10–11 and level of self-reported delinquent acts
involving property at age 12–13 (%)

Delinquent acts involving property at 10–11	Delinquent acts involving property at 12–13			
	None	Some	A lot	Total (n)
None	81	13	6	100 (1,269)
Some	68	26	7	100 (159)
A lot	63	20	17	100 (110)

Source: Sprott et al., 2001.

age 10 or 11 will be troublesome at age 12 or 13, when they can offi-
cially be designated as 'young offenders.' The National Longitudinal
Study of Children and Youth interviews a sample of Canadian youths
every two years. Tables 3.1 and 3.2 look at the relationship between the
level of self-reported aggressive behaviour (Table 3.1) and property
offending (Table 3.2) at age 10 to 11 to the level of self-reported acts at
age 12 to 13 (Sprott et al., 2001, Tables 7 and 8).

These two tables can be seen as illustrating two phenomena. First,
there is a fair amount of stability in offending. Those youths who were
heavily involved in offending (violent or property) when they were 10
or 11 years old were much more likely to be involved in high levels of
offending when they were 12 or 13 years old than were other youths.
However, significant numbers of youths who were relatively high
level offenders at age 10 or 11 were reported *no* offending two years
later. Thus, just because a youth commits offences early in his or her

Table 3.3 Cases entering youth court, by type of offence, for 12-, 14-, and 16-year-old youths (Canada, 1999–2000)

	12-year-olds n (%)	14-year-olds n (%)	16-year-olds n (%)
All types of cases	3,095 (3.0)	14,838 (14.5)	25,342 (24.8)
Minor property[a]	979 (4)	3,831 (15.7)	5,876 (24.1)
Break and enter	371 (3.6)	1,578 (13.3)	2,587 (25.1)
Minor assault	606 (5.9)	1,843 (18.0)	2,160 (21.1)
Major violence[b]	4 (0.7)	36 (6.5)	162 (29.3)

Source: Canadian Centre for Justice Statistics, 2001b.
[a] Minor property = theft under $5,000, possession of stolen property, mischief.
[b] Major violence = murder, manslaughter, attempted murder, aggravated assault, aggravated sexual assault.
Note: Each of these age groups represents just over 16% of Canada's youth population.

life, we should not assume that he or she will forever be a high-level offender.

Most of these youths obviously do not find themselves involved in any official way with the youth justice system. Thus it is useful, as a somewhat separate issue, to look at the kinds of matters that bring young people into the criminal justice system. We know, from existing court data, that younger children are brought into the court system at a much lower rate than are older children. Table 3.3 shows data on cases brought to court for 12-, 14-, and 16-year-old youths. Since those under 12 cannot be brought to youth court, we cannot look at data for them. However, a comparison of the cases brought to court across Canada for these three ages of youth can give us a hint of what would happen if Parliament were to decide to bring younger youths in to the justice system.

Young people are under the jurisdiction of the youth justice system for six years. An average of about 1/6 (about 16.6 per cent) of youths, then, are at each year of age, from 12 to 17, inclusive. However, 12-year-olds are responsible for only 3 per cent of all youth court cases, whereas 16-year-olds are responsible for 24.8 per cent of all youth court cases. The relationship with age is most notable when one looks at major violence. Fewer than 1 per cent of all cases (0.7 per cent) entering court for major violence involve 12-year-olds. In contrast, 29.6 per cent of the cases of 'major violence' involve 16-year-olds.

Table 3.4   Cases entering youth court, by type of offence, 12-year-olds and all ages (Canada, 1999–2000)

	12-year-olds n (%)	All ages n (%)
Theft under $5,000	588 (19)	14,514 (14)
Possession of stolen property	98 (3)	4,738 (5)
Failure to appear	249 (8)	11,078 (11)
Failure to comply with a disposition	91 (3)	13,517 (13)
Subtotal	1,026 (33)	43,847 (43)
Other thefts	106 (3)	4,536 (4)
Mischief/damage	293 (9)	5,103 (5)
Break and enter	371 (12)	10,285 (10)
Minor assault	606 (20)	10,235 (10)
Total: sum of 8 offences	2,402 (78)	74,006 (73)
All cases	3,095 (100)	102,061 (100)

Source: Canadian Centre for Justice Statistics, 2001b.

If one wanted to extrapolate from the data in Table 3.3 to youths under age 12, the following propositions might be considered.

- Younger children are responsible for a very small number of criminal cases of all types.
- Very young children appear to be particularly unlikely to be involved in serious violent cases. Across Canada, 12-year-olds were involved in only 4 of the 553 cases involving major violence during 1999–2000.

It is likely that if Canada did decide to make 10- and 11-year-olds subject to the criminal law (i.e., the Youth Criminal Justice Act), very few such cases would end up in youth court, and almost all of these would be minor in nature. In particular, a minuscule number of cases would involve serious violence. Court would most likely be used for relatively minor cases. As shown in Table 3.4, 12-year-olds in youth court are there largely for very minor matters. Table 3.4 examines all 3,095 cases involving 12-year-olds showing up at the court door in 1999–2000.

The right-hand column of Table 3.4 shows that almost three-quarters of the 102,061 cases involving youths of all ages brought to the youth court in Canada involve one of eight offences. None of these eight offences involve serious violence. The cases involving 12-year-olds present much the same overall picture. However, compared with youths as a whole, 12-year-olds are more likely to have as their 'principal charge' a minor assault and are, relatively speaking, less likely to be in court for a 'failure to comply with a disposition.'

Both of these differences make sense. There is a relatively high level of concern about violence, even minor violence. In the school system, this is operationalized as 'zero tolerance' policies, where even 12-year-olds may be referred to the police and charged for very minor acts of violence. 'Failure to comply with a disposition' is underrepresented, in part because a youth must first acquire a disposition before he or she can be charged with breaching it. For many 12-year-olds, there may not be time within their first young offender year to receive a disposition and violate it. So much to do, so little time to do it.

What Kinds of Cases Involving the Very Young Were Brought to Court under the Juvenile Delinquents Act?

It is important to remind ourselves of the kinds of matters that, under the JDA, were being dealt with by the youth courts involving children younger than age 12. Full data on this are, of course, available in reports from the Canadian Centre for Justice Statistics. A summary of a small portion of these data for all of Canada in 1983 is provided in Table 3.5. It should be remembered that the *maximum* age varied between 16 and 18 years across the provinces. Hence the 'total' number of delinquencies (in this case, *charges* brought to court rather than *cases*, as in more recent Young Offenders Act data presented in this book) would have been larger had it included all of those under the age of 18. Nevertheless, the table provides us with a picture of how the criminal law was used to deal with very young children when it was legally available for this purpose.

The data presented in Table 3.5 illustrate a number of important points. First, 10- and 11-year-olds were involved in a very small portion of delinquencies that the courts were dealing with – in 1983 it was only 1.4 per cent. Second, the argument that the youth justice system would carefully pick the most serious cases to bring into youth court is strongly challenged by these data. There were, in 1983, 1,625 delinquencies dealt with by the juvenile courts involving children aged 10

Table 3.5   Types of delinquencies that were dealt with in court in 1983 for (1) all youth, (2) 10- and 11-year-olds, (3) delinquencies of 10- and 11-year olds as a percentage of delinquencies of that type for youth of all ages (percentages in parentheses)

Delinquency	(1) All ages	(2) Age 10 & 11	(3) Age 10 & 11/all ages
All delinquencies	115,915 (100)	1,625 (100)	(1.4)
Violence	3,338 (2.9)	55 (3.4)	(1.6)
Theft and possession of stolen property	36,539 (31.5)	781 (48.1)	(2.1)
Break and enter	28,777 (24.8)	421 (25.9)	(1.5)
Robbery	1,290 (1.1)	10 (0.6)	(0.8)
Mischief	6,046 (5.2)	204 (12.6)	(3.4)
Various other	39,925 (34.4)	154 (9.5)	(0.4)

Source: Canadian Centre for Justice Statistics, 1983.

and 11. Only fifty-five of these (3.4 per cent of the delinquencies involving 10- and 11-year-olds) involved violence. Forty-eight per cent involved theft or possession of stolen property.

For the most part, the 10- and 11-year-olds being dealt with in the youth courts in 1983 were there for property crimes (over 85 per cent of the delinquencies involving 10- and 11-year-olds were for theft, break and enter, or mischief.)

In 1983 there were also a few delinquencies involving children under 10 years old – 235 in all. Nine of these were for assaults. Almost all of these delinquencies involving 7-, 8-, and 9-year-olds (209 of them or 89 per cent of the delinquencies attributed to children 7 to 9 years old) were for property crimes.

In other words, when very young children could be brought to court for criminal matters, they were not being brought there for what appeared to be exceptionally serious acts. It is worth remembering that 1983 was a year after the government of Canada released a statement 'setting out the policy of the Government of Canada with respect to the purpose and principles of the criminal law.' This policy statement, entitled The Criminal Law in Canadian Society, stated that 'the criminal law should be employed to deal only with that conduct for which other means of social control are inadequate or inappropriate' (Government of Canada, 1982, p. 52). A few years earlier, the Law Reform Commission of Canada (1976) had made a similar statement. At the time, neither statement was seen as controversial.

Police Discretion with the Very Young

Unfortunately, it is not very meaningful to compare offences committed by the very young (i.e., those 11 years old or younger) recorded by
the police before and after 1984, when the change took place in the age
of criminal responsibility. The reason for this is simple: a knowledgeable citizen (e.g., a school principal) might have brought an offence
apparently committed by a 10- or 11-year-old to the attention of the
police prior to 1984 because they knew that the police could deal with
it under the criminal law. The same person, after 1984, may have
looked for other civil, social welfare, or community approaches to the
problem rather than calling in the police.

Conly (1978) examined data from twelve police departments on
youth who were apprehended for offences during the month of
December 1976. The number of very young who were apprehended for
offences was very small. More interesting was that a very small portion of them were actually charged and brought to court. The police,
even when they could take children under age 12 to court, apparently
were not very enthusiastic about doing so. The data are presented in
Table 3.6.

What Offences Did Those under 12 Commit under the Young Offenders Act?

That a young person cannot be charged does not mean that the police
do not respond to a call and record that an offence has taken place
involving a young person apparently under the age of 12. The Canadian Centre for Justice Statistics released a report in 1992 describing
criminal occurrences involving those under 12 years old.

The study involved an examination of police occurrence reports in
twenty-seven police forces across Canada for varying lengths of time
(between four months and about three and a half years) ending in
mid-1992. It is an important study because it gives us one rather
detailed picture of what events are like that are brought to the attention of the police but which cannot, in law, be dealt with under the
criminal law. There are severe limits on these data: the reporting of
information about offenders who were under 12 was voluntary. In
addition, the time period of reporting for the participating jurisdictions varies considerably. Therefore, we do not know how representative these reports of offences are of Canada as a whole. Another study

Table 3.6 Apprehended juveniles charged, by age group

Age (years)	Apprehended	Charged n (%)
7–11	636	76 (12)
12–13	1,269	368 (29)
14–15	2,324	1,019 (44)
16–17	970	779 (80)
All ages[a]	5,179	2,242 (43)

Source: Derived from Conly, 1978.
[a] 'All ages' include a few youths for whom exact ages were not available.
Note: In 1976 many of the major municipal areas were in provinces with a maximum age under the Juvenile Delinquents Act of 15; hence, there were few 16- and 17-year-old juvenile delinquents.

of some of these matters (Roberts, 1999) was based on 1997 data. Youths under 12 do not appear to feature very prominently in police reports of crime.

- In the 971,000 incidents which occurred in the twenty-seven jurisdictions during the period ending in 1992, there were 406,662 persons described by the police as offenders. About 1.2 per cent (4,757) of these people were under 12. About 20.8 per cent were young offender age (aged 12 through 17, inclusive). In other words, looking at all offenders, young children apparently committing offences are not a large part of the crime problem. These data are fairly similar to those reported by Roberts (1999) from data obtained from the Department of Justice, Canada, on a subset of police forces in 1997. Of the 345,390 suspects identified by the police in that study, 1.5 per cent were children under 12, and an additional 24.1 per cent were youths 12–17, inclusive.
- Focusing on those offenders under 12, it is not surprising to find that the majority (about 60 per cent) were 10 or 11 years old. Almost all (89 per cent) were boys.
- Eight per cent of the offences recorded as having been committed by these 'under 12s' were violent offences. In about 1 per cent of the incidents, the police described the offences committed by the under

12s as sexual assaults. The 1997 data (Roberts, 1999) show an identical percentage. Another 1 per cent of the incidents involving these children were described as being an assault with a weapon or causing bodily harm. Another 5 per cent were described as the lowest level of assault ('common assault'). The 1997 data show a somewhat higher proportion of assaults, perhaps because of sampling or different categorization of the offences. As one would expect, however, most (64 per cent) of the violent incidents involving those under 12 years old were classified as common assault.

- Serious violence sometimes does occur. In three of the 4,757 incidents (0.06 per cent of the incidents) the police described the offence as aggravated assault. The 1997 data are quite similar. Of the 5,169 suspects under age 12, four were aggravated assault, and one young person under 12 was involved in a homicide.
- Weapons were used in only 8 per cent of the offences. Among the 4,757 incidents, four involved guns and twenty-nine involved knives.
- Five per cent of the *assault incidents* involved a physical injury defined as 'more than trifling or transient in nature and that required professional medical attention at the scene or transportation to a medical facility' (CCJS, 1992, p. 9).
- For the most part the victims of the assaults were either acquaintances (82 per cent) or members of the offender's family or close friends (6 per cent). Strangers were rarely chosen as victims (12 per cent of assault incidents).
- The largest portion of these very young offenders were described as either having committed mischief (41 per cent of the very young offenders) or some other property offence (46 per cent). Robbery was said to be the offence in only seven (0.2 per cent) of the 4,757 incidents.

These glimpses at offending by the very young give a fairly consistent picture. Most of the incidents involving this group and recorded by the police are fairly minor. There are, however, a very small number of very serious incidents that, if the youth were over 12, would almost certainly result in a court hearing.

The Few Serious Offences Committed by the Very Young

There is no doubt that some of the offences by those under 12 years old are serious. Furthermore, although it is not part of our recent history, we can never be sure that some very young children will not commit horrific acts like those that have received a great deal of publicity elsewhere in the world. But we have to keep the serious incidents in perspective. The 1992 study (CCJS, 1992) described criminal incidents involving over 4,757 children under 12 years old. Some of these incidents were very serious. In addition to the three that the police described as being aggravated assault, four of the 4,757 incidents involved firearms and about fifteen involved an injury requiring professional medical attention. The question is not whether serious crimes do occur. Rather we should be asking what is the best way of dealing with the range of 'criminal' matters that young children commit.

These sources of data about young children who offend – those actually brought to court in the dying days of the Juvenile Delinquents Act, those under the Young Offenders Act who were apprehended but found to be under the minimum age of 12, as well as the data from 12-year-olds who are prosecuted under the Young Offenders Act – suggest that serious offences committed by very young children are very rare.

The Trade-offs: How to Deal with the Very Young Offender

Even when one focuses on the very rare cases involving more serious offences one has to raise the question whether it makes sense for society to contemplate using the *criminal law* to deal with these very young children. There is probably general agreement that society must have a way to intervene in those very rare cases involving serious offences committed by those under 12 years old. The question is how one does it, rather than whether it is done.

If, for example, a young child is misbehaving in a way that could cause serious harm, does it make more sense to find an appropriate way of punishing the child or should an attempt be made to try to control and rehabilitate the child? Similarly, a young person who is uncontrolled by his or her parents, who runs away, and who also shoplifts should probably be treated for the more serious problems that are occurring rather than focusing on the shoplifting. For one thing, the 'offence' may not warrant the type of serious intervention that might be appropriate if a child welfare orientation were seen as being more relevant. In addition, if the focus of the intervention is on the offence rather than on the nature of the problem, then we may find that in the long run we are less well protected.

It is interesting to note that in a survey of 148 police services across the country (eighty-six provincial and municipal forces, forty-eight RCMP detachments, and thirteen Aboriginal police services) the majority of police officers surveyed indicated that they did not view the problem of crime involving children under 12 as serious (Augimeri, Goldberg, & Koegl, 1999). It is reported that 'most officers do not rate the problem of crime committed by children under 12 as serious. Most of the calls for service involving children under 12 are categorized as 'behavioural problems' rather than 'criminal acts' (ibid., p. 12). It is interesting to note, however, that few (23 per cent of police services surveyed) had specific policies for dealing with children under 12 who commit offences.

What Do Very Young Aggressive Children Look Like?

One of the reasons that there is reluctance to criminalize the behaviour of very young children is the belief that these are children who have already had difficult lives and that they would be harmed even more by criminal justice punishment. The alternative view regarding the most troublesome young children is a hypothesis suggested by Baumeister, Boden, and Smart (1996, p. 8): 'The major cause of violence is high self-esteem combined with an ego threat.' As Sprott and Doob (2000, p. 127) suggest, 'the characterization of violent youth as being self-satisfied could easily be used to support increasingly punitive criminal justice responses to these youth.' Sprott and Doob therefore examined data about a sample of Canada's most aggressive 10- or 11-year-old children based on analyses of the National Longitudinal Study of Children and Youth. In this survey, children provided information about various things including their own feelings and social relationships. In addition, the adult most knowledgeable about the youth (typically the mother) provided information to the survey. Finally, the school teacher who apparently knew the child best filled out a questionnaire about the child.

With three different sources of information about the child's aggressive behaviour (from the child himself or herself, the parent, and the teacher) as well as three different views about the child's feelings and social relationships, there were nine different possible combinations that one could look at. As it turned out, the pattern of results was the same no matter which combination of perspectives was used. In Tables 3.7 and 3.8 we have presented the relationship between the parent's assessment of the roughly 10 per cent most aggressive children and the

Table 3.7 Relationship between a child's self-reported feelings and a parent's identification of the child's aggressiveness. Percentage (and in parentheses number on which the percentage is based) of the 'most aggressive' girls and boys and 'other' boys and girls reporting each 'feeling'

Child's self-report of feelings	Girls		Boys	
	Most aggressive	Other	Most aggressive	Other
I don't feel as happy as other children	54.4 (100)	32.8 (1,279)	35.0 (196)	32.5 (1,181)
I feel miserable	48.7 (98)	36.0 (1,275)	46.3 (191)	34.0 (1,176)
I feel left out at school	36.4 (102)	17.0 (1,284)	27.4 (198)	14.8 (1,186)
I have trouble enjoying myself	49.3 (97)	29.0 (1,272)	34.8 (189)	25.1 (1,190)
I have a 'negative' self-image	51.9 (99)	27.8 (1,257)	48.6 (191)	28.8 (1,142)

Source: Doob and Sprott, 2000.

Table 3.8 Relationship between a child's self-reported social interactions and a parent's identification of the child's aggressiveness. Percentage (and in parentheses number on which the percentage is based) of the 'most aggressive' girls and boys and 'other' boys and girls reporting each 'negative' type of relationship

Child's self-report of social relationships	Girls		Boys	
	Most aggressive	Other	Most aggressive	Other
Negative relations with family	47.6 (101)	25.6 (1,269)	49.1 (211)	25.6 (1,172)
Negative relations with friends	42.6 (104)	22.9 (1,308)	54.6 (219)	28.9 (1,219)
Perception of parental rejection	47.5 (95)	30.7 (1,244)	47.2 (185)	35.5 (1,136)
Perception of teacher being 'fair'	51.2 (102)	68.8 (1,295)	56.1 (202)	63.1 (1,199)
Other children say mean things to you	18.9 (101)	8.7 (1,285)	21.8 (200)	7.7 (1,189)
Other children 'bully' you	19.2 (99)	7.5 (1,274)	24.7 (197)	12.4 (1,189)

Source: Doob and Sprott, 2000.

child's self-report of feelings (Table 3.7) and social relationships (Table 3.8).

On each of the eleven dimensions listed in Tables 3.7 and 3.8, the most aggressive 10- to 11-year-olds are the children who are least likely to be happy, and most likely to have a negative self-image and to have negative relations with family, friends, teachers, and other children. As Sprott and Doob (2000, p. 131) concluded: '[A reason] not to criminalize the misbehaviour of 10- and 11-year-olds is that these are children who are much more likely than other children to indicate that they feel miserable, left out, rejected by parents, bullied by other children, etc. Presumably, were their misbehavior dealt with in a punishment oriented criminal justice system, they would add 'the state' to the list of people or institutions that had rejected them as children.'

What Does the Public Think about Criminalizing Behaviour of Those under 12?

If the decision about the minimum age of criminal responsibility is ultimately a political one, and if politicians, on crime issues, prefer to follow rather than lead, a reasonable question to ask is what would happen if the politicians were to follow the general Canadian public. The answer to this appears to depend on whether one gives members of the public a reasonable question.

A 1999 national poll asked Canadian adults to 'imagine this situation. A 10-year-old boy has just committed a serious violent offence. How appropriate do you think it would be to have him charged with this offence and dealt with by the court? He then could be sentenced to serve a sentence in a prison for youth' (Sprott & Doob, 2000, 124). If one takes this question as being one that elicits the public's view of what should happen to 10-year-old offenders, the results are simple: 70 per cent thought that charging the youth would be very or somewhat appropriate. The important feature of this question, however, is that it does not offer a respondent any alternatives. It asks, in effect, do you think that the youth should be charged or do you think nothing should happen. Against a 'choice' of 'do nothing,' almost any response to a 'serious violent offence' looks good.

In reality, however, there are other choices. A youth could be dealt with through the child welfare or mental health system. In order to give respondents a real choice – the policy choice that is relevant – respondents were then asked a follow-up question: 'Another option, instead

Table 3.9 Relationship between initial support for a criminal justice approach and, when provided choice support for a mental health / child welfare approach as response to 10-year-old who has committed a serious violent offence (%)

Initial view: charge the child	Subsequent view: mental health approach		
	Prefer	Oppose	Total % (n)
Very appropriate	62.1	37.9	100 (354)
Somewhat appropriate	80.2	19.8	100 (429)
Inappropriate	86.2	13.8	100 (341)

Source: Sprott & Doob, 2000.

of having the youth charged with the offence and taken to court, would be to have the ten-year-old boy dealt with by the mental health system or the child welfare system. He could immediately be sent for treatment in a locked facility to deal with the problems that led him to behave violently. Do you prefer or oppose this approach instead of having the youth dealt with by the courts?'

Approximately 77 per cent of the people surveyed preferred a social welfare or mental health approach to charging the youth and dealing with him in the youth justice system. Put differently, support for a criminal justice approach to under-age offending fell from 70 per cent to 23 per cent when a choice of criminal justice or a child welfare approach was provided. Even people who initially believed that charging the child would be 'very appropriate' preferred the mental health choice when given the option. Table 3.9 shows the relationship between the responses to those two questions. Of the people who initially believed that it would be 'very appropriate' to deal with the child in the justice system, 62.1 per cent preferred the mental health approach when given the choice. Over 80 per cent of the people who believed it would be 'somewhat appropriate' or 'inappropriate' to deal with the child in the justice system preferred the mental health approach when given the choice.

Thus, although on a broad level there appears to be widespread public support for dealing with violent young children in the youth justice system, that support diminishes substantially when people are given a choice of ways with which to deal with the child. As Doob and Sprott (2000, p. 131) concluded: 'Ultimately, the decision of whether to criminalize their aggressive behavior is likely to be a political one rather than one based on utilitarian principles. If politicians were to listen carefully to members of the public, they would hear that there is, in fact, very little support for a criminal justice intervention when alternatives are offered. Thus, from a political perspective, one reason not to criminalize the behaviour of 10 and 11 year olds is that the public, when given a choice, prefers a welfare approach over a criminal justice approach.'

Have the Provinces Adequately Addressed the Issue of How to Deal with Children under Age 12 Who Offend?

Full legislative and administrative responsibility for the child welfare system lies with the provinces. The importance of provincial laws increased in 1984 for two reasons. First, the scope of behaviour falling under the YOA included only those acts which were violations of federal law. Provincial and municipal laws were no longer included and there was no longer a 'catch all' category of behaviour like 'sexual immorality or similar form of vice.' Second, what otherwise would be offences by those 11 years old and younger were no longer subject to criminal law.

Generally speaking, provincial legislation focuses on traditional child welfare issues, such as children suffering or at risk of physical or sexual harm or neglect. The Ontario law, that is, the Children and Family Services Act, which came into effect in 1984, covers all children in the province under the age of 16. In part because of the void left in the criminal law for youths under age 12 who might commit offences, a 'youth in need of protection' typically includes a broad definition of harms from which provinces wish to protect children. Thus, in Ontario the child can be found in need of protection if

the child is less than twelve years old and has killed or seriously injured another person or caused serious damage to another person's property, [and] services or treatment are necessary to prevent a recurrence and the child's parent or the person having charge of the child does not provide, or refuses or is unavailable or unable to consent to, those services or treatment;
or
the child is less than twelve years old and has on more than one occasion injured another person or caused loss or damage to another person's prop-

erty, with the encouragement of the person having charge of the child or because of that person's failure or inability to supervise the child adequately (Section 37(2)(j) and (k))

The Ontario child welfare law is not dramatically different from other provincial laws. And, like the federal criminal legislation, it has an explicit, but not very strong, statement endorsing the principle of minimal interference. Under 'purposes' it states that 'so long as they are consistent with the best interests, protection, and well being of children' there is the necessity 'to recognize that the least disruptive course of action that is available and is appropriate in a particular case to help a child should be considered' (Children and Family Services Act, Ontario, Section 1(2)2). 'Considering' a course of action does not, obviously, require that it be chosen.

If a child is found to be in need of protection, there is, again, a presumption in favor of the least disruptive intervention or a community placement (e.g., with a relative, neighbor, etc.; Section 57). Nevertheless, the fact remains that, on the balance of probabilities, a youth can be placed into the care of the state where that youth has committed offences and the parents appear to a court to be unable to supervise the youth adequately.

Hence, although Canada's criminal law does not address the offending of youths under age 12, the state can, and does, apprehend and hold in secure settings, youths under age 12 who commit offences. The problem, of course, with welfare interventions is that the concerns about due process are likely to be less salient in a child welfare intervention than in a criminal intervention, and the protections for the youth are likely to be less strong. For example, limits on how long a child can be held are likely to be more fluid than they would be under a 'definite sentence' form of youth criminal law.

The manner in which the child welfare or mental health systems of many provinces is administered may mean that young children who commit offences and who are under 12 years of age at the time are not dealt with adequately. It is easy to suggest that young children who offend should be dealt with outside of the criminal justice system. However, if there is a void, the question that one might wish to ask is whether the criminal justice system is better than no system at all? Bala and Mahoney (1994) reviewed, in the early 1990s, the various responses to criminal behaviour of children under 12, focusing on mental health and child welfare legislation. They *tentatively* conclude, 'that present legal responses are not totally adequate and serious consideration should be given to lowering the age of criminal responsibility to ten, with restrictions to ensure that a criminal response is used in an appropriate, restrained fashion. It must be recognized that merely changing the law will likely have little effect in terms of reducing criminal behaviour of children in this age group unless steps are also taken to ensure that appropriate services are available, services that recognize that children under 12 have different needs and capabilities from older youths and must be treated distinctly.' (ibid., pp. 44–5)

Nicholas Bala (1994, pp. 256–7) makes a similar point in another paper: 'The preferable approach for offending behaviour by children under 12 is for provinces to establish regimes that focus on their welfare, but provide for social protection through allowing long-term intervention in appropriate cases. To the extent that this has not happened, it may be necessary to consider a less satisfactory criminal response ... For offenders under 12, any youth justice response should be a last resort, with clear restrictions on removal from parental care, and provisions to ensure that these children are not placed with older offenders.'

Another question might be asked, however, if provincial child welfare resources are not adequate to respond to youths who offend at the moment (because, for example, they are focused primarily and understandably on children who themselves are at serious risk), do we have any reason to believe that a criminal system would be more effective in its response?

One of the serious problems with criminalizing behaviour of those under 12 years old is that it is almost certain that large numbers of very minor offenders would be brought into the criminal justice system. The data from 1983 presented in Table 3.5 suggest that we were not, in Canada, very successful in being selective in our use of the justice system for those under 12 years old.

Conclusion: The Trade-off

In the end, the age of criminal responsibility must be set arbitrarily with the knowledge that a 'trade-off' is involved. A very low age may satisfy those who favour punishment in most cases of transgressions and who mistakenly believe that control through the criminal justice system is the only, or even the primary, form of control available to the state. The irony is that a low age of criminal responsibility may also satisfy those who believe that the best way of connecting 'at risk' youths with social and psychological services is through the mechanism of a criminal charge. A low age of criminal responsibility may, conceivably, connect youths with service systems that are inadequately funded. The theory appears to be that by charging a youth, the justice system can connect the youth with needed services faster than would happen in the child welfare system. In effect, however, what a 'criminal justice' approach may be doing is simply jumping someone to the front of queue, thereby bumping to the back of the social service queue another youth who had not committed any offence. It would appear that a more sensible approach might be to provide adequate services for existing systems.

One might suggest that it is, in a sense, an admission of failure to make young children subject to criminal law control largely because no one is willing or able to intervene more appropriately. If one's goal is to attempt, at least at first, to find a way of avoiding future serious problems, a system in which the main tools are punishment appears to be a rather unimaginative approach to early delinquencies.

More importantly, the issue appears to be a question of *what* is done and what services are available. In the final analysis, it may be less important whether the law enabling intervention is criminal law created in Ottawa or child welfare law created separately in each province.

CHAPTER FOUR

The Nature of Youth Crime

When looking for the best way to respond to youth crime, or when trying to reduce the level of youth crime in a community, it is important to know exactly what one is dealing with. Solutions created to deal with one form of a problem may be inappropriate for dealing with other problems. Physicians, for example, do not generalize about 'disease' or 'injury.' They treat specific diseases and specific injuries. Surgery may be the best way of treating one condition; doing nothing may be the 'best practice' in dealing with another. When looking for ways in which society should respond to youth crime, then, it is necessary to respond to each problem as it presents itself.

What, then, do we mean when we talk about 'crime'? Clearly one way to think about what we mean by crime is to look at the definitions that exist in the Criminal Code. Another starting point might be to think about normal behaviour on the part of youth growing up. Let us think about two 'incidents' which might be called crime.

1 A 5-year-old gets mad at her mother who is putting her to bed early and throws something at her.
2 A 6-year-old takes a cookie out of a 'bulk store' bin and eats it. His father doesn't see him. The cookie is not paid for.

Both children know that what they have done is wrong. Both of these acts, if they were committed by older people, *could* be considered to be crime. Focusing on the legal definition of a crime or on the age of criminal responsibility can distract us from the decision process by which behaviour is defined as 'criminal.'

When trying to describe 'crime,' it is useful to think about the development of deviance or criminal behaviour in children. The National Longitudinal Survey of Children and Youth is a large national survey which began, in 1994–5, collecting data on a representative group of children across Canada, from birth to age 11. Every two years since then, Statistics Canada has returned to each child's family and collected additional data on his or her development. Part of the survey involves asking the person most knowledgeable about the young children (typically their mothers) about physically aggressive behaviour. From their data, we can get a picture of the development of early aggressiveness in a representative group of Canadian children. The authors of a report on a study of early aggressiveness point out: 'If physically aggressive behaviour is a phenomenon that develops over time as the effects of media, family adversity ... accumulate, we would expect older children to show more aggressive behaviour than young children ... However, if we assume that most children become better socialized as they grow older, we would expect that both boys and girls would become less aggressive as they age' (Tremblay et al., 1996, pp. 128–9).

It turns out that the results support the latter hypothesis:

> The physical aggression of boys and girls decreased in older age groups. Boys possessed higher physical aggression scores than girls in every age group, including the group of children age 2 to 3 years ... The age at which the largest proportion of children were reported by parents to 'sometimes' or 'often' 'hit, bite, or kick' was at 27–29 months. The frequency of this aggression then decreased steadily with age for both boys and girls. By the age of 11 years, less than 13.7% of boys and 8.3% of girls were reported to sometimes or often 'hit, bit, or kick' others ... These results suggest that the majority of children in Canada benefit from the socializing impact of their families and other socialization agents in their environments. (ibid., pp. 129–30)

We do not, of course, bring very young children into the justice system. It is useful to remember that youths, by the time they enter adolescence, are considerably less aggressive than they were earlier in their lives.

There are, unfortunately, some complexities in this idyllic picture. The first and most obvious one is that some youths persist into adolescence and adulthood in their level of aggressiveness. Moffitt (1993, 1997) has referred to this small group of youths – she estimates it to be fewer than 10 per cent of males – as 'life course persistent' antisocial offenders. She differentiates this small group of seriously aggressive children from a much larger group of youths who offend in adolescence. This second group is usually referred to as 'adolescent limited' offenders. As the term implies, the latter are youths whose offending behaviour begins and ends in adolescence. Their offending behaviour is largely limited to non-violent offences against property. 'Adolescent linked' offenders, Moffitt suggests, are normal adolescents who also do things that society considers to be offences.

Some evidence suggests that the development of a child into a 'life course persistent' offender is a result of a complex interaction between biological and social factors (Moffitt, 1993, 1997). This does not mean, however, that social factors are irrelevant to the development of a life course persistent offender. For boys, it would appear that being disadvantaged at birth (e.g., low birth weight) *and* during childhood combine to create a risk of early onset, life-course persistent antisocial behaviour. Hence, the adverse impact of low birth weight could be reduced or eliminated through social means. As one research study concluded: 'Supportive environments and early interventions stand a fighting chance at diminishing the consequences of birth-related difficulties, and such approaches may have an even more demonstrable impact on inner-city youths' (Tibbetts & Piquero, 1999, p. 869).

From the perspective of youth justice, both types of offenders are important. Clearly, life-course persistent delinquent behaviour needs to be addressed primarily from a preventive perspective. Adolescent limited delinquency, however, appears to be a product of normal development. A sensible youth justice system would, therefore, be premised on the understanding that most offenders who come in contact with it will grow out of their offending.

Measuring Youth Crime

If much youthful offending is a result of normal development, and if normal children tend to show aggressive behaviour that decreases over time, then it follows that the problem of measuring 'delinquency' in youths can be thought of as the problem of describing, in quantitative terms, much of what normal youths do. Normal youthful behaviour appears to involve acts like pushing, shoving, threatening, and minor acts of theft. The justice system, then, can hardly be expected to be adequate in describing the extent of these behaviours. One would not expect the records of the justice system to reflect most of what youths do, just as one would not expect health records to contain many of the less-serious colds, flu, or stomach disorders that many people experience in a year.

Measuring youth crime, then, is not straightforward. Nobody in our society has the job of measuring crime per se the way meteorologists measure rain. Instead, various people in our society collect *indicators* of crime. All of these indicators are imperfect. The reasons for this are easy to understand, once one realizes that the youth justice system can best be described as a set of institutions that respond to crime. What are loosely referred to as official 'crime statistics' are simply counts of events at different stages of the following process.

1 *An incident occurs.* Some crimes never get further than this in the process. Possession of prohibited drugs, for example, or impaired driving, may never be 'noticed' or thought of as crimes. A youth threatens another, but neither thinks of it as a crime.

2 *Someone must notice it.* A minor crime such as a scratch on a car or a broken window or a stolen item has to be noticed before it can be recorded. For example, the threat, 'If you say that again, I'll knock your head off' that one youth shouts at another is heard by a teacher.

3 *It must be defined as a crime.* Something can be damaged purposefully (a crime) or by accident; an item can be misplaced or stolen. The teacher decides that the threat she heard is serious. It is important to remember that identifying something as a crime does not mean that we know who has committed this act. The theft of something from a car is likely to be discovered long after the offender has left the scene. In cases of violent crimes, there is usually some knowledge of the offender (at least in terms of the offender's gender, and perhaps a rough idea of how many were involved and roughly speaking how old they were). But for much crime, the victim and, if it gets reported, the police, do not know, and never know who did it.

4 *Someone, often the victim, must successfully report the incident to the police.* In the 1999 Statistics Canada victimization survey (Besserer & Trainor, 2000), it was found that 63 per cent of assaults and 38 per cent of household break and enters or attempts were not reported to the police. Clearly, if crimes are not reported to the police, they cannot be counted by them. Thus, our first 'official' measure of crime does not include a large number of potential 'crimes.'

5 *The police must not only decide something is a crime, they must record it as such.* Many minor offences (e.g., minor vandalism or disturbances)

may be dealt with completely informally. The police may not record the minor incident since, from their perspective, there may be no reason to do so. In other instances, it will not be completely clear what the offence is. For example, an incident may fall easily into the broad category of 'assault.' But whether it is an assault causing bodily harm or an aggravated assault may not be clear from the victim's account. The decision is a discretionary one on the part of the police officer. Is a youth who threatens to 'knock your head off' and punches another youth in the face guilty of assault or attempted murder?

6 *A suspect may or may not be identified.* In many cases, the case will not go further than this, because the police may not have a suspect and therefore will not be able to charge anyone for the offence. Or if they have identified a suspect but not been able to locate this person, the case would not go further. In terms of 'standard' Canadian crime statistics, the incident might be recorded as an offence, but even if the victim named the suspect and that person was known to be age 12–17, it would not be recorded as a youth crime in the measures most commonly referred to as 'youth crime' statistics – youths charged with an offence, or cases in youth court.

7 *A suspect may or may not be charged.* If the police are able to identify and locate a suspect, they *may* then decide to charge this person with one or more offences that may or may not be the same as the offence (or offences) recorded described on the original incident report. If the suspect is a youth, this will be reported to the Canadian Centre for Justice Statistics (Statistics Canada) as a 'youth charged' with a particular offence. This measure is sometimes referred to as 'youths charged.' Its relationship with earlier stages of this process is problematic. As is described in Chapter 7, it is well established that many cases are screened out of the system by the police. Hence, there are many youths identified by the police but not charged. Changes in charging policy or practice at this stage can have a large impact on the number of 'youths charged' with offences.

8 *The offender will, presumably, be brought to court.* However, it is possible that the case will be referred to some form of alternative measures program. Depending on the jurisdiction, this could be a 'precharge' or a 'post-charge' decision. It is unclear whether youths referred for alternative measures after they are charged invariably remain in the 'youth court' data as having entered the court system. If a youth completes alternative measures, obviously a finding of guilt does not occur.

9 *A youth court 'case' is typically recorded for the youth entering the court system.* A count and description of these cases is important because it tells us about the cases we are processing in the formal court system.

10 *The accused person may or may not be found guilty of an offence.* Even if the youth is found guilty, it may or may not be for the offence that was originally charged.

Self-Report Measures of Offending by Youths

There are, of course, other ways of describing youth crime than relying on the police or the youth justice system. Criminologists, for example, have used 'self-report' measures of crime for quite some time. In these studies, young people are often asked to indicate (usually anonymously) whether they have committed any of a series of acts that could be considered to be criminal. The typical finding is that most young people commit crimes. For example, in a study of vandalism, it was found that 90 per cent of elementary school students and 89 per cent of high school students admitted to committing one or more act of vandalism in the year prior to being surveyed (Task Force on Vandalism, 1981).

Self-report studies of delinquency differ dramatically in the specificity of the questions that are asked. In general, the more specific and numerous the questions, the more offending will be reported. The study by Ontario's Task Force on Vandalism (1981) asked twenty-nine questions on vandalism alone. Thus, for example, if a youth is asked whether he or she damaged anyone's property, a certain portion will admit to damaging property. If, on the other hand, they are asked a set of specific questions about property damage (e.g., broken windows, scratched or otherwise damaged cars, limbs broken off trees, written graffiti on public or private property), a higher number of incidents will be reported overall. In general, these measures are useful as indicators of the *relative* levels of offending within a given study.

In a recent survey of over 3,000 Toronto high school students (Tanner & Wortley, 2002), the proportion of youths admitting having committed most of these acts in the year prior to being surveyed might be seen as being high, but was not dramatically different from rates obtained in other studies (see Table 4.1). Rates for males are higher in almost all instances, though the differences between males and females tends to be less in the less serious kinds of offences (e.g., theft of food or drink, minor thefts, using the public transit system without paying).

Table 4.1   Toronto high school students who report having engaged in various offences in their life and at least once in the past year (%)

Type of offence	At some time		Ten or more times		At least once in the past year	
	Female	Male	Female	Male	Female	Male
Breaking into automobile	4.4	14.4	1.1	4.4	2.2	8.0
Automobile theft	1.9	8.2	0.3	2.6	1.0	5.0
Bicycle theft	3.8	21.0	0.5	6.4	1.6	10.8
Break and enter home / business	2.9	10.8	0.1	2.9	1.4	6.5
Selling illegal drugs	8.1	19.0	3.1	10.9	6.2	15.5
Vandalism / property damage	31.0	51.9	2.7	11.7	21.4	31.8
Theft of food or drink	49.7	55.5	11.6	21.6	25.1	33.3
Other minor theft (under $50)	41.6	53.3	6.9	17.0	19.1	30.1
Other major theft (over $50)	10.9	23.6	2.2	8.6	5.1	14.5
Used transit without paying	42.7	47.8	7.8	18.0	25.4	32.7
Computer hacking	5.6	20.6	1.0	7.2	3.8	14.8
Used false identification	20.3	29.5	6.5	14.8	16.1	24.4
Begged for money	5.0	4.5	0.9	0.7	2.7	3.3
Squeegeed	0.9	2.3	0.4	1.0	0.4	1.6
Had sex for money	0.8	3.3	0.2	1.0	0.5	2.6
Graffiti / 'tagged' property	22.9	28.2	4.0	9.2	13.2	17.2

Source: Tanner and Wortley, 2002.

The general point illustrated by the data in Table 4.1 is that it is quite common for youths to do things that could be considered to be criminal offences. In 2002, for example, almost one-third (32.7 per cent) of the males in this survey and a quarter of the females (25.4 per cent) had used a transit system without paying.

Regional Variation in Youthful Offending

If one is interested in comparing 'youth crime rates' for different parts of the Canadian population, self-report measures such as these are probably the best available indicator. As we will see in detail in Chapters 7 and 9, there are large differences among provinces in the rate at which young persons are brought to court and, subsequently, placed in custody. The suggestion is sometimes made that these reflect provincial differences in rates of *offending* rather than differences in the manner in which the provincial justice systems respond to offending by youth.

Table 4.2   Regional variation in self-reported delinquency among 12 and 13-year-olds

	Region	Level of delinquency, %			
		None	Some	A lot	Total (*n*)
Violent offending	Atlantic	60	28	12	100 (469)
	Quebec	68	23	9	100 (378)
	Ontario	55	32	12	100 (499)
	Prairies	47	39	14	100 (462)
	B.C.	60	31	9	100 (144)
Property offending	Atlantic	68	23	8	100 (461)
	Quebec	68	19	13	100 (373)
	Ontario	63	28	9	100 (494)
	Prairies	61	27	12	100 (456)
	B.C.	69	24	8	100 (144)

Source: Sprott et al., 2001, Table 2.

In the National Longitudinal Study of Children and Youth, youths from age 10 onwards fill out a confidential report about their own behaviour and feelings. Looking at the delinquency reports of children aged 12 and 13 across the country (see Table 4.2), it is clear that there is some regional variation. However, this variation is minor compared to the variation in the kinds of cases going to youth court (described in more detail in Chapter 7).

Victimization Surveys

Another method of obtaining a description of crimes committed by youths is to examine directly the experiences of victims. As has been shown in a number of contexts, victimization surveys (such as those carried out by Statistics Canada approximately every five years, most recently in 1999) can provide extremely useful information about crime and the victimization experience. They also illustrate, as noted above, one of the problems in using official measures (e.g., police or court statistics) to assess the nature and extent of youth crime: Many victimizations are not reported to the police.

Residents of Canada are apparently very cooperative in telling Statistics Canada about their own personal victimizations. Although we can, through victimization surveys, estimate the incidence and prevalence of

Table 4.3   Age of offender as reported by Canadian victims, age 15 and older (%)

Estimated age of the offender (years)	Victimizations apparently committed by this age group	Canadian population (age 12 or older) of this age
≤ 17	23	9
18–24	29	11
25–34	23	17
≥ 35	25	63
Total	100	100

Note: Multiple offender incidents are characterized by the apparent age of the youngest offender.
Source of crime data: CCJS, 2000, General Social Survey, GSS-13.

specific crimes, we often do not know whether they were perpetrated by a youth or by an adult. Only in those cases where the victim was present is it possible for the victim to estimate the age of the offenders. These data are, however, worth looking at since they give a picture of offenders from the perspective of ordinary victims, even though this perspective may not lead to a representative picture of offenders.

Table 4.3 demonstrates that, in comparison with the portion of the Canadian population that is age 12 and higher, young people are identified as offenders by victims (age 15 and over) in a disproportionately high number of criminal victimizations.

Two things are apparent from the data in Table 4.3. First, those 35 years old and older are, as one might expect, not likely to be identified as offenders. They constitute 63 per cent of the Canadian population age 12 or over, but are described by victims as being responsible for only 25 per cent of the incidents. Young offender–age youths (those 17 and under) on the other hand, are considerably more likely to be involved as offenders than their portion of the population would suggest. Young offender–age youths constitute 9 per cent of the Canadian population that is above age 12 but are identified by victims as being the offender in 23 per cent of the incidents. However, the young offender rate is no higher, relatively speaking, than that of young adults, age 18 to 24. In fact, in a way, this table overestimates the rela-

Table 4.4   Relationship between age of the victim and the victim's estimate of the offender's age (in single-offender incidents) or youngest offender's age (in multiple offender incidents), given as a percentage

| Estimated age of the offender | Age of victim (years) | | | | Total (n) |
	15–17	18–24	25–34	≥ 35	
17 or younger	45	22	13	20	100 (739)
18 or older	8	32	28	33	100 (2,477)

Source for crime data: CCJS 2000, General Social Survey, GSS-13.

tive involvement of young offenders in crime, because in the case of multiple offenders involved in a criminal incident only the youngest is contained in the table. It underestimates the rate of involvement of young offenders in another way, however, since those under age 15 were not part of the survey. Young offenders, may be involved in a good bit of crime, but perhaps not more so than young adults.

These same data can be used to examine the relationship between the age of the offender and the age of the victim. Table 4.4 should be read as follows. There were 739 incidents with an offender estimated to be age 17 or younger. In 45 per cent of these incidents, the victim was aged 15 to 17. There were 2,477 incidents where the offender was estimated to be 18 or older. In only 8 per cent of these incidents was the victim between 15 and 17. Young people, it would seem from the reports of victims, are likely to victimize other young people. Older offenders, not surprisingly, victimize older people. Older people may be afraid of youths, but it would appear that they really should focus their fear on people closer to their own ages.

Police Statistics about Crime

We have already noted that many offences do not get reported to the police. Hence, those committing these unreported offences are unlikely to appear in official statistics about crime. But even if a crime is reported to the police, this does not mean that the report is of much use in describing youth crime. An obvious problem in using police statistics as a measure of youth crime is that the proportion of crimes 'cleared' by the police (i.e., crimes where the police are satisfied that they have a suspect) not only varies enormously, but in some cases is quite low. In the case of vandalism, only 34 per cent of incidents in which individual Canadians are the victims got reported to the police in 1999 (Besserer & Trainor, 2000). In that same year (1999), only 18 per cent of vandalism incidents are labelled as 'cleared' by the police (CCJS, 2000). In the case of household break-and-enters, 17.5 per cent of the cases reported to the police are 'cleared' by the police. In crimes against persons, substantially more are cleared. In about 73 per cent of cases, the police are able to name a suspect; in sexual assaults (only about 10 per cent of which are reported to the police in the first place), the police are able to name a suspect in about 65 per cent of the cases. In homicides the police are able to name a suspect in a very high proportion (75 per cent) of the cases.

One other rather simple artifact makes youths appear to be more responsible for crime than they probably are. Compared with adults apparently committing the same crime, it appears that youths are more likely to be apprehended. Snyder (1999) examined data on robbery in seven U.S. states. Using details of robbery incidents reported by the police, Snyder found, not surprisingly, that robberies apparently involving juvenile offenders were more likely than robberies involving only adults to have more than one offender. Hence, for any given robbery, those involving youths provide the police with more possible suspects than do robberies involving adult offenders. Moreover, a sophisticated analysis showed that 'controlling for other incident characteristics, these data find that juvenile robbery offenders are 32% more likely to be arrested than are adult robbery offenders' (ibid., p. 157). In other words, one reason that the justice system may overestimate the proportion of crime committed by youths is that youths are more likely than adults to get caught. Snyder concluded that 'both juvenile arrest and clearance statistics over-represent the juvenile responsibility for robbery in the United States ... This bias may have increased in recent years as a result of a the intense national focus on juvenile violence and the related increase in law enforcement attention to juvenile violent crime' (ibid., p. 160). The study demonstrates how cautious one has to be in interpreting reports of crime or arrests as they are contained in official records of crime.

Police Discretion

If an offence is reported to the police, and a youth is apprehended by the police for apparently committing the offence, that does not necessarily mean that a charge is laid by the police. In the case of young people, the decision not to charge is specifically mentioned as an option in the Young Offenders Act. Section 3(d) indicates that 'where it is not inconsistent with the protection of society, taking no measures or taking measures other than judicial proceedings under this Act should be considered for dealing with young persons who have committed offences.' Even before the Young Offenders Act became law, it was well established that many offences that came to the attention of the police did not end up in court (Conly, 1978; Doob & Chan, 1982).

The Youth Criminal Justice Act strengthens considerably the policy to reduce the reliance on the youth court. It provides a number of different options other than the court to hold the youth accountable for his or her actions. Thus, it is not surprising that the Youth Criminal Justice Act states that 'a police officer *shall*, before starting judicial proceedings under this Act against a young person alleged to have committed an offence, consider whether it would be sufficient ... to take no further action [or use one of a number of other non-court actions]' (Section 6(1), emphasis added). Besides requiring police to consider whether it is necessary to take a youth to court, the Youth Criminal Justice Act provides rather clear guidance to police which, in effect, encourages non-court approaches to offending youth. Measures outside of the formal court system ('extrajudicial measures') such as warnings or referrals to community programs are 'presumed to be adequate to hold a young person accountable for his or her offending behaviour if the young person has committed a non-violent offence and has previously not been found guilty of an offence' (Section 4(d)). The youth justice system has tended to focus on the youth's background of offending at least as much as the offence. Thus, it is important that the new law states that non-court alternatives can be used, even if they have been used before, and even if the youth has been found guilty on a previous occasion (Section 4(d)). If the offence is minor, and non-court approaches 'are adequate' to hold the youth accountable, then the law states that they should be used. All of this means that, if the legislation is followed, fewer, and perhaps somewhat different, cases will be brought to court. These changes are more likely to reflect the youth justice system than they are to reflect the behaviour of Canadian youths.

Under the Young Offenders Act, in all provinces and territories except Ontario, youths could also be dealt with by way of somewhat more formal 'Alternative Measures' (under Section 4 of the Young

Offenders Act) *before* they were charged. Hence, for these provinces, the only way that one can easily determine how many youths were apprehended for offences is by looking at police reports. Whether or not a young person whose offences are disposed of by way of alternative measures is recorded in the court statistics apparently depends on the procedure in place in that location for dealing with youths under that section of the Young Offenders Act. The Youth Criminal Justice Act includes the possibility of these more formal measures, though they are now called Extrajudicial Sanctions.

The result of these discretionary decisions is that records of offending collected from police ('youths charged') statistics or youth court statistics cannot give us an accurate view of the amount of crime committed by youth. We have noted that there are simply too many places where substantial amounts of youth crime are not captured by the statistics. We are not being critical of *any* of these statistical measures. They give important descriptive information about the operation of the youth justice system. Each set of statistics has very important purposes, but these purposes are limited.

The difficulty is, of course, that when one looks at, or reads in the newspaper, statistics about 'youth crime' the most readily available statistics about youth crime simply *do not* describe youth crime. Instead, they give a picture of the *end* of the filtering process, rather than the beginning. Many people have made decisions about whether a case should get into court. And, of course, the data are quite clear: those cases in court are not, and should not be, representative of all youth crime. Most people would probably agree that only a subset of youth accused of crime should go to court. And most people would probably agree that the most serious cases, for example, those involving serious violence or those where the offender persists in criminal activity, are good candidates for court. As we will see later in this chapter, however, most cases now going to court are relatively minor.

The problem is that police statistics and youth court statistics are the data most easily available. Hence, for example, in some of the debates that took place in the three years that the Youth Criminal Justice Act was before Parliament, there were assertions, from time to time, that the 'Quebec system' of youth justice was 'more effective' in dealing with youth and that Quebec, as a result has a 'lower youth crime' rate. The evidence that was typically alluded to Quebec's effectiveness was that few cases, relative to the rest of Canada, are brought to court in Quebec. The evidence that the 'Quebec system' has a lower crime rate was, typically, that fewer cases are brought to court. Thus, the statement that 'the Quebec system is more effective in reducing youth crime than youth justice systems elsewhere in Canada' is often, in reality, a statement that 'The lower rate of use of youth court in Quebec results in a lower use of youth court.' We are not suggesting that there is anything wrong with a reduced use of the youth court for young offenders. In fact, our own view would be that Quebec is being sensible in its parsimonious use of the youth court. That is quite different, however, from suggesting that the limited use of youth court in Quebec, as compared to the rest of Canada, reflects lower youth crime rates in that province.

As we have already seen (Table 4.2), self-report data for violent crime among 12- and 13-year-olds *do* suggest that Quebec rates are lower than those in other regions of Canada. This, we would suggest, is more likely a function of Quebec social policies having to do with young people *before* they turn 12 than of policies concerning young offenders who, by definition, are over 12. Violent offending by youths age 12 to 18 is almost certainly more a reflection of the experiences of these youth in their first 12 years of life than it is of the characteristics of their youth justice system. Programs that support youth (as we will see in Chapter 11) may well be effective in reducing violence. To the extent that property crime among youth is largely the responsibility of 'adolescent limited' offenders, it is noteworthy that Quebec rates of property offenses for the youngest young offender–age youths are comparable to or higher than the rates in the rest of Canada.

The important point here is to be wary of the implication that youth court or police data reflect ordinary youth crime.

Youth Court Statistics

In addition to these problems, one has to consider that the number of youths charged and going to court may not reflect the number of incidents. Two or more youths may be charged with a single incident. For example, in 1999–2000 sixty-seven youths entered the court system where the most serious charge was a homicide offence, but there could easily, in some cases, have been two youths charged in connection with a homicide involving one victim. Similarly, a single youth could be charged with one or more offences (e.g., the murder of two people) or a youth could be charged with a variety of offences. A 'case' in youth court (the normal unit of count) is defined as a set of one or more charges against a single individual entering a court on the same day. Two co-accused youths, then, constitute two separate cases, even if they were to be tried together in youth court. The youth court case will typically be described in terms of its most serious charge. Hence, the youth appearing in court facing charges of aggravated assault and breaking and entering will be described only in terms of the assault, whether the charges arose out of the same or different incidents.

Youth court data tables (CCJS, 2001b), then, describe in a reasonable and fairly straightforward way the cases that come to court. The relationship, however, to steps lower down in the 'official statistics' process is, obviously, much less than perfect.

Multiple Offending by Youths

It should be clear that 'counting' youth crime by looking at either the number of youths who are charged by the police or at youth court figures – that is, at offences that have passed the first seven stages in the statistics-compiling-process outlined earlier in this chapter – is problematic, in large part because changes in decision practices for the earlier steps can dramatically affect what happens at these latter stages. Another way in which youth crime is over-estimated, relative to adult crime, is something that has already been alluded to: youths are more likely to offend in groups than are older people. Young people tend to want to spend a lot of their free time with other young people. Not surprisingly, they also tend to commit offences when together. Youths reporting acts of vandalism, for example, indicated that about 64 per cent of the acts of vandalism were committed with friends (Task Force on Vandalism, 1981, p. 252).

One incomplete measure of the greater tendency of youths as compared to adults to offend in groups comes from victimization surveys. In the 1999 Statistics Canada victimization survey (CCJS, 2000), victims of crimes were asked how many offenders there were. When one looks at the victims' responses to this question as a function of the victim's estimate of the age of the youngest offender (or the only offender, if there was only one offender), it is evident that youths, much more than adults, are likely to offend in groups.

In looking at Table 4.5, it is important to remember that for many victimizations, no offenders were seen by the victim and therefore estimates of the offenders' ages were not reported. Even though they are obviously estimates, the data support the conclusion that young offenders are dramatically more likely to commit crimes in groups

Table 4.5 Relationship between the number of offenders reported by victim as being involved in a criminal incident and the age of the youngest (or only) offender, given as a percentage

Estimated age of youngest offender (years)	Number of offenders				
	1	2	3	≥ 4	Total (n)
17 and under	52	14	11	24	100 (727)
18–24	72	10	6	12	100 (927)
25–34	86	9	2	3	100 (749)
35 and older	94	5	<1	<1	100 (797)

Source for crime data: CCJS 2000, General Social Survey, GSS-13.

than are older offenders. For young offenders there were four or more offenders in almost one-quarter (24 per cent) of the cases. If 'three makes a group and four makes a gang,' it is not surprising that young people who offend will often be described as being in a gang. If all of those who were involved in the commission of a particular offence were to be apprehended and charged, therefore youths would tend to be over-represented in court relative to the number of offences they commit. Older offenders seem to be able to commit crimes alone that youths would prefer to do in groups.

In addition, when older people commit offences in gangs (e.g., the accountants at Arthur Andersen, or the managers at Enron or World-Com), they typically are not described as a gang. Apparently a 'gang of accountants' does not conjure up the fear that a gang of adolescents does. The term 'swarming,' for example, is sometimes applied to groups of youths who commit thefts or robberies in groups conjuring up the image, perhaps of a swarm of killer bees. The unsecured creditors of WorldCom, however, were not described as having been 'swarmed' by a gang of senior WorldCom executives when WorldCom's CEO reported that the company that he heads had 'uncovered an additional $3.3 billion in improperly reported earnings from 1999 and 2000' (Sidgmore, 2002) – additional to an equivalent amount previously 'uncovered' as having been reported inaccurately. Apparently illegal behaviour by youths is described in terms such as 'gangs' and 'swarming' when it involves tens or hundreds of dollars, but illegal behaviour ('improper' behaviour, one should perhaps say) by their elders involving billions of dollars is not.

From the victimization surveys, it would appear that the age groups of those who offend in groups tend to be relatively homogeneous. In 45 per cent of the incidents involving two or more offenders where the youngest offender was identified by the victim as being under 18 years old, the oldest offender was also identified as being under 18. What is more important, however, is that in an additional 47 per cent of these group incidents involving at least one youth, the oldest offender was described by the victim as being between 18 and 24 years old. In other words, in 92 per cent of the groups of offenders that included at least one youth, the oldest offender was estimated as being no more than 24 years old. Young people, when they do offend in groups, tend to do so with people roughly their own age.

A largely similar picture comes from a detailed study of group offending based on police (Revised Uniform Crime Reporting) data from across Canada during the 1990s. Carrington (2002), looking at incidents where people were identified by the police as offenders, notes that the proportion of incidents that involved multiple offenders was only 24.5 per cent when the offender (or oldest co-offender) was between 12 and 17 years old. However, for incidents where the oldest co-offender in the incident was 18 or over, multiple offenders were involved in only 9.3 per cent of incidents. These figures, as he points out, give a lower estimate of group offending by youth than many other studies. There are various reasons why these studies might differ on the absolute level of co-offending among youth. However, the generalization that co-offending is more likely among youth clearly still holds. The likelihood of co-offending appears to be approximately equal for males and females. Generally speaking, co-offending seems to peak at about age 10 and drops off dramatically until offenders are in their mid-20s, at which point it levels off. This pattern holds for most types of offences. In other words, for almost all types of offences co-offending is higher for children and adolescents and lower for adults. Carrington (2002, p. 303) points out: 'This result strongly suggests that, for most crimes, co-offending is not determined by the functional requirements of the type of crime: common crimes such as robbery, burglary, possession of stolen property, theft, etc., can apparently be committed just as well by lone offenders as by groups of different sizes, and the involvement of a group is consistently associated with younger offenders. Thus, the developmental theory of group crime is supported over the functional theory.'

How Should We Interpret the Picture of Youth Crime That We Get from Looking at the Kinds of Cases That Go to Youth Court?

We will be discussing the question of 'youth crime trends' in more detail in Chapter 6. What is necessary to remember at this point is that as we change our assessments of what *should* go to court, it is likely that the police, being generally responsive to the public's assessment of what is and is not serious, will change the 'mix' of cases going to court. For example, in one small-scale study carried out in Toronto of young offenders age 12 through 15 (Doob & Meen, 1993), it was found that in 1982–4 (the last years of the Juvenile Delinquents Act) 7.7 per cent of the cases before the Toronto juvenile court involved violence. In the first couple of years of dealing with young people under the Young Offenders Act, the proportion of cases involving violence was 10.1 per cent. By the end of that decade (1989–90), however, the proportion of violent cases in the Toronto courts had risen to 23.8 per cent. In 1999–2000 across Canada, the proportion of cases entering the youth courts that were 'violent' (22.5 per cent) was quite similar to the Toronto figures from a decade earlier.

How is the apparent increase that took place in the first few years of the Young Offenders Act to be interpreted? One could interpret it as reflecting changes in the kinds of offences that young people commit; but the data could reflect changing standards of how much violence is acceptable or of what constitutes violence: the point at which a fight becomes an assault, or the point at which a verbal threat becomes a crime may have changed. Therefore, it would be simplistic to assume, without further evidence, that this increase in cases coming to court reflected a parallel increase in the underlying behaviour of youths in Canada. A good portion of this change likely has to do with shifting public and police values about what is important to take to court.

Violence obviously is an important public concern. It is reasonable to expect that the police would be responsive to these concerns and bring more violence to court. However, to understand even what goes to youth court, one must look at these cases reasonably carefully. Table 4.6 shows data for the most serious ('principal') charge facing youths entering the youth courts in Canada during 1999–2000. These data are obviously more important as a measure of the kinds of cases that are brought to the youth justice system than as a measure of the kinds of things that Canada's 2.45 million youths age 12 to 17 do in a given year. However, a careful examination of the cases that are brought to court reveals that many of them are not very serious. Of the cases going to youth court, 43 per cent involve minor property offences (19 per cent of all cases have minor thefts or possession of stolen property as the only or the most serious charge), or they involve 'administration of justice' offences (24 per cent have failure to appear in court or failure to comply with a disposition – apparently, the most common 'disposi-

Table 4.6   Types of offences (principal charge) in
youth court cases, Canada, 1999–2000

	Cases in court n (%)
Theft under $5,000	14,514 (14)
Possession of stolen property	4,738 (5)
Failure to appear	11,078 (11)
Failure to comply with a disposition	13,517 (13)
Subtotal	43,847 (43)
Other thefts	4,536 (4)
Mischief/damage	5,103 (5)
Break and enter	10,285 (10)
Minor assault	10,235 (10)
Total: Sum of 8 offences	74,006 (73)
All cases	102,061 (100)

Source: Canadian Centre for Justice Statistics, 2001.

tion' not to follow is a probation order). To repeat, 43 per cent of the
cases going to youth court involve only a relatively minor offence. As
Table 4.6 shows, almost three-quarters of all cases going to youth court
in Canada involve a small number of *relatively* less serious offences.

Obviously, some very serious offences do end up in youth court.
Table 4.7 examines these. What is notable about the serious categories
of offences (e.g., assault or sexual assault) is that the less serious types
of offences are much more common than are the more serious cases.
For example, there were 10,235 common assaults, but only 415 aggravated assaults, entering the court system.

It is also clear that findings of guilt (or transfers of these matters to
adult court) are even more rare for very serious violent offences than
they are for the less serious offences. Youths sometimes do commit
very serious offences, and they do get found guilty for these offences.
But it is important to recognize that serious violent offences are relatively rare.

Table 4.7 shows that there were 102,061 cases brought to youth court
in Canada in 1999–2000. Guilty findings were registered in 68,236. Violent cases constituted 22.5 per cent of all of the cases that went to court
and 20.2 per cent of the cases where a finding of guilt was registered.

Table 4.7   Violent cases by type of offence that went to court and where offender was found guilty or transferred to adult court (number, and in parentheses, percentage for this type of case)

	Cases to court	Cases found guilty or transferred
All cases	102,061 (100)	68,236 (100)
Violent cases	22,937 (22.5)	13,808 (20.2)
Homicide	67 (0.07)	38 (0.06)
Attempted murder	66 (0.06)	8 (0.01)
Sexual assault (I)	1,313 (1.3)	620 (0.91)
Sexual assault causing bodily harm / weapon	53 (0.05)	18 (0.03)
Aggravated sexual assault	5 (<0.01)	2 (<0.01)
Common assault	10,235 (10.0)	6,572 (9.6)
Assault causing bodily harm / weapon	4,479 (4.4)	2,496 (3.7)
Aggravated assault	415 (0.41)	188 (0.28)
Robbery	3,109 (3.0)	1,921 (2.8)
All other violent offences	3,195 (3.1)	1,945 (2.9)

Source: Canadian Centre for Justice Statistics, 2001.

Serious violent cases, either going to court or where the youth was found guilty, constituted a very small minority of all cases. For example, fewer than one-half of 1 per cent of all cases going to court involved aggravated assault (0.41 per cent of all cases), and an even smaller percentage of the cases where a guilty finding was registered had aggravated assault as the most serious charge (0.28 per cent). Robbery, another offence which can involve serious threats of violence, constitutes only 3 per cent of the cases coming to court and 2.8 per cent of the cases involving a finding of guilty. Common assault, the most serious charge in about 10 per cent of cases, typically involves the use of force where no bodily injury occurred, and therefore while it is violent, typically it is not considered to be a serious violent offence.

It is plausible to assume, based on research on the police (e.g., Carrington, 1998; Doob & Chan, 1982; Conly, 1978), that the police are more likely to charge serious offenders than minor offenders. These data, then, suggest that serious offences are very rare.

The youth court data for 1999–2000 should be interpreted with the number 2.45 million in mind. This is the number of youths age 12 to 17 in Canada for that year. Hence, in noting that 415 youths were charged in 1999–2000 with aggravated assault, we should keep in mind that this is 415 out of 2.45 million.

Finally, it is worth observing that about two-thirds of cases brought to youth court involve a finding of guilt for one or more offences. For cases entering court involving violence, only about 60 per cent result in a finding of guilt. For very serious cases (e.g., homicide, attempted murder, aggravated sexual assault, and aggravated assault), however, the number of cases with guilty findings is somewhat lower than this. For example, there were sixty-six cases that entered the court structure with attempted murder as the principal charge, but only eight cases in which a guilty finding was registered with this as the most serious charge of conviction. Hence, the 'charge' and 'bringing to court' statistics tend to show youths as more involved in violent crime (especially serious violent crime) than do the 'findings of guilt' statistics.

Gender

One of the strongest and most consistent correlates with offending is the gender of the offender. As shown earlier in this chapter (see Table 4.1), on self-report measures, girls typically report lower levels of offending than do boys. The same pattern holds for cases going to court. What is most interesting is that within categories of offences (e.g., violence) girls are less likely to be involved in serious forms of violence. The offending patterns in court statistics, for a selected number of offences, are shown in Table 4.8.

Two sets of conclusions might be drawn from Table 4.8. First, for each of the offences (or categories of offences) listed, girls are involved in a minority of the cases going to court. Girls constitute about half (49 per cent) of the young offender age population. In none of these offences do they account for half of the offences. Second, within each category of offence (e.g., violence), the more serious the offence, the greater the under-representation of girls. For example, for the most serious violent offences (murder, manslaughter, attempted murder, and aggravated assault), girls account for 12 to 15 per cent of the cases going to youth court. For the least serious violent offence (minor assault), girls constitute 31 per cent of the cases. For property offences, the same relationships hold. Girls are the accused in only 9 per cent and 11 per cent of the cases of theft over $5,000 and cases of breaking and entering respectively. They account for 27 per cent of the minor theft cases. Finally, girls are relatively rarely involved in cases of escaping custody (14 per cent of the cases involve girls), but are relatively more likely to be involved in the less serious administration of justice cases (failure to appear or breach of a term of a disposition).

Table 4.8   Relationship between girls accused in a case and the severity of the principal offence charged, Canada, 1999–2000

Offence	Accused in the case	
	Girl n (%)	Boy
All cases	21,507 (21)	80,554
Break and enter	1,052 (10)	9,233
Theft over $5,000	143 (9)	1,510
Theft under $5,000	3,886 (27)	10,628
All property offences	7,622 (19)	33,500
Murder, manslaughter	8 (12)	59
Attempted murder	9 (14)	57
Aggravated assault	62 (15)	353
Assault with weapon or causing bodily harm	822 (18)	3,657
Minor assault	3,167 (31)	7,068
All violent offences	4,913 (21)	18,024
Escape custody	107 (14)	663
Failure to comply with a disposition	3,502 (26)	10,015
Failure to appear	3,094 (28)	7,984

Source: Canadian Centre for Justice Statistics, 2001b.

It should be noted that there is also a problem when comparing 'percentage changes' of groups with different initial base rates. As Sprott and Doob (2003) point out, in the context of an analysis of gender differences in crime trends during the 1990s,

Both boys and girls saw increases in YOA offences. There have been speculations of gender discrimination with the increasing proportions of girls in YOA offences (failure to comply with a disposition in particular) compared to boys (see Reitsma-Street 1999). However, it is not clear that girls have seen larger increases in this offence than boys. If one looks that the percent increase, girls have seen a larger increase than boys have. In 1991/2 girls were found guilty of YOA offences at a rate of 14.1 per 10,000 and in 2000 they were found guilty at a rate of 23.4 per 10,000 – a 66% increase. Boys, on the other hand, were found guilty of YOA offences at a rate of 45.2 per 10,000 in 1991/2 and in 2000 they were found guilty at a rate of 64.3 per 10,000 – a 42% increase. However, percentage increases or decreases can be misleading if the starting points are different. A different way of examining this, then, would be to look at the rate change over time – girls saw a rate increase of 9.3 (14.1 to 23.4) in YOA offences while boys saw a rate increase of 19.1 (45.2 to 64.3).

Whether one says that the rate of finding girls guilty is increasing more substantially than the rate of finding boys guilty depends on the denominator one uses. (pp. 78–9)

The lesson from this illustration is clear: one has to look carefully at the data that are presented to know what 'crime' measures or changes in crime rates really mean.

Conclusion

There is no direct way of measuring crime. Official crime statistics – such as the number of youths charged or the number or type of cases going to court – give an indication of the kinds of matters that are receiving criminal justice processing, but, because they are the result of discretionary decisions, they should not be seen as direct measures of 'crime' as such. For example, since many crimes are not reported to the police and many of the crimes that are reported are never solved, an 'offender' is never identified.

Changes in the apparent level of youth crime, a topic to be further explored in Chapter 6, may reflect changes in the behaviour of youths (e.g., changes in their rates of offending or in the manner in which they offend), or they may reflect changes in the decisions of adults on whether to charge a youth who is apprehended.

One of the problems in 'counting' youth crime is that youths, much more than older people, tend to offend in groups. It would appear that youths are more likely to be apprehended for offending than are older people. Relative to their offending, youths may be over-represented in official 'crime' statistics.

Nevertheless, when victims are able to identify the people who victimized them, the information they provide suggests that young offenders (those 17 and under) and young adults (those 17 to 24 years old) are over-represented among offenders. Victims age 15 to 17 are much more likely than older victims to identify another young person as the person who victimized them. Generally speaking, it would appear that young people victimize those who are close to them in age.

Eight offences or groups of offences account for almost three-quarters of the cases going to court. None of these involve serious violence. Within the category of cases involving 'violence,' the statistics make obvious that those youths who are apprehended by the youth justice system are dramatically more likely to be charged with minor than major forms of violence.

When youths are asked about their own offending behaviour, many admit to at least some offending in their lives. Most of this offending is, however, relatively minor in nature. As we have already noted, much of this offending is done in groups.

It is important to remember the process by which youth court statistics are created. The most commonly used statistics on youth crime – police reports of 'youths charged' and youth court statistics – are much more important as indications of discretion to charge youths and take them to court than as measures of crime.

CHAPTER FIVE

Youth Crime, Special Issues: Gangs, Schools, and Recidivists

In Chapter 4 we presented an overview of what we know about 'youth crime' in Canada. The picture that emerges is of a substantial amount of minor offending, combined with a small proportion of serious offences. In this chapter we examine three parts of the youth crime picture: gangs, recidivism, and crime in schools. We have grouped them in one chapter for a very simple reason: It appears that these aspects of youth crime, along with violence (covered in more detail in Chapter 6) receive special attention when concern is raised about the general issue of youth crime. They have been the focus of much attention and debate in the past decade. Equally important, these areas are likely to be less well understood than are other aspects of youth crime.

Groups and Gangs

In Chapter 4 we noted that youths, much more than adults, are likely to offend in groups. It is important, therefore, not to equate offending in groups with 'gangs.' If one defines a gang as a relatively stable, somewhat organized, group with clear or formal leadership, most groups of young people that commit offences do not qualify as 'gangs.' Citing large numbers of studies, Reiss (1988) notes that 'offending groups are often treated as synonymous with gangs, the gang being territorially organized, age-graded peer group engaged in a wide range of activities and having a well-defined leadership. Most persons who engage in delinquency are not members of such highly structured groups' (p. 120). Reiss goes on to point out that 'offenders' criminal histories ordinarily are characterized by a mix of different types of offences and by a mix of offences committed alone and with accomplices.'

LeBlanc and Fréchette (1989) note that their data, from Montreal, 'show that the accomplishment of the crime is the work of micro-groups, flexible and transient; it is not the result of organized gangs in most cases.' They point out that the accomplices vary from criminal event to criminal event, but that, as with other more acceptable behaviour, the groups of young people tend to be roughly the same age.

We are not suggesting that gangs per se do not exist. Clearly, they do. In the United States, many cities have, from time to time, been faced with quite organized and territorially defined gangs. Although they tend to be less well studied in Canada, they also have existed in some of our cities. However, it is likely that *as a phenomenon*, gangs change over time and across cities (Spergel, 1990); they also may not account for a large portion of youth crime.

The problem of definition is illustrated in a survey of 5,935 Grade 8 students in forty-two schools (315 classrooms) in eleven American cities (Esbensen, Winfree, He, & Taylor, 2001). Differences in definition are important, as can be seen from the following proportions describing youth who under various definitions, may be considered to be 'gang members.'

- 17 per cent report ever being in a gang
- 9 per cent report currently being in a gang
- 8 per cent report being in a gang that does delinquent things
- 5 per cent report being in 'organized' gangs that have leaders, symbols, and initiation rights
- 2 per cent define themselves as being 'core' members of organized gangs

A similar range of definitions of gang membership was developed in a study of Vancouver gangs (Gordon, 2000). In Vancouver gangs have been seen as a significant social problem for over fifty years. It appears, at least in British Columbia, that many of the members of groups identified as gangs drifted into 'membership' just as young people 'drift' into membership in other groups like the Boy Scouts. 'The availability of choices is a key to understanding a person's involvement in gangs. If an individual has no access to, or is not encouraged to join, a mainstream group, an 'illegitimate' group may be chosen instead' (ibid., p. 43). The author of the Vancouver study suggests that the phenomenon of the gang should be 'viewed along a continuum ranging from groups of friends who spend time together and who occasionally get

Table 5.1   Current and former gang members reporting that they have engaged in various activities within
the gang context (*N* = 377)

Activity	%
Sold illegal drugs	39.3
Used alcohol and/or illegal drugs	56.2
Engaged in property crime	39.5
Fought against other gangs	56.8
Used the gang for protection	77.5
Played sports together	64.2
Socialized or hung out	82.8
Went to parties or clubs	73.2

Source: Tanner and Wortley, 2002.

into trouble, to more serious, organized criminal groups or gangs'
(ibid., p. 44).

Gordon's study examined all of those people in custody or on probation in the Vancouver area who were identified by correctional personnel as being or having been involved in gangs. The problem, however,
is that 'small groups of offenders were being referred to as 'gangs' when
the members of these groups did not see themselves that way' (ibid., p.
47). Indeed, the 'names' of gangs were sometimes imposed on a group
of offenders by the news media even when the members did not consider themselves to be a gang, but rather saw themselves as a group of
friends who sometimes offended. Excluding these cases, there were also
some 'real' gangs. The most organized ones might be described as being
'criminal business organizations' which consist largely of adults who
'engage in criminal activity primarily for economic reasons and almost
invariably maintain a low profile' (ibid., p. 48). 'Street gangs,' on the
other hand, consist mainly of young adults and perceive themselves as
a gang and acknowledge membership. 'Wanna-be gangs' are loosely
structured groups who engage in impulsive criminal activity (including
violence) and want to be seen as a gang.

In a very recent study of youthful offending in Toronto (Tanner &
Wortley, 2002), more than 3,000 high school students were asked about
gang membership. About 11 per cent (16.3 per cent of males and 6 per
cent of girls) indicated that they were current or former gang members.
On examination (Table 5.1), one sees that much of the 'gang' behaviour
attributed to youths is ordinary youthful behaviour.

Table 5.2   Youth reporting that they have belonged to
either a 'criminal' or a 'social' gang (N = 3,393)

Characterization of belonging	%
Never been a gang member	88.9
Former member of a social gang	2.0
Current member of a social gang	1.5
Former member of a criminal gang	3.4
Current member of a criminal gang	4.2
Total	100

Source: Tanner and Wortley, 2002.

The activities of the gangs, as described by the youths, reveal two
things. First, a sizable number of youths indicate that they committed
various forms of illegal behaviour. Second, the gang was also a social
organization. Indeed, in Table 5.2 although 11.1 per cent of youth are
or were gang members, 'criminal' gang membership involved only 7.6
per cent. In Table 5.2, a youth was described as being in a criminal
gang if he or she indicated that he or she had either sold drugs,
engaged in property offending, or fought against other gangs as part of
their regular gang activities.

In other studies, it would appear that the 'risk factors' for gang
membership (e.g., less cohesive or dysfunctional communities, family
disorganization, school failure, high commitment to delinquent peers,
early anti-social behaviour) are, in fact, 'risk factors' for offending
more generally (Howell, 1997). This is not surprising, since those who
commit offences are likely to be doing it in groups which, in turn, get
labelled as gangs.

Gangs and the Public

As Schissel (1997) points out, kids 'hanging around in groups' create
terror in many members of the public, who equate a group of young
people with a criminal organization. In addition, he points out that
mass media accounts, sometimes fed by police reports, equate 'gang
membership' with racialized or immigrant groups (ibid., pp. 58–71).
He notes that in Saskatoon in the mid-1990s, wildly different estimates
existed about the number of gangs in the city, the estimates being
based on graffiti and an increase in thefts of sports jackets (ibid.). Many

newspaper accounts described a group of youths as a gang while offering no evidence that its organization fit any definition of the term.

Because youths spend time with one another, and, as a result, tend to offend together, the raw materials for creating images of 'youth gangs' are often present in an urban environment. Some 'moral panics' involving gangs have been carefully studied. One 'case study' of the development of a 'youth gang problem' comes from McCorkle and Miethe (1998). In Las Vegas, Nevada, before the mid-1980s, there appeared to be no gang problem. Nevertheless, in 1985 two police officers were assigned to gather evidence on gangs. These officers announced in 1986 that there were 4,000 gang members in Las Vegas involved in crime.

Media coverage of gangs skyrocketed from fewer than twenty-five stories about gangs per year from 1983 to 1987 to approximately 140 to 170 per year in the period 1988–91. A poll in 1989 showed that most residents (89 per cent) thought that gang problems were worsening. Police sweeps were authorized and patrols (often by undercover police) of schools began. New statutes were introduced; consideration was given to banning gang membership, and penalties for 'gang-benefiting' crimes were increased. By 1992, the police had begun to declare a victory over the gangs. As laws were passed that gave police additional powers and large increases in police budgets were approved, the gang 'problem' disappeared from public view.

Police data suggested that during the late 1980s charges against youths identified by the police as gang members increased from about 3 to 7 per cent of those charged, but most of the increase occurred late in the period, around 1992 or so. Even prosecutors, however, were not comfortable with the labelling of young offenders as gang members, suggesting that the statistics regarding gang membership might be vastly exaggerated. When the concern erupted, youths identified as gang members accounted for only about 3 per cent of all reported violent crime in the county. The anti-gang legislation was, with a couple of exceptions, almost never used against gang members.

The group that benefited most from the view that 'gangs were out of control,' namely, the police, appeared to have created the moral panic. Stories of gangs came, not surprisingly, at a time when there was a budget crunch and when the legitimacy and fairness of the police were being questioned because of allegations of brutality (McCorkle and Miethe, 1998). Police spoke of the growing threat from gangs, the 'fact' that the police were 'out-gunned' by the gang members, and needed new resources and new legislation. The police presented a 'four-year plan' for increased resources to combat gangs. In the end, the panic disappeared: newspaper articles about gangs dropped off dramatically by 1994. But the police got their resources and their laws, and attention was diverted from ongoing police scandals. Throughout the whole panic period, even using the police department's own statistics, gang activity, if it increased at all, never accounted for more than 5 to 7 per cent of youth crimes. Gangs, even though they were largely imaginary, had an impact, but only on the criminal justice system, not on crime.

A very similar set of events occurred in Hawaii in the early 1990s (Perrone & Chesney-Lind, 1998). Although in the period 1992–6, there was no evidence of any substantial change in youth crime in Hawaii, newspaper coverage of gangs increased dramatically. During this time, there were almost twice as many stories about gangs as there were in 1987–91 and more than seven times as many stories focusing on juvenile delinquency. The majority of newspaper articles were quite unremarkable. However, when the articles did have a point of view, they often used terms like 'young killers' and included 'advice' from 'Los Angeles gang experts' that Hawaii 'has all the makings for a youth gang crisis' (ibid., p. 106). The gangs were described by the police as 'well organized in a paramilitary situation.' The media then 'set the stage for a war that had not yet occurred' (ibid., p. 107). However, juvenile arrests, other than for status offences, were not increasing during this time and survey data (of young people) suggest that gang membership was not increasing. Staus offences involve behaviour such as curfew violations or being a runaway from home that constitutes an offence only because of the person's 'status' as a youth. Status offences are not criminalized in Canada.

Not surprisingly, a statewide survey in 1997 showed that most people (92 per cent) thought that juvenile arrests had increased in the previous few years. Most of these people thought that the increase was large.

Implications of What Is Known about Gangs for Crime Control

Given these findings, it would be attractive to approach crime control by suggesting that strategies should be developed to identify and incapacitate those young people who recruit others into delinquency. However, given that relationships, networks, and delinquent groups are rather unstable and short-lived, such a strategy may be ineffective at best. Young people do commit offences in groups, and this makes 'incapacitation' strategies ineffective for another reason. Reiss (1988, pp. 121–2) points out that 'for about half of all robberies, the *same* robbery is part of the criminal history of more than one offender. Although there are on the average two offenders per robbery, in about one fourth of all robberies, the same incident enters the criminal history of three or more offenders ... The larger the size of any participant's offending group, the less, on the average, that individual's absence should diminish the number of offences.'

There are several important implications based on the finding that youth crime tends to occur in groups. First, the distinction between a group and a gang is sometimes more in the eyes of the beholder than it is in the eyes of those who are participating in offending. To a middle-aged person walking down the street, a rowdy bunch of 15-year-olds may well be a gang. From their perspective, however, they may simply be a group of kids all from the same school on their way to a party. If they commit an offence together – or a series of offences – it increases the likelihood that they will be described as a gang. It is interesting to remember that a group of people who do things together – sometimes with the whole group, and sometimes with just a subset of the whole group – does not normally become a gang until they are seen to be doing something illegal. This is not to say that gangs, groups of people who come together largely or exclusively to commit offences, do not exist. It is to say, however, that we should be careful in interpreting the term 'gang' when it is applied to a group simply because they are involved in at least one offence.

Second, if a group of young people commit offences together, the charging of one member of this group with a criminal offence, and, eventually, the incapacitation of this person for some period of time, may have no impact whatsoever on offending. If it is the 'group' that is committing the offences, the group may continue without the one person, or perhaps with somebody else. In other words, if 'incapacitation' of youthful offenders is a goal in certain circumstances, it should not be surprising that reduction of crime will not necessarily be the result.

Third, treatment of youthful offenders focused solely on their individual characteristics may not be effective unless it focuses on the group influences on the young person as well. In addition, treatment which takes place in custody (where the young person is separated from the natural influences of peers) may not prepare the young person for his or her return to the community.

Fourth, if one forgets that young people are sometimes charged along with others who have committed offences with them, we can easily misunderstand the nature of statistics coming from the courts. For example, two young people may commit a serious assault on a third person. The two youths might be charged with the most serious level of assault: aggravated assault. However, it may turn out that only one of them was really responsible. The second young person might have participated to some extent, but not in the brutal violence that could have justified the original charge. The first young person might be found guilty of the aggravated assault and receive a quite severe disposition. The second youth, given the actual role played in the offence, might well have the charge dismissed or be found guilty of a much less serious offence, or be found guilty of the original offence of aggravated assault but be treated quite leniently at the disposition stage of the proceedings. Knowing the full facts would make such a decision more understandable than would simply knowing what the original charge was and what the final dispositions were.

Finally, given that young people often commit offences in groups, we should keep in mind that our most accessible set of statistics about youth crime (the *Youth Court Survey* produced annually by the Canadian Centre for Justice Statistics) focuses on 'cases.' A 'case' consists of the set of charges against a single individual arriving in court on a single day. Two young people facing identical sets of charges (or different sets of charges) for exactly the same set of offences will count as two cases. Thus, two young people charged with the same break-and-enter into a single house, will show up as two cases. Looking at the cases in the youth court as an indication of the amount of youth crime in a community can therefore be deceptive. On the one hand, it may underestimate the amount of youth crime because many people are not apprehended or charged. It also may underestimate youth crime because one youth charged at one time with a large string of offences shows up as one case in the court statistics. On the other hand, the numbers of cases can overestimate the amount of youth crime because a single incident can involve more than one young person.

School Violence

In recent years, in part because of high-profile shootings in some American and Canadian schools, the issue of school violence has become a social issue. One result is that school systems in parts of Canada have created 'zero tolerance' policies for violence in schools. For example, Ontario's 'Code of Conduct' for youths in schools requires suspensions for such behaviour as uttering a threat, possession of illegal drugs, or providing alcohol to minors (e.g., a 19-year-old giving a can of beer to an 18-year-old friend). Are schools really that dangerous? It turns out that the peak times for youths to be involved in violence are the hours immediately after school, not during school (Office of Juvenile Justice and Delinquency Prevention, 1999). This is not, of course, very surprising. Although school age youths spend close to 20 per cent of their waking hours in school, and those with whom they are likely to engage in violence (other youths) are nearby, schools are, by and large, relatively well structured.

Gun violence in schools is, of course, the centrepiece of many mass media stories about schools. However, in the United States, it is estimated that the number of youths struck by lightning each year is about twice the number who are killed by gun violence in schools. Donohue, Schiraldi, and Ziedenberg (1999) examined data on school violence from a variety of sources, all of which pointed to the same rather simple conclusion: lethal violence in schools is rare. There are about 51.5 million students in American schools (U.S. Department of Education and the Department of Justice, 1998). In 1997–8 there were forty shooting deaths in U.S. schools, which is similar to the average number killed in each of the previous six years. The number of school shooting deaths is, however, an overestimation because the data included any deaths that occurred near or on the way to school. Thus, any deaths (suicides or homicides) of children or adults, committed by children or adults, were included. The authors estimated the rate of juveniles murdered outside of school to be forty times higher than the rate of murders in school.

Another way of putting the violent deaths occurring in schools in context is to look at murders of youths. In the United States, in the 1992–3 and 1993–4 school years, 7,357 children were murdered. During these same years, sixty-three students were murdered at school (ibid., p. 9). Said differently, fewer than 1 per cent of American children who were murdered during these two years were murdered at school.

Donohue et al. (1999) also reported results from victimization surveys administered to students between 1989 and 1995, which found that there was a 0.1 per cent increase in overall victimization. During that same time, however, the United States saw significant increases in the rate of juvenile arrests for serious violence. The authors also examined 'violence related' hospital emergency admissions of youths. Only about 6 per cent were said to have occurred at school. In contrast, 48

Table 5.3   Grade 12 students in U.S. schools reporting various victimizations, 1976–1996 (%)

Years	Injured with a weapon	Injured on purpose by unarmed person	Threatened with a weapon	Threatened by unarmed person
1976–80	4.7	12.0	11.6	20.2
1981–85	5.0	13.3	12.9	23.2
1986–90	5.2	14.0	12.7	24.3
1991–95	5.0	12.4	14.6	24.0
1996	4.8	11.7	13.3	21.6

Source: Kaufmann et al., 1998.

per cent of the injuries occurred at home, 29 per cent at work, and 15 per cent on the streets. Moreover, in a self-report survey in 1993, roughly 90 per cent of students surveyed said that they felt 'safe' or 'very safe' at school.

The data from U.S. schools on actual violence (much of the material in this section is from Doob and Sprott, 1999) are instructive, because it is not difficult to find suggestions that each new incident of highly publicized school violence represents 'another in a recent trend.' For the six-year period beginning in 1992–3 and ending in 1997–8, the number of school shooting deaths, across the whole of the United States, is as follows: 55, 51, 20, 35, 25, 40 (Donohue et al., 1999). It is difficult to find a sustained upward trend in these numbers.

However, it could be argued that homicides are unusual. It would, therefore, be useful to know about 'actual' day-to-day violence that occurs in schools. From 1976 to 1996, a representative group of students in their final year of high school throughout the United states was asked questions about victimization (Kaufman et al., 1998). If violence has been steadily increasing, we should see increases of self-reported victimization. Table 5.3 shows the percentage of students reporting various victimizations, averaged over 5-year intervals. There is some year-to-year variation, with no clear substantial, or consistent, increases over the years. There does, however, appear to be a small increase in some indicators from one period to another. For example, we see that in 1976–80, 12 per cent of youths reported being injured without a weapon, while in 1986–90, 14 per cent of youths reported being injured without a weapon. An increase such as that does not

Table 5.4   Students in U.S. schools reporting bringing weapons on to school property (%)

Bringing weapons on school property	1992	1993	1994	1995	1996	1997
Grade 12 youth reporting carrying a weapon ≥ 1 day in past 4 weeks	6.2	7.9	6.1	6.4	5.7	N/A
Grade 12 youth reporting carrying gun ≥ 1 day in past 4 weeks	N/A	N/A	3.1	3.2	3.3	N/A
Grades 9–12 reporting carrying a weapon ≥ 1 day in past 30 days	N/A	11.7	N/A	9.6	N/A	8.5

Source: Kaufmann et al., 1998.
N/A = not available.

demand *changes* in policies to address youth violence. Nor does it indicate an 'epidemic' of violence in schools. At the same time, however, the absolute level of victimizations – whether 12 per cent or 14 per cent – strikes us as being quite serious.

We can investigate violence in schools not only from self-reported victimizations, but also from students' self-reports of bringing weapons to school. Kaufman et al. (1998) also present data from surveys where high school students were asked whether they had carried a weapon onto school property at least once in the previous four weeks. These questions were asked in only a few recent years (see Kaufman et al., 1998, for details). As Table 5.4 demonstrates (and consistent with Table 5.3), there is no clear or consistent increase in reports of bringing weapons to school. Again, although we see year-to-year variation, no clear trend appears.

While victimizations in U.S. schools and bringing weapons to school do not appear to be increasing, one thing is increasing in schools: fear of victimization. Kaufman et al. (1998, p. 75) asked questions about how fearful students are while at school. Unfortunately, these data are available only for the years 1989 and 1995. Nevertheless, comparing those two years we see an increase in the proportion of students who report being afraid on the way to or at school (Table 5.5). The presence of a gang is, of course, of some concern. It should be remembered, however, that an increase in the proportion of students reporting that

Table 5.5   Students, age 12–19, reporting 'fear' of violence (%)

	1989	1995
Feared attack or harm at school	5.5	8.6
Feared attack or harm on the way to and from school	4.4	6.7
Avoided one or more places in school	5.1	8.7
Reported street gangs present at school	15.3	28.4

Source: Kaufmann et al., 1998.

there were gangs in their schools was not accompanied by noticeable increases in violent victimizations.

Concerns about crime are present and the fact that measurable numbers of students fear being attacked or harmed at school should be taken seriously. Students' fear, as well as victimizations, should be addressed, whatever the level. However, which provides a better description of violence in schools: self-reported school victimization data or students' fear?

Unfortunately, we do not have equivalent detailed longitudinal data on victimizations in Canadian schools. In the absence of any data to the contrary, and given that overall levels of police reports of violent crime are not increasing in Canada, it would appear unlikely that there is any substantial upward trend in Canada. Not everyone takes this view. Gabor (1999, p. 389) notes:

My own national study of violence in the schools lends further support to the notion that violence and intimidation among our youth rose from the mid-1980s to the mid-1990s. Officials from 260 school boards and 250 police departments were surveyed [in the mid-1990s] across the country ... Close to 80% of both police personnel and educators contacted felt that the problem of violence in the schools had grown over the ten-year period leading up to the survey. Most of the remaining respondents felt that the problem had remained the same over the ten-year period. Not one police official and just two percent of the educators felt that the problem was less serious than it had been a decade earlier.

The differences between the position that Gabor takes and the position taken here are important. We would prefer to rely on data related more directly to offending than data from school boards which, clearly, are not even directly observing what is happening in the schools. We would not question that there may have been increased police involvement in schools as a result of an understandable concern about violence in schools and policies to require police involvement. The question is whether one accepts the impressions of those who have some association with schools as evidence of what is happening over other evidence.

Even though there are relatively low levels of lethal violence perpetrated in schools, and even though students appear to feel safe in schools, the response to the media 'hype' about the 'violence' crisis has been to cut after-school programs, put police officers in schools, expel students for minor acts of violence, and try youth as adults. For example, the number of suspensions and expulsions in the United States increased from 3.7 per cent of students in 1974 to 6.8 per cent in 1998 (Schiraldi & Ziedenberg, 2001). Part of the problem may be in determining what constitutes 'violence.' An 8-year-old boy in East Sable River, Nova Scotia, was suspended from school for pointing a breaded chicken finger at a class mate and saying 'bang' (*National Post* 'Grade 2 boy,' 2001). Interestingly, because he is under 12, and, therefore, not criminally responsible for his violent use of a chicken finger, he was named in the newspaper article. In addition, his 'criminal' record of similar 'crimes' was reported: he had previously pointed his own finger at someone and said 'bang,' a crime that had also earned him a day's suspension. Chicken fingers are, apparently, a favourite weapon for 8-year-olds. An Arkansas boy had been suspended from school earlier that same year for pointing an identical item at a teacher. He, however, uttered the threat, 'Pow, pow, pow.' Had these youths been above the age of criminal responsibility, they could have been charged criminally.

One thing that should be kept in mind when considering the suspension of youths from schools is that the exclusion or suspension of children from the educational processes has been criticized on various grounds, including that it appears to increase the likelihood of delinquent behaviour by youth as well as the probability that youth will drop out of school (Schiraldi & Ziedenberg, 2001). In the United States, suspensions are strongly associated with race: African Americans are nearly twice as likely to be suspended from school as whites (ibid.).

Recidivism

Recidivism – some form of re-offending – is the measure most often focused on when studies of the outcome of some criminal justice process is examined. People often want to know what the 'recidivism rate' is for a group of offenders who go to court, or who spend time at a boot camp, or who are given some kind of special treatment. Unfortunately, the concept of recidivism or re-offending is not that simple.

Imagine we are studying youths who have been taken to youth court for the first time. If someone were to ask, 'What is the recidivism rate of these youths?' this would seem like a fairly simple question. It is not. First, some of these youths will certainly not be found guilty in the first instance. Youth court data for 1999–2000 (CCJS, 2001b) suggest that about two-thirds of the cases brought to and disposed of in youth court will result in a guilty finding. Since the others will have not been found guilty or will have had their charges dismissed, it does not really make sense to talk about 'recidivism' for these youths.

In turning to those youths who were found guilty, we have one obvious problem to face. Data from self-reported studies would suggest that almost all youths have done *something* that might be constituted as an offence. In Chapter 4, for example, we reported that close to 90 per cent of youths admitted to at least some form of vandalism in the year prior to being surveyed. Given these and other self-reported data, it would seem that 'recidivism' measured by this kind of survey would be very high: at least 90 per cent, if measured carefully.

What happens if the measure focuses on 'official' measures of criminal involvement, such as being found guilty a subsequent time in court within a certain time period? Two factors immediately have to be considered. First, for a youth to be found guilty in court, a large number of discretionary decisions have to have been made. As outlined in Chapter 4, a number of steps have to occur before the youth is brought to court, let alone found guilty. Second, a youth can be apprehended by the police, admit the offence, but still be dealt with informally outside of the system or by way of alternative measures. Hence, 'recidivism' measured by youth justice system statistics is going to reflect decisions made before the youth appears in court.

Moving beyond these problems, one also sees that what 'counts' as recidivism makes a difference. Imagine that you were to hear that the recidivism rate (measured for a stated period in a stated way) for serious violent sexual offenders was 20 per cent. It would be easy to think that they were subsequently committing violent sexual offences, but this is unlikely to be the case. For example, Lee (2000) examined the subsequent findings of guilt of 597 British Columbia male youths whose first offence involved offences against the person or weapons offences. She showed that about 19 per cent of the first subsequent findings of guilt for this group involved another offence against the person or weapons offence (estimated from Lee, 2000, Figure 48). For the 121 girls in her sample, the comparable figure was about 36 per cent. In other words, if youths whose first offence involved violence or weapons offences do come back to court and are found guilty, they are more likely to be subsequently found guilty of a property offence than an offence against persons.

Comparisons across jurisdictions make official measures of recidivism even more problematic. As will be discussed in Chapter 7, there is enormous variability in the number of cases that are brought into youth courts. This finding has three implications:

1 If a jurisdiction (e.g., a province or a city) were to screen out minor cases and take youths to court only if they were serious or repeat offenders, then the youths in court in that jurisdiction would tend, on average, to have more serious criminal records than would the youths in jurisdictions that took every offender to court. Consider, for example, a jurisdiction that was selective in its use of youth court. It would have a mechanism for screening out minor offenders. The result is that those who did end up in court would be the 'worst' youths. A comparison of the court caseload, then, of a jurisdiction where youth court was rarely used with one where youth court was used for almost any offender (serious or minor) would show a higher proportion of serious offenders in the jurisdiction with few youth court cases. This would be an automatic result of having few minor offenders, rather than having large numbers of serious offenders.

2 Recidivism rates, as measured by court data (e.g., findings of guilt), could be lower in those provinces that are more selective in their use of the courts, especially if they are selective in bringing youths who commit minor offences repeatedly into the court system. Imagine two jurisdictions. In one jurisdiction youths are apprehended and charged each time they offend. Almost everyone in that jurisdiction would, then, have a long criminal record. A jurisdiction that used court more selectively would have few youths with long criminal records.

3 Youths who live in communities with high levels of police enforcement are more likely to be described as recidivists, since they will be more likely to be apprehended.

The concept of recidivism is inherently problematic. It is often talked about as if it depended solely on the youth. It also depends on the behaviour of those controlling the youth justice system. At a minimum, one has to be very careful about how recidivism is defined.

One of the most comprehensive studies of youth court recidivism in Canada comes from Lee (2000), who examined the court history of all youths born between 1972 and 1974 who came into the British Columbia youth court system at least once. The main analysis focused on those who had been found guilty at least once – eliminating, therefore, the 21 per cent of boys and 31 per cent of girls who were brought to court at least once but were never found guilty (ibid., p. 9).

Lee's data shows that the more times a youth is brought to court, the higher the likelihood of recidivism. She presents data on re-conviction within six months, one year, and two years of the disposition, (ibid., pp. 19–20),[1] some of which is reproduced in Table 5.6. Because Lee's data deal only with youth court careers, the two-year recidivism data report only on youths who were less than 16 years old at the time of any given disposition, because older youths were not subject to the youth justice system for the full two years after the disposition.

The data in Table 5.6 show that the more times a girl or a boy has been to court the higher the likelihood is of his or her coming back into the system. For example, the six-month recidivism data show that about 22 per cent of male offenders and about 20 per cent of female offenders come back into the system after their first disposition in youth court. For youths who have been handed their eighth disposition, however, the six month recidivism measure is up to 46 per cent for boys and 54 per cent for girls. Not surprisingly, the longer a youth is at risk the higher the recidivism rate: two-year recidivism rates are considerably higher than six-month recidivism rates for both girls and boys.

---

1 The number of cases for these observations varies dramatically. There were, for example, 9,709 male and 2,393 female youths who received their first disposition in time to be able to be tracked in the youth system for six months. Only 116 male and thirty-nine females received their tenth disposition in sufficient time to be tracked for six months in the youth court system. Only twenty-three boys were able to be tracked for two years after their tenth disposition. An insufficient number of girls who had that much experience with the youth court system were available to track past their seventh disposition.

Table 5.6   Rates of recidivism (as percentage, and in parentheses number that the percentage is based on) for young offenders by disposition number, time to first offence after this disposition, age, and gender

Disposition	Recidivism at 6 months (age 12–17)		Recidivism at 2 years (age 12–15)	
	Boys	Girls	Boys	Girls
1st	22 (9,709)	20 (2,393)	50 (4,564)	38 (1,345)
2nd	37 (3,580)	39 (684)	78 (1,456)	65 (342)
3rd	41 (2,145)	42 (367)	86 (745)	72 (180)
4th	43 (1,315)	47 (209)	89 (435)	84 (85)
5th	43 (832)	47 (127)	90 (273)	87 (54)
6th	42 (554)	54 (87)	91 (164)	87 (38)
7th	45 (371)	57 (58)	94 (94)	84 (25)
8th	46 (239)	54 (39)	91 (58)	[a]
9th	54 (161)	[a]	94 (33)	[a]
10th	47 (116)	[a]	96 (23)	[a]

Source: Data derived from Lee, 2000, Figures 9 and 10.
[a] Small numbers of cases for girls preclude estimates of recidivism for those groups.

Table 5.7   Relationship between recidivism rate for boys and girls at 1 year after disposition and the number of times they have been sentenced (disposition number), for youth of various ages at sentencing (percentage, and in parentheses number that the percentage is based on)

Age (years)	First disposition		Second disposition		Third disposition	
	Boys	Girls	Boys	Girls	Boys	Girls
12 or 13	41 (835)	35 (209)	70 (181)	71 (31)	87 (71)	[a]
14	38 (1,508)	33 (479)	67 (490)	70 (128)	81 (224)	63 (65)
15	37 (2,221)	29 (657)	58 (785)	51 (183)	68 (450)	59 (105)
16	34 (2,507)	19 (578)	54 (1,039)	49 (183)	59 (661)	45 (95)

Source: Data derived from Lee, 2000, Figures 14 and 15.
[a] Small numbers of cases for girls preclude estimates of recidivism for this group.

The younger a youth is at the time of the disposition, the more likely he or she is to return to the youth justice system as an offender. Table 5.7 presents the data for one-year recidivism after the first, second, and third time that the youth was sentenced. Again, the likelihood of recidivism goes up with the number of previous dispositions. Table 5.7 also shows that as the age of the offender increases, the likelihood of recidivism goes down.

As Lee (2000, p. 29) points out, the data (in Table 5.7) suggest that 'recidivism rates are lowest at the first disposition and lowest of all at the first disposition at older ages when the numbers of offenders are largest. This indicates that general application of scarce or expensive resources at *first* dispositions, especially for older offenders, would not be cost effective.'

The type of case (e.g., if it is violent, or an offence against property) does not seem to be very important as a predictor of recidivism rates. Similarly, whether a youth received a sentence involving custody or a sentence where probation was the most significant disposition did not appear to matter.

How Different Are Recidivist Offenders?

Recidivists, it turns out, do not seem to commit much more serious offences than do youths who are in court for the first time. A national study (Doherty & de Souza, 1996) involving most of Canada's jurisdictions found that the offences committed by youths in court for the first time are not dramatically different from the offences committed by those in court for the second or subsequent time. This was a study of youths found guilty in youth courts across Canada[2] in 1993–4. A youth found guilty on at least one charge on a previous occasion was considered to be a recidivist.

As can be seen in Table 5.8, recidivists tended to be found guilty of quite similar offences as those for which they were in court for the first time.

The data for boys reveal that the most serious charges for first offenders are not very different from those for recidivists. For girls, however, the data are slightly different. Recidivist girls are less likely than first offence girls to be found guilty of theft under $5,000 and common assault and more likely to be found guilty of the residual category of

---

2 Youths from Ontario and Nova Scotia were not included because complete youth court records for the youths found guilty in these provinces could not be obtained. Findings of guilt for 'post-disposition administrative offences' were not included. (The excluded offences included such things as failure to comply with a disposition, escaping custody, and being unlawfully at large.)

Table 5.8   Offences of conviction for first-time offenders and recidivists (in parentheses, as percentage of all offences)

	Male offenders		Female offenders	
	First-time offenders	Recidivists	First-time offenders	Recidivists
Relatively minor offences				
Common assault	1,325 (9.2)	902 (7.9)	700 (21.0)	284 (17.5)
Theft under $5,000	2,375 (16.5)	1,924 (16.8)	1,110 (33.4)	403 (24.8)
Possession of stolen property	947 (6.6)	1,085 (9.5)	162 (4.9)	90 (5.5)
Mischief to property	1,040 (7.2)	720 (6.3)	123 (3.7)	72 (4.4)
Sub-total	5,687 (39.4)	4,631 (40.5)	2,095 (63.0)	849 (52.2)
More serious offences				
Other violence	2,186 (15.2)	1,201 (10.5)	272 (8.2)	144 (8.9)
Break and enter	3,184 (22.1)	2,753 (24.1)	256 (7.7)	117 (7.2)
Theft over $5,000	590 (4.1)	717 (6.3)	74 (2.2)	41 (2.5)
Other property	642 (4.5)	477 (4.2)	183 (5.5)	118 (7.3)
Sub-total	6,602 (45.8)	5,148 (45.0)	785 (23.6)	420 (25.8)
Drug offences	710 (4.9)	423 (3.7)	78 (2.3)	44 (2.7)
Other offences	1,421 (9.9)	1,235 (10.8)	368 (11.1)	312 (19.2)
Total	14,420 (100)	11,437 (100)	3,326 (100)	1,625 (100)

Source: Derived from Table 1, Doherty and de Souza, 1995.

'other offences.' (Unfortunately, we do not know which offences contributed most to this residual category. Our source of data is a published report that does not indicate which offences were most highly represented here.)

The relatively high degree of similarity of offences between youths who are first offenders in court and those who are recidivists in the study by Doherty and de Souza is similar to a more detailed study of persistent offenders in England. Hagel and Newburn (1994) considered youths who had been arrested three or more times. Starting with this population, three definitions of 'persistence' were applied to the pool of 531 youths who had been arrested three times in a year (number of arrests, number of offences attributed to them, number of offences *known* to have been committed by them). An attempt was made to identify the 10 per cent most persistent youthful offenders. The only problem was that sixty-nine different youths were identified by one or more of these criteria, but only thirty of these sixty-nine were identified by all three criteria. As Hagel and Newburn point out, 'these are the juveniles in whom the police, the courts, the press and the public are particularly interested' (ibid., p. 101). Their offences were the same as those of other juveniles; there were just more of them: 'It is not the case that these persistent offenders were committing the more violent or serious offences' (ibid., p. 102).

Hagel and Newburn also noted that, if one looked at persistence over time, and one used as a measure of persistence 'frequency of known and alleged offending over a three month period,' those who would be defined as persistent varied across time: 'It was rare for [offenders] who met the criteria in each quarter to be the same individuals' (ibid., p. 103), and 'offending, particularly persistent offending by juveniles, is a relatively transitory activity' (ibid., p. 105). The overwhelming finding bears repeating: 'Persistent offenders ... whichever of the three definitions was used – did not seem to be strikingly different from the full sample, with the tautological exception of the frequency of their offending' (ibid., p. 119). They noted that 'very serious offences – grievous bodily harm, aggravated burglary, rape and sexual offences – did not represent in total as much as one percent of all offenses attributed to persistent young offenders – a pattern that is typical of juvenile offending generally' (p. 120). Hagel and Newburn pointed out that 'any definition of persistence will inevitably be arbitrary' (ibid., p. 122). They concluded that 'not only is the process of attempting to define persistence deeply problematic, but because there is a degree of arbitrariness in the way some offenders rather than others become defined as persistent, creating a custodial sentence for that group raises issues both about equity and about efficient resource use' (ibid., p. 123).

Thus, it would appear that we cannot reliably identify who is likely to be a persistent offender. Definitions can be created and applied, but equally reasonably sounding definitions would identify different groups of offenders. Persistent young offenders, by any definition, may have committed more offences, but the offences that they commit, on average, are no more serious than the offences committed by others. A special regime for such offenders may look good as long as one does not look carefully at the effects.

Unfortunately, many criminal justice programs or initiatives attempt to use 'recidivism' as the measure of whether of not a particular program has 'succeeded.' In this chapter we have discussed how problematic the concept of recidivism is. If the criminal justice system uses the most restrictive definition of recidivism – how often a young person gets processed by the criminal justice system in a given period – then many programs seem less than successful. If we broaden our views however, about what success can mean – that a youth feels better about himself, or that a youth still commits crimes, but less frequently, for example, then perhaps the criminal justice system can make some meaningful, albeit limited, impact on youths' lives.

Conclusion

The three topics that we have examined in this chapter, gangs, school violence, and recidivism, have one important thing in common: they are all areas of special concern to the public when youth violence is being considered. Each of them, however, turns out to be more complex than one might imagine, and each of them is probably, objectively, less important in understanding youth crime than one might first imagine. Perhaps the lesson to be learned is the obvious one: We need to know what we are talking about before we draw conclusions about what needs to be done.

CHAPTER SIX

Trends in Youth Crime: Has Youth Crime Increased in the Past Few Years?

The level of crime in our society – and, more specifically, the level of youth crime in our society – is a political as well as an empirical issue. Those who suggest that crime is increasing are sometimes seen as using scare tactics in an attempt to find support for harsh criminal justice policies, on the assumption that harsh policies will cause crime rates to level off or decrease. Those who suggest that crime is not increasing are sometimes seen as attempting to minimize the impact of crime on victims or as suggesting that leniency is the appropriate response to crime.

As is pointed out in Chapters 1 and 11, our assessment of the empirical evidence is that the level of crime in society and the severity of the measures society uses in response to crime are quite independent. Within the ranges of penalties that are plausible in our society, then, the severity of the response of the criminal justice system to crime is not going to make a lot of difference to the amount of crime we experience.

The political reality, however, is that independent of whatever conclusions one might come to from a careful reading of the facts, it is likely that if crime is seen as increasing, additional pressure will be placed on Parliament and the youth justice system to 'do something about it.' And, 'doing something about it' usually means getting tougher.

It is easy to understand the source of this kind of pressure. In 1997 a representative sample of Ontario residents were asked whether they thought that crime in Ontario, and crime in their own neighbourhoods, was increasing, decreasing, or staying the same (Doob, Sprott, Marinos, & Varma, 1998). Overall 69 per cent of Ontario residents thought that crime was increasing in the province and 40 per cent thought that crime was increasing in their own neighbourhoods. They were also asked whether they thought that youth court sentences were too severe, about right, or not severe enough. As shown in Table 6.1, people who

Table 6.1   Relationship between perception of crime levels and perception of sentencing (percentage and number that the percentage is based on)

	Sentences		
	Not severe enough	About right or too severe	Total % (n)
Crime in Ontario			
Increased	89	11	100 (638)
Stayed the same	81	19	100 (231)
Decreased	66	34	100 (47)
Crime in neighbourhood			
Increased	90	10	100 (357)
Stayed the same	84	16	100 (486)
Decreased	73	27	100 (56)

Source: Doob et al., 1998.

thought that crime in Ontario or in their own neighbourhoods was increasing were more likely to hold the view that sentences in youth court were not severe enough. For example, 90 per cent of those who believed that crime had increased in their own neighbourhoods thought that sentences were not severe enough, whereas only 73 per cent of those who thought that crime in their neighbourhood had decreased thought that sentences were not severe enough.

Youth court judges have quite a different view of crime from that of the general public. In early 2001, only 7 per cent of these judges thought youth crime was increasing. Most (71 per cent) saw youth crime levels as unchanging (Doob, 2001).

Inferences about Changes in Youth Crime Rates: Other Countries

As pointed out in Chapter 4, we do not have definitive information about how much crime there is in a community, let alone how much youth crime. It follows that we do not have any definitive evidence as to whether youth crime has increased, decreased, or stayed the same in the past few years. It is difficult enough to estimate whether certain types of crime overall have increased, decreased, or stayed the same. But knowing whether the perpetrators of these offences are youths is even more difficult. Yet, when considering crime as a whole, there are some indications that levels of crime in many countries may have levelled off in recent years.

In this section, we look at youth crime trends in three countries, not because they are in any way 'representative' of youth crime around the world, but rather because the difficulties in assessing trends are particularly evident in these countries. There may be some countries where a reasonable inference might be that there have been increases. We have examined youth crime patterns in the United States, Japan, and Sweden largely because the controversies in assessing changes in youth crime seem remarkably similar in these countries to the controversies that exist in Canada. It is useful, therefore, to look at the data from other countries – and the statements being made about these data – before turning to the situation in Canada.

United States

In the United States there appeared to have been a relatively short-term increase in serious violent crimes committed by youths in the late 1980s and early 1990s. This short-term increase in violence was, not surprisingly, seen as a long-term trend. For example, in a paper 'based on an August 1995 briefing to [U.S.] Attorney General Janet Reno,' criminologist James Alan Fox (1996, pp. 2–3), after reviewing the changes in family structure and social policy that might be responsible for an apparent increase in youth crime suggests that:

> as if the situation with youth violence was not bad enough already, future demographics are expected to make matters even worse. Not only are today's violent teens maturing into more violent young adults, but they are being succeeded by a new and larger group of teenagers. The same massive baby boom cohort that as teenagers produced a crime wave in the 1970s has since grown up and has had children of their own ...
>
> By the year 2005, the number of teens, ages 14–17 will have increased 20% over its 1994 level, likely producing additional increases in crime and other social problems associated with an expanding youth population.

What is interesting about Fox's analysis is that his solution – 'reinvesting in schools, recreation, job training, support for families, and mentoring' – constitutes a very reasonable way of thinking about crime no matter what the 'trend' might be. Indeed, the approach to crime prevention he suggests is just as relevant whether youth crime is increasing, decreasing, or staying the same.

A more coherent analysis of youth crime trends in the United States comes from another criminologist, Frank Zimring (1998). In two chapters entitled 'A Youth Violence Epidemic: Myth or Reality?' and 'The Case of the Terrifying Toddlers,' Zimring examines U.S. data over a somewhat longer period of time and examines, among other things, age-specific crime rates. One important finding highlighted by Zimring is that the nature of the trends vary across crimes. Although in the United States rates of aggravated assault and homicide involving offenders ages 13 to 17 increased in the late 1980s, there were sharp reductions in the early 1990s. Similar trends were not found for robbery and rape. The increase in the homicide rate for young offenders which occurred in the late 1980s appeared to be completely the result of an increase in gun homicides. Interestingly, there was no comparable change in the homicide rates for offenders aged 25 to 34.

Zimring suggests that police behaviour appears to have changed with 'a greater police willingness to report and upwardly classify assault crimes and a greater willingness to arrest those who commit assaults' (ibid., p. 42). Victimization surveys carried out in schools in the United States show that 'involvement in serious assaults are virtually identical in 1982 and 1992' but police data show big increases.

Zimring is, however, less optimistic about our ability to predict 'because rates of serious offenses tend to be cyclical in unpredictable ways' (ibid., p. 45). But equally important is the fact that the trends are different for different crimes. Hence, one cannot talk about trends of violent crime since these vary across individual crimes. Although he acknowledges that demographic changes are important, he suggests that in the United States, the important factor in understanding overall crime rates is the 'age specific' crime rates. For example, in 1984, the homicide rate for males aged 13 to 17 was about ten per 100,000 inhabitants. Ten years later it was close to thirty-five. 'Age specific' crime rates are dramatically more important than minor changes in the age distribution of society.

Zimring notes that those who, like criminologists James Q. Wilson and John DiIulio, predict an army of 'terrifying teenagers' or 'superpredators' have used inappropriate and, in some instances, bizarre arithmetic to substantiate these predictions. Zimring describes the prediction of a 'predatory menace' of youths as a 'classic case of a compounded distortion' (ibid., p. 60). DiIulio is quoted as saying, in 1996, that 'Over the next 10 years more juvenile "superpredators" will be flooding the nation's streets' (cited in Howell, 1997). Building on such analyses, James Q. Wilson has suggested that 'just beyond the horizon, there lurks a cloud that the winds will soon bring over us. The population will start getting younger again. By the end of this decade [the

1990s] there will be a million more people between the ages of 14 and 17 ... This extra million will be half male. Six percent of them will become high rate, repeat offenders ... Get ready' (cited in Abrahamse, 1997, p. 6). It is not a pretty picture. It is also not an accurate picture. But it is an alarming picture.

Zimring points out that DiIulio's calculations would lead one to the conclusion that there are 'already 1.9 million juvenile superpredators on U.S. streets.' The difficulty with this statement, Zimring notes, is 'that happens to be more young people than were accused of any form of delinquency last year in the U.S.' (1998, p. 62).

Abrahamse (1997) points out that in California in 1996, young males (ages 15 to 24) made up about 7 per cent of the population. A 15 per cent increase in their numbers – the estimate used by those who are pushing the 'superpredator' imagery – will mean that they would constitute about 8 per cent of the population (ibid., p. 7). His findings are quite clear: 'Demography is *not* destiny' (ibid., p. 1). The estimate that one gets for crime in the future depends, not surprisingly, more on the crime rates of different cohorts of children than on the (rather small) variation in the proportion of the population that they constitute. Violence rates are highly age specific. Homicide arrest rates in California in 1981, for example, were about twenty-five per 100,000 for the highest group (20-year-olds) and about half that for 40-year-olds. In 1994, things had changed dramatically. The peak occurred earlier (age 18) and was much higher (about forty-eight per 100,000 18-year-olds). But the rate for 40-year-olds was much the same (or a bit lower) as it had been thirteen years earlier. The problem is that different birth cohorts do vary in their (eventual) crime rates. There have been times when rates have increased as much as 3 per cent over the previous birth cohort for years at a time. Over a long period of time, this amounts to a substantial increase. Decreases (from one birth cohort to the next) have also occurred. Abrahamse concludes that what lies in store for a community 'depends on the upbringing of young [people in the community] - today' (ibid., p. 2). He cautions that 'if, from this time on, every birth cohort is substantially more violent than the previous one, California [or any jurisdiction] is destined to experience a troubling wave of violence, commencing early in the next century.' There is room for optimism, however, because 'one element in the equation that matters – the future behavior of today's children – is one that could be modified' (ibid., p. 11).

These analyses are corroborated by Levitt in an analysis that separates out the effect on crime of demographic changes from the effects of changes to the age-specific rate of offending. He concludes that 'changes in the age structure through 2010 will work very weakly in favour of lower crime in stark contrast to the frequently made assertion that the United States is in the beginning stages of a demographically driven crime wave' (1999, p. 592). The experience in recent years of dramatic changes in the age-specific crime rates of certain groups in the United States suggests that it is these changes that are much more important in understanding changes in overall crime rates. Social programs which have an impact on the level of involvement in crime of those entering the crime-prone years are, obviously, much more important than the shifts in the age structure of our society.

Japan

The situation in Japan is not too different in one way from that in other countries: people seem to believe that youth crime is on the increase. Hamai (1999) notes that in a national survey carried out for the Prime Minister's Office in Japan, 94 per cent of respondents indicated that they believe that serious crimes committed by juveniles are increasing, with most of these respondents believing that the increase is large. At the same time, the overall number of offences recorded by the police as having been committed by youths has, if anything, gone down since the mid-1980s. The most important exception to this general trend is robbery. But robberies, in Japan, constitute fewer than 1 per cent of offences involving youths cleared by the police. Hamai (1999) notes that Japanese robbery rates (for young people and for adults) are dramatically lower than in the West – about one-twentieth of those in the United States, England and Wales, Germany, or France. Notwithstanding low rates by international standards and questionable figures supporting the inference that there is an increase in youth crime, Hamai (1999, p. 10) points out that 'Based on the understanding that juvenile delinquency is increasing and becoming serious, the National Police Agency urged its police agencies to strengthen their capability of dealing with juvenile offending and issued guidelines to combat juvenile offending in August 1997. This approach must have contributed to apprehending more juvenile offenders since then.'

Sweden

Europe has sometimes been classed along with the United States as showing an increase in youth crime, and, in particular, youth violence. Pfeiffer (1998, p. 255), for example, has suggested that 'an increase in youth violence has been apparent in the United States and in ten European countries.' Pfeiffer includes Sweden, even though the data are anything but clear. Estrada (2001) recently reported that the figures leading to the inference that there is an increase in violence committed by youths reflect a somewhat selective view of the facts. Thus, for example, Pfeiffer shows large increases in police reports of theft and assault and suggests that medical records (of those requiring medical attention for assault) contradict the hypothesis that these are differences in reporting rather than behaviour. Estrada points out that the comparisons that are presented (e.g., 1995 vs 1986) are not representative of overall trends. By putting these figures in a somewhat less selective context, however, one sees that 'the mid-1980s stand out as a low point' in hospital admissions as a result of violence. For example, 'for 15–19 year olds, admissions during the 1990s lie at exactly the same level as they did during the second half of the 1970s' (Estrada, 2001, p. 644).

School violence follows a pattern we have seen in North America. Estrada's description of the situation in Sweden could well be applied to Canada or the United States:

> There is evidence of a change in the way acts of violence in schools are viewed and in attitudes toward the kind of responses such acts should be met with. During the first half of the 1980s, a fairly clear line is drawn between more and less serious forms of physical violence. Less serious incidents would in general not be reported to the police, but would rather be dealt with internally by the school. During the second half of the decade, on the other hand, there is already evidence of a tendency to advocate contacting the police even in the event of less serious forms of disorder. During the 1990s, this tendency becomes more pronounced. (ibid., p. 649)

Not surprisingly, in Stockholm between the early 1980s and the late 1990s, the school moved from being the source of only 29 per cent of the assaults reported to being the source of violence reports in 60 per cent of the cases. School violence cases 'accounted for more than 80% of the increase in recorded cases [of violence]' (ibid., p. 650). Victimization data of youths aged 16 to 24 show no linear trends in the levels of violence requiring medical attention or bodily injury. There is, however, a good deal of year to year variation.

An examination of media stories about youth crime shows quite a different pattern. In 1986, 'a new image is presented of the young perpetrator. He is portrayed as polite, emotionally cold and unpredictable. He assaults others for kicks. The social factors are pushed into the background ... The image of the juvenile offender [that has been established by 1987] is that of a calculating "super-predator," a hardened young delinquent whom society needs to protect itself against' (ibid., p. 648).

Inferences about Changes in Youth Crime Rates: Canada

It is useful, we think, to place the question of youth crime in the larger context of crime generally. The first bit of evidence about changes in victimization rates comes from victimization surveys carried out by Statistics Canada in 1988, 1993, and 1999 (see Gartner & Doob, 1994; Besserer & Trainor, 2000). In 1988, about 9,000 people participated in the survey; in 1993, over 10,000 people were questioned about their victimization experiences, and in 1999, over 25,000 Canadians were questioned about similar matters.

Respondents were asked detailed questions about a small subset of crimes. These crimes were, however, those that are most likely to occur to individuals personally (assault, sexual assault, robbery, and personal theft) or to their households (break and enters, thefts of household property, car thefts, and vandalism). The data were quite consistent: for the crimes where comparisons could be made, there was no evidence of increased victimization between 1988 and 1993 and between 1993 and 1999.

This is not to say that crime levels were low. In fact, almost a quarter of respondents indicated, in each survey, that they had been the victim of at least one personal or household crime. For many victimizations, especially property offences, the age of the offender is unknown. However, logically one has to realize that if there were a change in the rate of offending by one group (e.g., young people), there would have to be a compensatory change in the age-specific rate of offending for some other group. Otherwise, the overall rate of victimization could not be identical across the three surveys, which, in fact, it was.

From the victimization data, then, there is no evidence of an increase in crime, generally, and there is no reason to believe that youth crime had increased either.

Homicides and Other Crimes

Most criminologists appear to believe that homicides in Canada are unlikely to go either unreported or misreported in any significant way.

Figure 6.1. Homicide rate, Canada

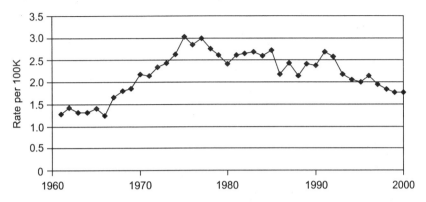

Source: Fedorowycz, 2001.

Homicide rates have varied quite a bit in the past forty years. Using the typical measure of homicides per 100,000 people in the population, the data show some quite distinct periods. From 1961 to 1965 they were quite low (a range of 1.28 to 1.43). By the mid-1970s, however, they had increased dramatically (1974–8 range from 2.63 to 3.03). By the early 1990s, the rates had generally drifted slowly downward (1990–4 range from 2.05 to 2.69). From 1996 to 2000, however, they were down even further (range, 1.76 to 2.14). The overall trend data are shown in Figure 6.1.

No matter how one looks at the data, when we examine homicide rates between the mid-1970s and 2000, it would be impossible to suggest that, over this period, there had been a clear increase. The rates for 1998, 1999, 2000, and 2001 (each of which was approximately 1.8 homicides per 100,000 in the population) are comparable to the rates we experienced in the late 1960s. Nevertheless, a 1997 Ontario survey (Doob et al., 1998) found that 66 per cent of respondents thought that homicide rates had *increased* in the previous twenty years.

Crimes reported to the police – and violent crime in particular – increased quite steadily until the early 1990s. Since the early 1990s, however, there has been a levelling off or decline in the rate of reported crime (see Figure 6.2). One can also see from Figure 6.2 that violent crime contributes little to the overall crime rate.

As pointed out in Chapter 4, police reports about crime require someone to bring these events to the attention of the police. We know that changes in police reports of crime can result from changes in the willingness of victims to report crimes. As police become more sensi-

Figure 6.2. Crimes reported to the police (all criminal code violations and all violence)

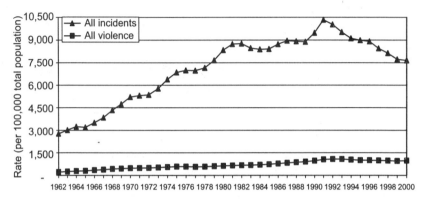

Source: CCJS, 1963–2001.

tive to victims of sexual assault – and as victims anticipate more sensitive treatment from the police – one might expect there to be increased willingness to report crime. Such increases in reporting will lead to increased rates of reported crime. Nevertheless, even if there were an increase in violent crime during the 1990s, it is clearly not evident in the official police records of crime.

Youth Crime

We have some very specific indicators of levels of youth crime. When one looks at youths named as suspects in homicide offences, it appears that the number of such cases has not changed much over the past twenty-five years. These data are important because when members of the public think about crime, they often think about homicide. And, although we do not have a direct measure of the number of homicides committed by young people, we do have a plausible proxy for it: the number of youths charged with a homicide offence. The data in Figure 6.3 demonstrate quite clearly that there is no overall pattern in the number of young offenders charged with homicide offences. What is clear from these data, however, is that there is enormous variability in the number of these events that occur from year to year. Thus, the largest number of youths charged with homicide occurred in 1975 and 1995 (sixty-eight youths charged) and the lowest occurred in 1984,

Figure 6.3. Number of youths named as suspects for homicide offences (Canada)

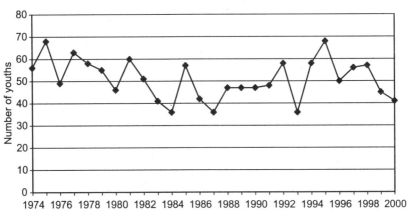

Source: Data provided to the authors by CCJS and Fedorowycz, 2001.

1987, and 1993 (thirty-five youths charged with homicide offences). These data are but one more illustration of the importance of looking at longer term trends rather than focusing on the number of very high profile offences.

Another factor that should be kept in mind is that the numbers in this figure relate to the actual *number* of youths charged, not some kind of abstract rate. For example, when we see, in 2000, that forty-one youths were named as suspects in homicide offences, we need to remember that this represents forty-one out of 2.45 million youths. Homicides involving youthful suspects are, by any measure, rare events.

The public, however, does not appear to know about these data. One anecdote from about 1996 involving the first author illustrates the problems of perceptions of ordinary members of the public:

> A 'researcher' for a national television news program telephoned me to see if I could appear on television to explain 'why young people were committing more murders now than 20 years ago, or so.' I pointed out that although we did not have good data on 'who was committing murders' we did have data on what she was probably referring to, since the call came shortly after the police had charged some young people with a homicide offence. I pointed out that I did have reasonably up-to-date figures on the number of youths charged with a homicide offence each year

since 1974 and there did not appear to be any simple linear trend though there is enormous year-to-year fluctuation.

She was quite clear in her response: 'That can't be so.' I explained that our impressions are sometimes in error in part because few of us 'count' these things, and then I gave her a short sales pitch for the data from the Canadian Centre for Justice Statistics. She wouldn't believe me: 'It just seems to me that 20 years ago, these things almost never happened.' Finally, in exasperation, and in conflict with lessons my mother taught me from an early age, I asked her her age. 'Twenty-three,' she answered. I pointed out that 20 years before this conversation she was three and I was over 30 but the reason I went to the statistics was that I didn't believe I could 'remember' well how many youths had been charged with homicide. She was very polite, telling me in the end, that she didn't think I was the right person for the interview since her boss 'knew' that youth homicides had increased. (Doob & Sprott, 1999, pp. 536–7)

Given the kind of information that the public gets about youth homicides it is not surprising to find that the vast majority of respondents to the 1997 Ontario survey referred to above (Doob et al., 1998) think that youth homicides are increasing in frequency. Whereas 'only' 66 per cent of respondents erroneously thought that the overall homicide rate was going up, 79 per cent thought that the rate of youths involved in homicides was increasing.

Much like the United States, fears have been raised regarding Canada's future demographic change and possible 'youth crime waves.' Data for the last thirty years demonstrate that these fears are unfounded. An analysis by Sprott and Cesaroni (2002) suggests that unlike the United States, the slight increase in homicide rates in Canada in the late 1980s and early 1990s was not concentrated in any single age group. In Canada, most age groups (15–19, 20–24, 25–29, and 30–39) saw slight age-specific homicide rate increases in the 1990–4 time frame. Moreover, while in the United States the homicide rates for the age groups 14 to 17 and 18 to 24 are currently higher than they were in the 1970s, only one age group (the 15 to 19-year-olds) in Canada is currently experiencing very slightly higher homicide rates than they exhibited in the 1970s. Demographics have accounted for roughly 14 per cent of the decrease in homicide rates in Canada in the past twenty-five years. This is quite similar to estimates for the United States from others such as Fox (2000) and Levitt (1999). Demography is not, apparently, destiny at least as far as homicides are concerned.

Figure 6.4. Youths charged by police for violent offences, Canada

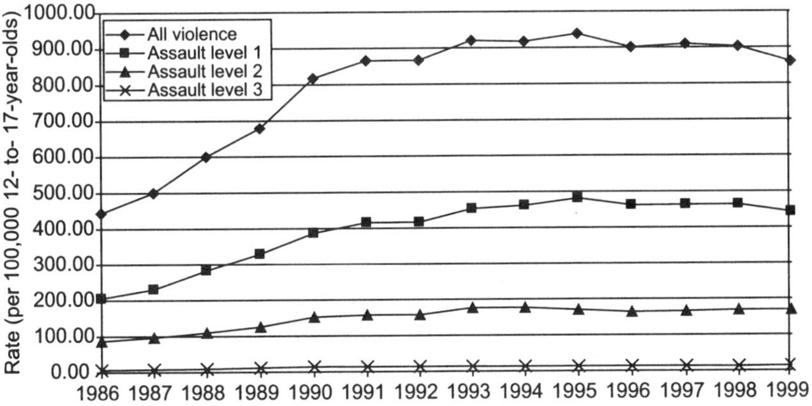

Source: Canadian Centre for Justice Statistics, 2001a.

Changes in the Level of Youth Crime?

Youth court statistics were incomplete, in Canada, between the advent of the YOA in 1984 and 1991. However, one can look at another measure of youths' involvement in the justice system: the number of youths named as having been charged by the police for violent offences (see Figure 6.4).

Figure 6.4 illustrates a rather dramatic increase in youths charged for any violent offence. These data are often cited by the police and others as an indication that 'the youth violence problem' is getting worse. This increase, however, is disproportionately driven by increases in the low-end cases of violence. As an illustration, we have included, in this same figure, the relevant rates for the three levels of assault in Canadian law. Level 1 assault ('common assault') accounts for dramatically more of the increase than does either Level 2 ('assault causing bodily harm or assault with a weapon') or Level 3 ('aggravated assault'). It was not until the mid-1990s that evidence could be found to suggest that 'violent youth crime' had levelled off.

During the early 1990s, the claim was often made that although the overall measures of youth violence did not show an increase, the 'quality' of youth violence was, nevertheless, becoming more serious. This is, of course, a rather surprising suggestion, because even in the first

Table 6.2   Changes in the distribution of youth court cases: all cases and violence cases, Canada, 1991–6

	1991–2	1992–3	1993–4	1994–5	1995–6	Change from 1991–2 to 1995–6
Cases to court (Row 1)	116,397	115,187	115,949	109,743	111,027	−5,370 (−4.6%)
Cases per 100,000 YO age youth (Row 2)	5,309	4,983	4,972	4,650	4,656	−653 (−12.3%)
Cases with principal charge of violence (Row 3)	19,824	21,653	23,374	23,010	23,084	+3,260 (+16.4%)
Violence cases per 100,000 YO age youth (Row 4)	904	937	1,002	975	968	+64 (+7.1%)
% cases with principal charge of violence (Row 5)	17.0	18.8	20.2	21.0	20.8	+3.8

Source: Doob and Sprott, 1998.

part of the 1990s it was evident that the overall rate of violent crime reported in police statistics was levelling off. Nevertheless, there was a basis for the claim that youth violence was getting worse (see Table 6.2). The data in the following tables (from Doob & Sprott, 1998) demonstrate that during this period of apparent increase in violence, the increase was rather selective.

It would be easy to assert from the data in Table 6.2 that although overall rates of 'youth crime' (as estimated from the number of cases going to court, Row 1) were going down, the proportion of this crime that involved violence (Row 5) was going up. More importantly, there was a 16.4 per cent increase in the number of violent cases involving youths as defendants in five years (Row 3). This change is non-trivial: there were 3,260 more cases involving youths charged with violence going into the court system in 1996–6 than there were in 1991–2. There were, however, in total more youths in Canada in 1995–6 than there four years earlier. Hence, the change in rate (Row 4) was much more modest. Nevertheless, the proportion of the cases going to youth court involving violence was also increasing, from 17 per cent of youth court cases to almost 21 per cent of youth court cases (Row 5).

How would one estimate the 'quality' of violence in these cases? There are some reasonable ways of looking at these figures. One would suspect, if the *police* were seeing more acts of very serious violence, then there would, in particular, be more serious charges being laid against these youths. Hence, if police-reported violence were qualitatively more severe than it had been, the growth should show up most clearly in the more serious forms of violence. We know, however, that it was not showing up in the youths charged with homicides (see Figure 6.3). Table 6.3 suggests that the evidence for increasingly severe forms of violence coming into the formal system was not there.

Looking first at the data in Row 1, it is clear that the increase in minor assaults was considerable. Even when corrected for the number of youths in Canada in that year (Row 4), there is a substantial increase in common assaults. For the most serious assault cases (Row 3 for the number of cases, and Row 6 when expressed as 'rates'), however, there is no evidence of an increase. The middle-level assault cases fall between these two extremes.

The comparable data (Table 6.4) for girls show the same overall trend: a large increase for minor assaults, and a decrease for the most serious type of assault.

The hypothesis that the 'quality' of youth violence got worse as the level of overall reported violence has levelled off certainly does not find support in the data that should reflect changes, had they occurred.

When one looks at a slightly longer time period, with a somewhat different definition of 'serious violence' the picture is not much different, but it illustrates a problem in understanding levels of youth crime. In Table 6.5, we have defined 'serious violence' as murder, manslaughter, attempted murder, aggravated sexual assault, and aggravated assault. Here, one could easily say that in the five-year period from 1994–5 to 1999–2000 there was a 41 per cent increase in findings of guilt (or transfers to adult court) for serious violence cases. From 1995–6 to 1998–9, a three-year period, there was a 77 per cent increase. Both of these sound like dramatic increases. One has to remember that these percentage increases obscure a rather important fact. We are talking about a very small number of youths who have been found guilty of serious offences. The increase in serious violence refers to the behaviour of roughly fifty to 100 youths out of 2.45 million youths in the country. One way of put-

Table 6.3   Changes in the distribution of youth court cases: three levels of assault, Canada, 1991–6

Type of offence	Number of cases					Change from 1991–2 to 1995–6
	1991–2	1992–3	1993–4	1994–5	1995–6	
Level 1: Minor assault cases (Row 1)	8,594	9,717	10,854	10,906	11,280	+2,686 (+31.3%)
Level 2: Assault with a weapon or causing bodily harm (Row 2)	3,431	3,685	3,836	3,745	3,695	+264 (+7.7%)
Level 3: Aggravated assault (Row 3)	308	311	309	317	312	+4 (+1.3%)
Level 1 per 100,000 YO age youth (Row 4)	392	420	465	462	473	+81 (+20.7%)
Level 2 per 100,000 YO age youth (Row 5)	156	159	165	159	155	−1.0 (−0.64%)
Level 3 per 100,000 YO age youth (Row 6)	14.0	13.5	13.3	13.4	13.1	−0.9 (−6.4%)

Source: Doob and Sprott, 1998.

ting these findings in context is shown in Table 6.6. There we can see that of the 2.45 million youths in Canada, very few are involved in serious violence as measured by charges which bring them to court or findings of guilt. Serious violence does happen, but it is relatively rare.

Changes in the Pattern of Involvement of Girls in Crime

From time to time in recent years, concern has been raised about the apparent increase in violence involving girls. Although typically sys-

Table 6.4   Changes in the distribution of youth court cases, girls only: three levels of assault, Canada, 1991–6

	Number of cases					Change from 1991–2 to 1995–6
	1991–2	1992–3	1993–4	1994–5	1995–6	
Cases with principal charge of violence (Row 1)	3,547	3,947	4,688	4,484	4,684	+1,137 (+32.1%)
Level 1: Cases of minor assault (Row 2)	2,354	2,774	3,277	3,127	3,272	+918 (+39.0%)
Level 2: Cases of assault with a weapon or causing bodily harm (Row 3)	532	573	706	659	658	+126 (+23.7%)
Level 3: Cases of aggravated assault (Row 4)	44	41	48	43	35	−9 (−20.5%)
Cases involving violence per 100,000 YO age girls (Row 5)	332	350	412	390	403	+71 (+21.4%)
Level 1 per 100,000 YO age girls (Row 6)	220	246	288	272	281	+61 (+27.7%)
Level 2 per 100,000 YO age girls (Row 7)	49.8	50.9	62.1	57.3	56.6	+6.8 (+13.7%)
Level 3 per 100,000 YO age girls (Row 8)	4.12	3.64	4.22	3.74	3.01	−1.11 (−26.9%)

Source: Doob and Sprott, 1998.

Table 6.5   Trends in youth violence: findings of guilt, (including transfers to adult court) for violence

Year	All youth cases	Minor violence	Common assault	Serious violence
1991–2	75,214	12,100	5,687	190
1992–3	77,308	13,777	6,684	190
1993–4	78,104	14,735	7,507	165
1994–5	74,092	14,441	7,448	167
1995–6	73,109	13,992	7,556	139
1996–7	74,889	14,293	7,636	183
1997–8	74,607	14,513	7,105	203
1998–9	72,052	14,427	6,898	246
1999–2000	68,236	13,808	6,572	236

Source: Canadian Centre for Justice Statistics, 2001b.
Serious violence = murder, manslaughter, attempted murder, aggravated sexual assault, aggravated assault.

Table 6.6   Violence offences among youth cases entering court, 1999–2000: Seriously violent Canadian youth?

1999–2000	Canada
Total youth	2.45 million
All youth cases	102,061
Violent cases	22,937
Serious violent cases[a] to court	553
Serious violent cases guilty or transferred	236
Murder, manslaughter cases	67
Murder, manslaughter cases guilty or transferred (26 + 12)	38

Source: Canadian Centre for Justice Statistics, 2001b.
[a] Serious violence: murder, manslaughter, attempted murder, aggravated sexual assault, aggravated assault.

tematic data are not used to illustrate these concerns, such data can be found. Figure 6.5 shows the proportion of all cases entering youth court, and all cases involving violence, where girls are the accused. What is clear is that over the past ten years, the proportion of cases in court involving girls has increased.

It would be easy to infer, therefore, that girls have become more 'criminal' and, in particular, have become more violent. Figure 6.5,

Figure 6.5. Percentage of all cases (and all violent cases) involving girls in Canada

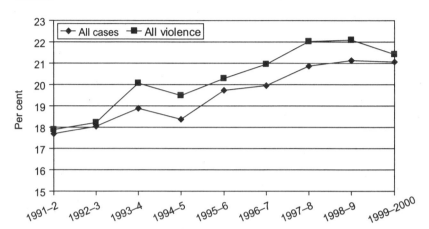

Source: Canadian Centre for Justice Statistics, 2001b.

however, has to be understood in light of Figure 6.6, which shows quite a different picture.

In Figure 6.6, we present the number of cases per 1,000 girls and boys going into court. The picture is quite a different one, although it based on the identical data. What is changing is not the behaviour of girls, but the behaviour of boys.

Somewhat cynically, one could suggest that Figure 6.6 demonstrates that girls are being blamed (in Figure 6.5) for something which really reflects changes for the better in boys. Figure 6.6 shows that the rate of being brought to court for girls, over the past decade, is fairly constant. Boys, however, are being brought to court at a lower rate now than they had been and, as a result, can be seen as making girls look relatively worse.

When one looks at the proportion of different levels of seriousness of violence that girls are responsible for (Figure 6.7), the picture becomes even more coherent. Girls are not involved in as much violence as are boys, and when they are, they are disproportionately likely to be involved in less serious forms of violence.

The proportion of cases of the least serious form of assault (common assault) involving girls is considerably higher than the proportion of cases of the more serious forms of violence (assault causing bodily

Figure 6.6. Rates per 1,000 youths of bringing girls and boys to youth court in Canada

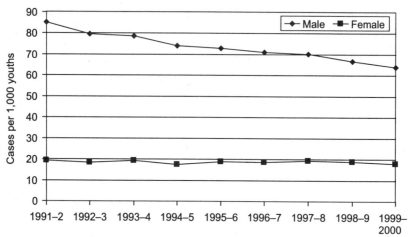

Source: Canadian Centre for Justice Statistics, 2001b.

Figure 6.7. Percentage of different types of violence that girls are 'responsible' for, Canada, 1991–2 to 1999–2000.

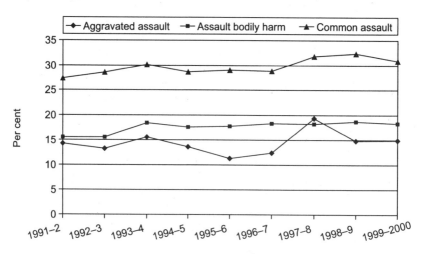

Source: Canadian Centre for Justice Statistics, 2001b.

Table 6.7   Relationship between girls and boys as the accused and the severity of the violence charged, Canada, 1995–6

Offence (principal charge)	Accused in violence cases	
	Girls and boys	Girls *n* (%)
Murder, manslaughter	44	2 (4.5)
Attempted murder	64	4 (6.3)
Aggravated assault	312	35 (11.2)
Assault with weapon or causing bodily harm	3,695	658 (17.8)
Minor assault	11,280	3,272 (29.0)

Source: Doob and Sprott, 1998.

harm, or aggravated assault). Generally, the more serious the violence, the less likely it is that a girl will be the suspect in a court hearing.[1]

Doob and Sprott (1998) performed a more detailed analysis of the phenomenon of girls being especially under-represented in serious violence. Their results for 1995–6 are shown in Table 6.7. For both males and females, the involvement in minor cases of violence vastly outnumber the number who arrive at court facing a serious charge. However, the proportion of cases coming to court involving girls goes down dramatically as one moves from common assaults (29 per cent of the cases involve girls as the accused) to murder or manslaughter (4.5 per cent of the cases involve girls as the accused).

Trends in Youth Crime and Trends in the Charging of Youths

Another indicator of trends in youth crime comes from a study by Carrington and Moyer (1994), which examined the increase in violent cases coming to youth courts in Canada after the Young Offenders Act was brought into place. They conclude that the increase was a result of

---

1 The anomaly in the 1997–8 data for aggravated assault illustrates a finding we have already discussed. What is anomalous about this one data point is that the proportion of accused youths who are girls is (slightly) higher than the proportion of assault causing bodily harm cases involving girls. A further examination of these data shows that there was not an unusually large number of girls in court on charges of aggravated assault. Instead, there was an unusually low number of boys.

a change in charging practices on the part of the police, rather than any change in the underlying behaviour of young people.

None of this suggests, however, that youth crime is not changing or that the changes that may be occurring are not disturbing to us. For example, a decade ago the term 'swarming' did not exist as a word applied to young people. Since then, however, 'swarming' as a term was first applied in Toronto to young people in large (and sometimes not so large) groups surrounding and robbing someone. It has also been applied to a method of stealing from stores whereby a group of young people enter a store and mill around in such a way that it is impossible to see whether items are being stolen. More recently the term was applied to a frightening experience that a couple of women had in being taunted and threatened (but fortunately not physically harmed) by a large group of belligerent youth. It may well be that these *forms* of crimes did not exist some time ago. It is likely, however, that some other forms of crimes that existed ten or twenty years ago are not very widespread now.

There are also assertions being made that the nature of particular crimes – particularly violent crime – is getting worse. Unfortunately, other than the homicide data already cited, we do not have a clear understanding whether this is the case. It may be, for example, that the carrying of weapons in schools has increased. It is also possible that behaviour which used to be acceptable in the past, adolescents carrying pocket knives to school, for example, simply is not acceptable any more. In other words, what used to be seen as acceptable is now considered an offence. This is, however, speculation.

When one looks at the published research on the question of whether crime has increased, the picture is not clear. Corrado and Markwart (1994) conclude from their analysis of police and court data that there has been a real increase in the amount of violence taking place among youth in the previous five to ten years. They specifically state that they believe it is a true increase in crime, rather than some change in police charging practices or in public tolerance – an argument that some people have advanced.

Carrington (1995) takes issue with Corrado and Markwart's analysis. He suggests that they have made a number of comparisons which exaggerate the increase in the number of youths apprehended for violent offences; he also suggests that the rates are, in fact, no higher than they have been in other years. What has changed is the manner in which we deal with violence.

There are some obvious examples of policies that could increase the amount of violence coming to the attention of the police and going to court. In Ontario, for example, some school boards have instituted policies whereby even minor violence (what used to be called 'schoolyard fights') is to be responded to by the school authorities. In many cases this means calling in the police. Such policies could, for example, explain the increased proportion of cases going to youth court that involve violence. Doob and Meen (1993) noted that the proportion of all cases that involve violence getting to the disposition stage of proceedings in the Toronto juvenile courts in the last years of the Juvenile Delinquents Act was only about 8 per cent. Looking at this same age group (those over 12 and under 16) in the first years of the Young Offenders Act, they found that the proportion of violence had increased to about 10 per cent. By the end of the decade, the proportion of violent cases had increased quite dramatically to about 24 per cent.

Is Youth Crime Increasing?

Where does this all leave us? Perhaps the most stark way of illustrating the two interpretations of the existing data would be to consider the following quotations:

> With the exception of homicide, the evidence and the arguments are convincing in supporting the view that there has been a real and substantial increase in youth violence in Canada in recent years, especially with armed robberies and more serious assaults, but also including other forms of youth violence such as common assault. (Corrado & Markwart, 1994, p. 354)

> A brief discussion is in order of the striking difference between our finding of no increase in all types of robberies – indeed, a decrease, albeit statistically non-significant, of 32% in robberies involving a firearm – and Corrado and Markwart's finding of increases between 100 percent and 267 percent in robberies by young offenders. The explanation, of course, lies in the method of comparison ... Robberies by young persons did increase substantially after 1986, but this was an unusually low year. By 1992, robberies by young persons had simply returned to their levels of the early 1980s. To conclude from this that the Young Offenders Act had reversed a downward trend in robberies by young persons would, however, be an error ... Rates of robberies by adults followed a similar trend during the

1980s, which could not have been due to the Young Offenders Act. (Carrington, 1995, pp. 68–70)

The increase in police-reported violent youth crime is considerably smaller than was suggested by Corrado and Markwart's analyses, is concentrated in mainly non-violent offenders against the person, and appears to be part of a larger social trend, not unique to young offenders. To what extent this trend in police-reported crime rates represents an increase in actual crime or an increase in reporting by the public and recording by the police, is difficult to say from these data. (ibid., p. 71)

In a later paper, Carrington examined charging practices for a twenty-year period from 1977 to 1996. It provides a very plausible explanation for a rather simple sounding finding: 'The per capita rate of young persons charged has increased significantly since the inception of the Young Offenders Act' (Carrington, 1999, p. 4). Using police data, Carrington attempted to overcome some complex issues in creating comparable measures over this whole period when the definition of a youth was changing (from age 7 to age 12 in all provinces and from 15 to 17 in some provinces).

Carrington suggests that there was 'a jump in charging [of youths by the police] in 1986 that did not occur in apprehensions of young person' (ibid., p. 18). The result was that there was a 27 per cent higher charge rate in 1986–96 than in 1980–3, as compared with a 7 per cent increase in the apprehension rate. In other words, the police exercised their discretion differently under the YOA than they had under the JDA: they charged a higher proportion of those youth who were apprehended. Quebec was the only province that showed a decrease in charge rates. What happened in the other provinces is that the YOA clearly changed police charging practice. It appears, from other analyses (Carrington, 1998, p. 24), that the increase in proportions charged 'applied over the entire YOA range ... and was therefore not simply due to the addition of 16 and 17 year olds.' As Carrington notes, 'there is no basis in fact for public concern about increased level of youth crime or the supposed failure of the YOA to control youth crime' (ibid., p. 25). The change that did occur is a change in the behaviour of adults (police charging practice) not a change in the behaviour of youths.

The last word on this matter goes to Corrado and Markwart and it is something that Peter Carrington could probably agree with. They make it clear that although the amount of youth violence may have increased this does not mean that it is 'out of control.' Corrado and Markwart (1994, p. 355) point out that 'while we believe the evidence supports the view that there has been a real and substantial increase in youth violence (other than homicide) in recent years, these changes must be put into perspective. While these increases may be real, the incidence remains relatively low. Violent crime is certainly not running rampant and non-violent crime remains the staple of youth crime.'

They take the position that the problem with society's response to crime is that it is both too harsh and too soft: it is too harsh in the way it deals with the majority of crime (non-violent crime) and too mild in the way in which it deals with serious violence. The point that they make is similar to that made by others: by dealing with all offences as if they were the same, adequate resources cannot be focused on the most serious cases.

One final point needs to be made about the homicide data we have presented: there is, very roughly speaking, one young person charged every week to ten days for a homicide offence. To the extent that our media report these events on a national basis, it means that the public has enormous opportunities to hear about homicides committed by youth. Thus, it is completely understandable – if the media are reporting youth homicides quite regularly – for people to believe that there is an increase. We remember these recent reports, and assume that it must not have been 'like that' a few years ago.

Conclusion

What can one conclude from all of these data? We would suggest that crime generally and youth crime in particular are probably not increasing. This does not mean that crime is not changing in form; it does suggest that overall the rates of criminal code offences actually occurring may not have changed much. It is important to remember that there is plenty of crime in our society that comes to the attention of the youth justice system. That there *may* not be any more of it than there was five, ten, or fifteen years ago may reassure us, but it should not distract us from the two separate goals of improving the youth justice system and of addressing the problem of youth crime.

CHAPTER SEVEN

Getting the Case to Court

As discussed in Chapter 4, for a case to end up in youth court, a number of decisions need to be made. Even after an event is noticed and identified as an offence, someone has to decide that it is worthy of formal intervention, and, typically, someone has to call the police. The question we are going to address in this chapter is a straightforward one: what happens to a case when it is brought to the attention of the police?

Under the Juvenile Delinquents Act there were no specific provisions for alternative measures or diversion programs but police often used their discretion to deal with youth informally. Certain sections of the Juvenile Delinquents Act, however, could be read as encouraging police discretion. For example, as we pointed out in Chapter 1, Section 38 indicated that 'the care and custody and discipline of a juvenile delinquent shall approximate as nearly as may be that which should be given by his parents, and that as far as practicable every juvenile delinquent shall be treated, not as criminal, but as a misdirected and misguided child, and one needing aid, encouragement, help and assistance.'

In addition, of course, Canadian police are not required to lay charges against every person (adult or youth) whom they believe may have committed an offence. Hence, it was, and still is, within the jurisdiction of the police to look for less formal ways of responding to a youth than to take them to court. As an alternative, the police may encourage the youth to apologize to his or her victim or the officer may escort a youth to his or her home and have a talk with the parents. Police departments in some locations developed more formal diversion programs which included warnings, requirements to do community service, and restitution to the victim (Pate, 1990).

What was clear in the years leading up to the replacement of the Juvenile Delinquents Act with the Young Offenders Act in 1984 was that in many locations only a small minority of youths who were apprehended by the police were actually brought to court.

The Decision Not to Charge a Young Person

The issue of police discretion in the handling of young offenders was fairly well researched in Canada and elsewhere in the 1970s. Conly (1978) carried out a study of police discretion in the charging of young offenders in a number of metropolitan areas. Probably the most important single factor that determined who was brought to court was the metropolitan area in which the young offender lived. The variation across areas was enormous, with a low of 17 per cent of young offenders apprehended for criminal matters being charged in one municipality (Hamilton, Ontario) and a high of 96 per cent charged in another (Calgary). The variation was not related to provincial policy; Edmonton, for example, had only 30 per cent of its youth apprehended for offending being sent to court.

The decision whether to charge a young person is probably a difficult strategic one. Police officers dealing with young offenders know that many young offenders are not likely to develop into adult criminals. They also understand that a first-time offender who has committed a minor offence is not likely to be punished very harshly by the youth court. Even if punishment might be desired, therefore, it is recognized that the court might not impose it. Police officers may also take into account the fact that youth courts have only limited resources available (both in court time and dispositional services). To use these limited resources on young people who are not in need of them may be counterproductive. Finally, from a strict 'crime control' perspective, police officers may make a sensible – and quite often valid – prediction that in terms of crime control there would be no long-term benefit to society by taking a young person to court.

A study carried out in the mid-1970s of the factors used by police officers to determine whether to charge young people (Doob & Chan, 1982) found that a combination of offence and offender characteristics correlated with the decision to charge. Not surprisingly, the seriousness of the offence was one of the predictors of the police officer's decision to charge. Other predictors included whether the young person had been previously apprehended (and either warned or charged) and the young person's behaviour when confronted with the police (e.g., whether the suspect readily admitted the offence).

Police officers were also responsive to the victim: offenders whose victims indicated that they wanted a charge laid were more likely to end up in court. A number of factors (seriousness of the offence, previous contacts with the police, the juvenile's 'actions' in response to being apprehended, and the victim's request) appeared to be the most relevant. At the time that this particular study was carried out, the policy of the police force being studied was to take into account the 'attitude' of the young person in making a decision to charge. Some people have questioned whether using 'attitude' to determine the outcome of a case is appropriate; the young person's attitude may be a reflection of his or her inability to respond in a manner the police officer perceives as appropriate more than it is an indication of future misbehaviour.

In a large-scale study of police discretion in police departments that participate in the 'incident based' crime reporting system, Carrington (1998)[1] found that 59 per cent of young persons apprehended by police were charged or recommended to be charged and 41 per cent were processed 'by other means.' 'Other means' can include a range of activities that begin with police discretion, including returning a youth home, warning or cautioning the youth, or referring the youth to an alternative measures program. Not surprisingly, the proportion of youths charged varied from province to province; these differences might not reflect police practices as much as the impact of the Crown, screening agencies, and programs that provide alternative measures. For example, in Ontario, alternative measures can only take place after a charge has been laid, and therefore would show up as a charge in police statistics.

Carrington's (1998) study was able to look at a large number of variables about the incident and the accused youth. Unfortunately, not all police forces contribute data to this program. Carrington reported data for seven jurisdictions, some of which were provinces and some of which were individual police departments. However, there were enough data available (94,221 incidents involving one or more youths) for the two years that Carrington studied (1992 and 1993) to allow for some understanding of what determined a youth's fate when apprehended by the police as a suspect in a criminal offence. There was con-

---

1 Based on data from the Revised Uniform Crime Reporting Survey. The study includes characteristics of the accused and of the incident for 94,221 young persons apprehended in 1992 and 1993 by police departments in towns and cities in New Brunswick, Ontario, Saskatchewan, British Columbia, and almost all of Quebec.

siderable variability across jurisdictions in the overall charge rate. In York Region, Ontario, only 43 per cent of the youths who were apprehended were charged, whereas in Vancouver 88 per cent were charged. Saskatchewan also had a relatively high (79 per cent) overall charge rate for apprehended youths. In the overall sample of police departments, 59 per cent of the youths were charged.

Two types of variables which have been shown previously to be related to the decision to charge were not available on the Uniform Crime Reporting (UCR) form: the demeanour of the accused and the accused's official record of offending. Previous research would suggest that these each add to our understanding of the police officer's decision. The factors that Carrington examined are probably best thought of as adding to our understanding above and beyond these two factors.

Carrington divided the factors that affected the decision to charge into three groups: those that had a high, moderate, and low impact on the decision (Carrington, 1998, Table 17). In an interesting and useful discussion, Carrington separated what he calls the 'individual' impact of a variable on the likelihood of charges being laid from the 'overall' impact. The individual impact is size of the impact of that variable on the decision to charge. As Table 7.1 shows, those charged with more serious offences were 14.8 per cent more likely to be charged than those charged with less serious offences.

The 'overall impact' on the decision is somewhat different. The police officer's notation that there was evidence that the youth had consumed alcohol or drugs had a rather large impact on the likelihood that charges would be laid against that youth. However, because so few youths were identified as having consumed alcohol or drugs, the overall impact of the variable on the decision to charge was rather minimal.

For the most part, there are few surprises in Table 7.1. Many of the factors that affect police decisions can be seen as being a function of the apparent seriousness of the offence (e.g., type of offence, weapon, type of incident, number of co-accused, value of property, level of injury, or adult present) or the youth's level of responsibility (age of the accused, use of alcohol or drugs). However, three predictors of the overall decision to charge warrant some additional attention.

Gender

Before controlling for other factors, there was a very slight difference suggesting that females were more likely to be charged than males (60.3 per cent of females charged vs 58.8 per cent of males). However, when

Table 7.1   The impact of various case characteristics on the likelihood of charges being laid against an accused youth

| Characteristic | Value associated with high likelihood of charge | Individual impact | | Overall impact rank (1 = highest) |
		Rank	Mean % difference from baseline	
High impact				
Most serious violation in offences against persons	Serious (homicide or other indictable)	1	14.8	1
Age of the accused	Older	2	10.9	2
Weapon	Firearm or other weapon	3	10.2	4
Moderate impact				
Consumption of alcohol or drugs	Identified as having consumed alcohol or drugs	4	9.7	Tied: lowest (11)
Type of incident	'Other' offences, e.g., administration of justice offences, rather than property or offences against persons	5	7.1	3
Victim-accused relationship	Stranger or unknown relationship	6	5.7	5
Aboriginal status	Aboriginal	7	5.6	9
Number of co-accused	Larger number	8	5.0	7
Value of property	High value	9	3.6	6
Low impact				
Level of injury to victim	Major injury	10	3.3	8
Offence is shoplifting	Shoplifting	11	2.7	10
Adult co-accused	Adult also apprehended in incident	12	2.4	Tied: lowest (11)
Gender	Male	13	2.3	Tied: lowest (11)

Source: Adapted from Carrington, 1998, Table 17. Baseline charge rate = 59%. Difference from baseline estimated adjusted for spurious relationships (i.e., differences that are best explained by other variables).

other characteristics of the case were controlled for – for example, region where the incident took place, age of the accused, type of incident, whether the incident involved shoplifting, and value of property – males were slightly more likely to be charged than were female young offenders. On the surface, it would appear that female young offenders were slightly *more* likely to be charged than males who were apprehended. This apparent harshness towards females was an artefact of other differences between females and males. For example, shoplifters are more likely, on average, to be charged (60 per cent charged) than are youths charged with other offences (54 per cent charged for other offences). Females accounted for 15 per cent of the total sample, but were the accused in 46 per cent of the shoplifting cases. Ignoring offence would suggest a higher likelihood of females being charged, whereas this is probably best thought of as an effect of offence, not gender.

Aboriginal Status

Even after adjusting for other variables, the difference between the overall charge rates of Aboriginal versus non-Aboriginal youths was maintained. Controlling for other variables, the likelihood of an Aboriginal youth being charged was .69, which was quite a bit higher than the likelihood of a non-Aboriginal youth being charged (.58). Aboriginal youth tended to be concentrated in locations with high charge rates (e.g., Saskatchewan).

Incident Involved Shoplifting

In this study, after controlling for various characteristics of the youth (e.g., region, gender, Aboriginal status, age, presence of a co-accused adult, presence of other co-accused youths) and of the offence (value of the property or other indications of offence seriousness) there was still an impact of whether the incident involved shoplifting. Given that shoplifting constituted about 18 per cent of all cases, this tendency to treat shoplifting cases more harshly than one might otherwise expect increases the youth court case load measurably.

It is evident from all of the information that is available on the decision to take a youth to court that it is not a routine mechanical event. The various pieces of research which have been carried out in Canada on this topic indicate that a large number of characteristics of the youth, the incident, and the interaction between the youth and the police officer affect the decision. Under the Young Offenders Act, little guidance was given to the police officer on how this decision should be made. Hence, there is no obvious standard against which the data we have just summarized might be compared.

The Young Offenders Act

Unlike the Juvenile Delinquents Act, which was largely silent on the question of whether a young person who apparently offended should be brought to court, the Young Offenders Act made it quite clear to the police and others that there were choices other than bringing a case to court. Under Section 3(1)(d) of the Young Offenders Act, the police were given the discretion to deal with cases, where appropriate, completely outside the youth justice system. Specifically, the YOA tells the police that 'where it is not inconsistent with the protection of society, taking no measures or taking measures other than judicial proceedings under this Act should be considered for dealing with young persons who have committed offences.' In addition, Section 3(1)(f) indicates that 'in the application of this Act, the rights and freedoms of young persons include a right of the least possible interference with freedom that is consistent with the protection of society ...' These sections, in effect, legitimize a practice in place in all provinces and territories. Police, everywhere, do not bring formal charges against all those youths who have committed offences. But the Young Offenders Act did not go one step further and explain how the decision should be made.

It is interesting to note that, when the Young Offenders Act became law, the proportion of those youths (in provinces where data were available) who were charged after being apprehended by the police jumped from about 55 per cent prior to 1984 to about 65 per cent in 1986.[2] These two proportions were quite stable both before and after the Young Offenders Act became law (Carrington, 1999). As Carrington points out, 'It seems likely that this jump in charging of apprehended youth was due to the YOA, since it occurred immediately after

---

2 The qualification 'in provinces where data were available' is important in understanding the *absolute* level of the proportion charges. Data for this decision are more broadly available than for the detailed analysis carried out by Carrington (1998), but neither set of data is complete. What is important here is that the proportion charged increased dramatically.

the YOA came into effect and the charge ratio was stable over the rest of the two decades examined' (ibid., p. 18). He notes that 'the jump in police charging was especially pronounced in Saskatchewan and Ontario ...' (ibid., p. 26). Quebec, on the other hand, 'experienced a continuous decline in the charge ratio after 1988' (ibid.).

The law was being administered in a manner that encouraged the charging of youths who apparently had committed minor offences. The Young Offenders Act did not require that charges be laid, but for reasons that are not well understood, it seemed to have happened. Obviously, it could have been the change in the law that was the cause of the increased use of the formal youth justice system, or it could have been societal changes that occurred during this same time (e.g., changes in levels of tolerance for adolescent misbehaviour) or some combination of other factors.

Alternative Measures

The Young Offenders Act formalized one form of diversion from the youth court by designating a procedure whereby youths who admitted their offences could be referred (either pre- or post-charge) to a designated program referred to as 'alternative measures.' The legislated criteria are vague. They can be used only if 'the person who is considering whether to use such measures is satisfied that they would be appropriate, having regard to the needs of the young person and the interests of society' (Section 4(1)(b)).

One possibility is that by formalizing what had previously been done informally (through police exercising their discretion not to charge), more youths ended up being charged. Hence, while formal alternative measure programs may have increased in numbers since the implementation of the YOA, it is not clear that they have been successful at what they were designed to do – divert youth from formal processing in the youth justice system. In fact, it appears that police have sometimes become more reluctant to use their discretion or informal means to deal with youth.

All jurisdictions have designated programs for dealing with young offenders by way of alternative measures under Section 4 of the Young Offenders Act. The Act lays out various legal safeguards for the young person. Most jurisdictions (the exceptions being New Brunswick, Ontario, and the Yukon) allow youths to be referred both before and after they have been formally charged. In Ontario and the Yukon youths are referred to programs after charges have been laid; in New Brunswick programs operate at the pre-charge stage only (Stevenson, Tufts, Hendrick, & Kowalski, 1998).

There are a variety of alternative measures programs currently operating in Canada, including the following:

- apologies – through written or personal contact with the victim
- essays or posters – with focus on crime prevention.
- restitution or compensation – financial compensation to the victim
- personal services – provided where appropriate and desired by the victim
- educational programs – such as 'Shoplift' which educates youth on the impact of shoplifting on the community
- community service – for non-profit organizations, in the community (hours vary considerably)
- various social skills improvement courses, or, in Aboriginal communities, programs which attempt to impose traditional consequences on the young person (Stevenson et al., 1998)

The most frequent type of alternative measure in Canada appears to be community service (22 per cent) followed by apologies (13 per cent) (Kowalski, 1999). There is some variation across provinces and territories in the type of alternative measure commonly used. For example, in the Yukon supervision (32 per cent) is the alternative measure most commonly used, while in Quebec (40 per cent) it is social skills improvement, and in Manitoba (30 per cent) it is a parental action letter (ibid.).

The Use of Alternative Measures

Unfortunately, we know very little about the manner in which decisions are made to refer a young person to an alternative measures program. Part of the problem is that there is no obvious way in which such decisions are 'captured' by existing statistical programs. If a young person is dealt with by way of alternative measures *before a formal charge is laid*, then the case would not normally show up in youth court statistics (assuming that no subsequent charge was laid with respect to the same matters). Furthermore, if a young person is referred by the police to an alternative measures program, this decision would not differ in police statistics (Uniform Crime Reporting) from the situation where a police officer deals with a case with a simple warning. However, in some jurisdictions, charges can only be laid if they are first approved by the Crown. If the police recommend a young person be charged in these jurisdictions, the UCR data will show the youth as 'charged' even if the Crown subsequently places the young person in an alternative measures program.

Alternative measures are generally used for less serious offences and for young people without a criminal record. Of alternative measures cases 70 per cent involve property-related crime – over one-half involve theft under $5,000 (Kowalski, 1999). Although few jurisdictions can provide data on prior criminal history, those that do indicate that less than 1 per cent of youth who participate in alternative measures have prior findings of guilt (ibid.).

In 1997–8, 89 per cent of youth successfully completed all alternative measures that they agreed to, and another 1 per cent partially completed these measures (ibid.). Compared with their numbers in the population, Aboriginal people are somewhat over-represented in alternative measures programs. However, given that Aboriginal youths are over-represented among those charged, it should not be surprising that they are somewhat over-represented in alternative measures programs. What is not known is whether they are over-, under-, or equally represented as a proportion of those who come in contact with the police.

Extrajudicial Measures under the YCJA

Principles designed to address the need to screen cases out of the court system form a key part of the Youth Criminal Justice Act. When the plans to develop the Youth Criminal Justice Act were announced in May 1998, the document released by the Minister of Justice indicated that 'alternatives to the formal youth justice system are an important component of the youth justice strategy for the less serious and temporary behaviour that accounts for the majority of youth crime. They allow for effective early involvement to correct antisocial behaviour ... [They] hold great promise as appropriate, effective and efficient responses to crime. Communities and youth justice committees have important roles to play in youth court alternatives' (Department of Justice, 1998, pp. 19–21).

Unlike the Young Offenders Act, the Youth Criminal Justice Act includes detailed principles and options for dealing with cases outside of the court system. Measures outside the formal court system ('extrajudicial measures') such as warnings and referrals to community programs etc. are 'presumed to be adequate to hold a young person accountable for his or her offending behaviour if the young person has committed a non-violent offence and has previously not been found guilty of an offence' (Section 4(c)). In addition, 'extrajudicial measures should be used if they are adequate to hold a young person accountable for his or her behaviour' (Section 4(d)).

It is consistent with the overall philosophy of the act, then, that the YCJA states that non-court alternatives can be used even if they have been used before, and even if the youth has been previously been found guilty (Section 4(d)). If the offence is minor, and non-court approaches 'are adequate' to hold the youth accountable, then they are to be used. Police are told that they 'shall' consider non-court approaches in all cases before starting judicial proceedings (Section 6(1)). However, perhaps because of the provincial, rather than federal, responsibility for the administration of justice, the failure of a police officer to consider non-court approaches does not invalidate any charge that is laid against the youth (Section 6(2)). Finally, a section on 'extrajudicial sanctions' is quite similar to 'alternative measures' under the Young Offenders Act.

The intent of these sections of the YCJA is to encourage the use of less formal responses to youthful offending.

Public Acceptability of Dealing with Youths Outside of the Formal System

It is clear that a concern for those whose jobs depend on the public acceptability of youth justice policies is that dealing with young offenders outside of the court system might be seen as a 'lenient' approach to crime. In the press release announcing the first reading of the Youth Criminal Justice Act in March 1999, for example, the Minister of Justice listed the fact that the new act would 'allow for and encourage the use of a full range of community-based sentences and effective alternatives to the justice system for youth who commit non-violent offences' as point number 12 in a list of thirteen 'new' points of the legislation she was introducing (Department of Justice, Canada, 1999, p. 2). One suspects that she was not comfortable advertising that one of the purposes of the new act was to keep youths out of court.

She need not have been so worried. In one Ontario survey (Doob et al., 1998), people were asked how appropriate it was for a minor property offence (a theft of goods valued at $25 from a local store) to be brought to court. One group was asked, simply, how appropriate it was for the case to be fully processed by the court. A second group was

Table 7.2   Assessment of procedure for dealing with a minor theft by a young offender (percentage, and in parentheses, number)

Procedure described	View of procedure			
	Inappropriate	Neutral	Appropriate	Total
Court	46.7	18.2	35.2	100.0 (165)
Court with information about costs	43.6	28.2	28.2	100.0 (163)
Family group conference	5.7	19.5	74.7	100.0 (174)

Source: Doob et al., 1998.

presented with the same outcome (court processing), but were also told that the cost of court processing was about $1,500. The third group was presented with an alternative to court where, a form of 'family group conference' was described as follows: 'The young person is dealt with outside of the court system. The young person and members of his family and the store owner are brought together at a meeting to discuss the offence and come to a written agreement about what the consequences should be for the young person. If the offender does not do what is agreed upon, he can be brought to court.'

They were then asked, on a 10-point scale, to indicate how appropriate they found it to deal with a case like this in the manner that was described. Dividing the scale into three categories, the overall findings are shown in Table 7.2.

The family group conference was seen, by far, as being the most appropriate way of dealing with the problem. Furthermore, close to half of Ontario residents see it as completely inappropriate to deal with minor thefts in court.

One finding that was a bit surprising, however, was the fact that making the cost of court processing salient did not affect the overall ratings. The following tables, however, show that this 'no difference' (between the two court conditions) is a bit more complex than it first appears.

In looking at those who thought that sentences for youths were too lenient (see Table 7.3), we see a rather interesting pattern. First of all, for those who think that sentences are not harsh enough, we see the same pattern that was evident above:

• Dealing with the offender in a family group conference was seen as the appropriate way of dealing with the case.

Table 7.3 Appropriate procedure for dealing with a minor theft by a young offender, according to those who think that youth court sentences are too lenient (percentage, and in parentheses number)

Procedure described	View of procedure			
	Inappropriate	Neutral	Appropriate	Total
Court	47.8	16.9	35.3	100.0 (136)
Court with information about costs	38.8	27.9	33.3	100.0 (129)
Family group conference	6.8	19.5	73.7	100.0 (133)

Source: Doob et al., 1998.

Table 7.4 Appropriate procedure for dealing with a minor theft by a young offender, according to those who think that youth court sentences are about right or too severe (percentage, and in parentheses number)

Procedure described	View of procedure			
	Inappropriate	Neutral	Appropriate	Total
Court	35.3	29.4	35.3	100.0 (17)
Court with information about costs	52.2	34.8	13.0	100.0 (23)
Family group conference	–	20.0	80.0	100.0 (25)

Source: Doob et al., 1998.

- Taking the case to court was seen, overwhelmingly, as being inappropriate or at best somewhere in the middle.
- Making the cost of court processing salient had no real impact on the respondents.

However, when one looks at those who think that sentences are about right or too severe, a somewhat different pattern emerges (see Table 7.4). A family group conference still constitutes the more appropriate means of dealing with the offender. However, this group of people are sensitive, it seems, to costs: telling them that it will cost $1,500 to process the offender in court makes the court be seen as even less appropriate.

It should be remembered, of course, that those who think that sentences are too harsh or about right constitute a minority of respondents. For them, not only is the family group conference the approach that is

Table 7.5   Judges' views on proportion of cases that could be dealt with outside of court, Quebec and rest of Canada (percentage, and in parentheses number)

	Cases that could be dealt with adequately outside court			
	Most–all	About half	Few–none	Total
Quebec	9.1	18.2	72.7	100.0 (22)
Rest of Canada	14.6	41.7	43.7	100.0 (206)
Total	14.0	39.5	46.5	100.0 (228)

Source: Doob, 2001.

seen as appropriate, but making the cost of a court hearing salient reduced the rated appropriateness of the court option.

Judges' Views of the Cases before Them

We have already noted, in Chapter 4, that many of the cases going into youth court are quite minor in nature. In a January 2001 survey of Canadian youth court judges (Doob, 2001), respondents were asked to indicate what proportion of the cases before them 'could have been dealt with just as adequately (or more adequately) outside of the youth court (e.g., informally, by "diversion," or by use of alternative measures if they had been available),' One province, Quebec, looked quite different from the rest. But across Canada, more than half of the judges thought that the majority of cases before them could have been better dealt with outside of the court (see Table 7.5).

Table 7.5 demonstrates that outside of Quebec, 14.6 per cent of youth court judges thought that most of the cases they were seeing could be dealt with adequately outside of youth court. However, an additional 41.7 per cent thought that about half of the cases before them could be adequately dealt with outside of the courts. Said differently, more than half (56.3 per cent) of the judges outside of Quebec thought that at least half of the cases they were seeing in youth court could be handled just as well outside of the formal court system.

Not surprisingly, these figures were much lower in Quebec. Quebec judges, it appears, were more likely to feel that it was useful to bring the cases before them into the formal court system. One of the obvious reasons for this is that Quebec brings far fewer cases to youth court than is done elsewhere in Canada. This can be seen in Table 7.6.

Table 7.6   Youth court cases per 100 youths in the jurisdiction, 1999–2000

Jurisdiction	Cases per 100 youths
Canada	4.17
Newfoundland	3.64
Prince Edward Island	2.71
Nova Scotia	4.12
New Brunswick	3.73
Quebec	1.96
Ontario	4.28
Manitoba	7.00
Saskatchewan	9.41
Alberta	6.14
British Columbia	3.64
Yukon	13.81
Northwest Territories	10.09
Nunavut	4.29

Source: Canadian Centre for Justice Statistics, 2001b.

As Table 7.6 demonstrates, there are huge differences across jurisdictions in Canada in the rate in which cases are brought to youth court. These differences are unlikely to be the result solely of differences in the rate of offending. It is unlikely, for example, that Quebec youths offend at a rate that is half that of Ontario. Some jurisdictions, it seems, bring more cases to youth court than others.

Judges would appear to attribute the overuse of the court, in part, to the inadequacy of alternative measures or other non-court measures. It was not clear whether these responses referred to an inadequacy in the *number* of available non-court programs or the frequency in which these programs were *being used*. Nonetheless, the point was simple: those judges who indicated that large numbers of the cases they were seeing could be dealt with outside of the court were most critical of the unavailability and/or under-use of alternative measures programs (see Table 7.7).

This relationship holds when one looks separately at the views of Quebec judges, on the one hand, and judges in the rest of Canada, on the other. (Note, however, that almost all Quebec judges were content with the availability of alternative measures.)

The basic problem appears to be easy to describe. Quebec was the only region in Canada where a majority of judges thought that alterna-

Table 7.7   Relationship between judges' views on adequacy of alternative measures and judges' views on proportion of cases that could be handled outside court (percentage, in parentheses number)

Cases that could be dealt with adequately outside court	Adequate alternative measures?			
	Definitely yes	Probably yes	No, don't know	Total
Most / almost all / all	6.3	9.4	84.4	100.0 (32)
About half	7.5	15.1	77.4	100.0 (93)
Few–none	34.6	36.4	29.0	100.0 (107)
Total	19.8	24.1	56.0	100.0 (232)

Source: Doob, 2001.

tive measures were adequate (see Table 7.8). Judges who sat in more than one community were asked about the largest and the smallest communities in which they sat. The results for the two sizes of communities were similar.

Overall, it would appear that in every region of Canada other than Quebec, a substantial portion of the youth court judges thought that many (half or more) of the cases coming before them could have been dealt with 'just as adequately (or more adequately) outside of the youth court.' Even in Quebec, where judges were most likely to believe that adequate alternative measures or other 'non-court' programs in the community existed, approximately a quarter of the judges indicated that many of the cases they were hearing could be dealt with outside of the court. The proportion holding this view was considerably higher for the rest of Canada.

Alternative Measures and the Community

The delivery of alternative measures services varies across the country – some provinces/territories administer these programs through the various government departments, probation officers, or youth workers. Some jurisdictions use community and/or non-profit organizations, and some use volunteer committees such as Youth Justice Committees. Section 69 of the Young Offenders Act states that in any province of territory, the Attorney General 'may establish one or more committees of citizens, to be known as Youth Justice Committees, to

Table 7.8   Judges' perception of adequacy of alternative measures (largest or only community), by region in Canada (percentage, and in parentheses number)

| Region | Adequate alternative measures? | | | Total |
	Definitely yes	Probably yes	No, don't know	
Atlantic	6.7	33.3	60.0	100 (30)
Quebec	87.5	12.5	–	100 (24)
Ontario	10.3	25.0	64.7	100 (68)
Prairies	16.4	25.5	58.2	100 (55)
B.C.	13.2	20.8	66.0	100 (53)
Territories	25.0	–	75.0	100 (4)
Total	20.1	23.5	56.4	100 (234)

Source: Doob, 2001.

assist without remuneration in any aspect of the administration of the *Act* or in any programs or services for young offenders.'

Although committees to advise on alternative ways of handling youths have existed for many years in many forms, Youth Justice Committees are seen in First Nations communities as a particularly important way by which to respond to high rates of youth crime and recidivism among Aboriginal youth. The first formal Youth Justice Committee in Manitoba was established in Roseau River First Nation in 1975 in response to youth violence in the area (Paiement, 1996). By the mid-1990s, formalized Youth Justice Committees were operating in at least five jurisdictions in Canada (Newfoundland, Manitoba, Alberta, Ontario, and the Northwest Territories). In Manitoba, it is estimated that 60 per cent of alternative measures cases are dealt with by justice committees, and in Newfoundland the majority of alternative measures service delivery is the responsibility of youth justice committees (Moyer, 1996). In Nova Scotia and New Brunswick, the final decision to divert (after the Crown recommendation) as well as service delivery is the responsibility of diversion committees (ibid.).

A Youth Justice Committee may have virtually any number of members and often includes people from the business community, schools, churches, cultural organizations, and individual parents (Paiement, 1996). Committees generally focus on first-time, non-violent offenders, and either alone or in conjunction with a probation officer are respon-

Figure 7.1. Use of alternative measures and court, 1997–8, by province or territory*

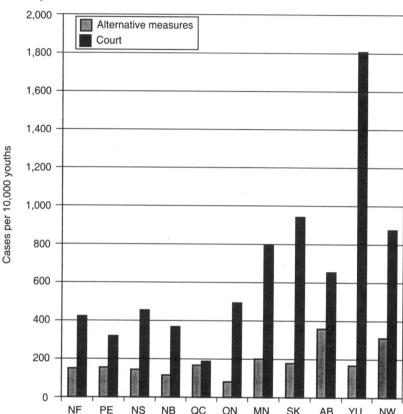

Source: Kowalski (1999).

*Data were not available for B.C. and Nunavut.

sible for ensuring that the terms of the alternative measures agreement are completed (ibid.).

It should be no surprise that there is a good bit of variation across provinces in the use of alternative measures for youths. Figure 7.1 shows the rates of taking youths to court and referring youths to alternative measures.

Two things are apparent from Figure 7.1. First, the rates of using courts appear to vary considerably more than the rates of using alternative measures. The second rather clear finding is that the relationship between the relative use of court and alternative measures is not very strong. Generally speaking, there is a slight tendency for those jurisdictions that make high use of youth court to be ones that make high use of alternative measures. But some provinces, most notably Ontario, make relatively high use of youth court and rather low use of alternative measures. This is not surprising. In the early days of the Young Offenders Act, Ontario did not set up any alternative measures programs. In fact, Ontario successfully defended this policy in a case (R. v S.(S.)) that went to the Supreme Court of Canada. After establishing that it did not have to establish alternative measures programs, Ontario voluntarily began establishing them for relatively small numbers of cases.

Comparisons with the United States

The federal government's 1998 White Paper outlining the reasons for bringing in what eventually became the Youth Criminal Justice Act and the act itself both imply that youth courts are over-used in Canada. A figure presented (Department of Justice 1998: 20) in the *Strategy for the Renewal of Youth Justice* (1998) suggests that the United States, Great Britain, and New Zealand all divert more youths from the courts than does Canada. A more detailed comparison of the rate of bringing cases to court is provided by Sprott and Snyder (1999). An updated version of these data (provided by Jane Sprott) shows that during the 1990s, the rate of bringing cases to court (per 1,000 youths in the community) was slightly higher in the United States than in Canada for violence (Figure 7.2), comparable for property offences (Figure 7.3), and much lower in Canada than the United States for drug offences (Figure 7.4). From the data in these three figures, it would appear that the biggest difference between the United States and Canada is in the use of youth court for drug offences. For some reason – differences in offending, enforcement practices, charging practices, or diversion practices – there is a large difference between the use of court for drug offences, but not for violent or property offences.

Pretrial Detention

Under the Young Offenders Act, the justification for the *pretrial* detention of a young person – who legally is innocent of the charges – were the same as for adult defendants:

Figure 7.2. Canada–U.S. comparison on rates of bringing cases to youth court for violent offences.

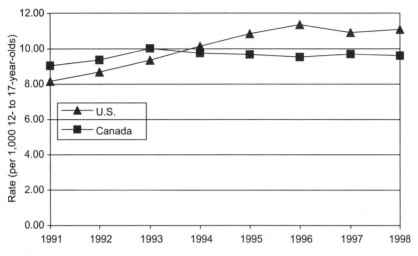

Source: Sprott and Snyder, 1999; updated by Sprott.

Figure 7.3. Canada–U.S. comparison on rates of bringing cases to youth court for property offence.

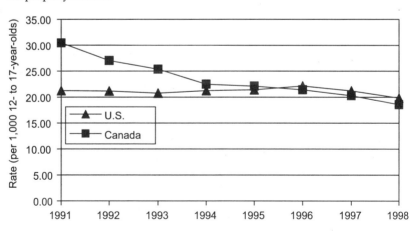

Source: Sprott and Snyder, 1999; updated by Sprott.

Figure 7.4. Canada–U.S. comparison on rates of bringing cases to youth court for drug offences.

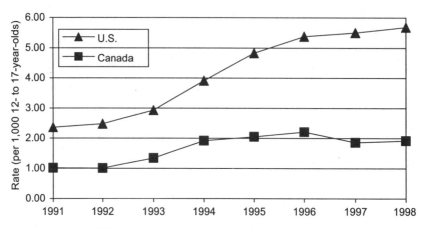

Source: Sprott and Snyder, 1999; updated by Sprott.

- 'Detention is necessary in order to secure his or her attendance in court.'
- 'Detention is necessary for the protection or safety of the public ... having regard to all circumstances including any substantial likelihood the accused will, if released from custody, commit a criminal offence or interfere with the administration of justice.'
- 'Where the detention is necessary in order to maintain confidence in the administration of justice, having regard to all the circumstances, including the apparent strength of the prosecution's case, the gravity of the nature of the offence, the circumstances surrounding its commission and the potential for a lengthy term of imprisonment' (Section 515(10) of the Criminal Code)

Generally speaking, it is presumed that the young person should be released rather than held. However, the onus is on the accused to demonstrate why the detention is not necessary in certain cases, most commonly if the accused is being charged for an offence while awaiting trial for a different offence.

Young people are entitled to a detention hearing to determine whether detention is required, and generally there is a requirement that this occur within twenty-four hours of the young person being detained.

Under the Young Offenders Act, the one legal difference between

Table 7.9   Detention cases where 'responsible person' raised in court, by region (percentage, and in parentheses number)

| Region | Proportion where responsible person raised in court | | | | | |
	All, almost all	Most	About half	A few	Almost none, none	Total
Atlantic	3.3	23.3	13.3	36.7	23.3	100 (30)
Quebec	4.2	25.0	29.2	25.0	16.7	100 (24)
Ontario	13.7	11.8	11.8	21.6	41.2	100 (51)
Prairies	11.1	16.7	16.7	25.9	29.6	100 (54)
B.C.	20.8	24.5	28.3	18.9	7.5	100 (53)
Territories	–	25.0	25.0	50.0	–	100 (4)
Total	12.0	19.4	19.4	25.0	24.1	100 (216)

Source: Doob, 2001.

bail decisions for adults and bail decisions for children is that there is a special provision (Section 7.1) indicating that youths who otherwise would be detained prior to trial can be released to the care of a 'responsible person' if the judge deems it appropriate. In the period leading up to the introduction of the YCJA, some concern was expressed that this section was rarely invoked, at least in some locations.

In a cross-country survey of youth court judges' views of the youth justice system (Doob, 2001), it would appear that the invocation of the responsible person section varies enormously across judges, and, to some extent, across provinces. British Columbia judges were most likely to indicate that this possibility is raised regularly in court, while judges from the Atlantic provinces and Ontario were least likely to indicate that it is raised regularly in court (see Table 7.9).

These findings are corroborated by the findings in a study by Varma (2002). In none of the 118 bail hearings that she observed was the issue of a responsible person even raised. In the youth court judges' survey, one judge noted that one reason that the 'responsible person' provision is not raised is that 'the kids who are detained are 'out of control' of their parents and/or child protection agencies.' The Young Offenders Act is silent on whether it is permissible to detain a youth for child welfare reasons, although it does indicate that a youth should not be *sentenced* to custody for his or her own good (Section 24(1.1)(a)).

When asked, youth court judges across the country varied somewhat in how frequently they indicated that a youth was detained prior to

Table 7.10   Cases where detention necessary for welfare reasons, by region (percentage, and in parentheses number)

| Region | Proportion where detention necessary for welfare purposes only | | | |
	Half or more	Few	Almost none, none	Total
Atlantic	23.3	43.3	33.3	100 (30)
Quebec	8.3	50.0	41.7	100 (24)
Ontario	33.3	40.4	26.3	100 (57)
Prairies	44.4	27.8	27.8	100 (54)
B.C.	25.0	48.1	26.9	100 (52)
Territories	50.0	50.0	–	100 (4)
Total	30.3	40.7	29.0	100 (221)

Source: Doob, 2001.

trial *only* because the youth had 'no adequate place to stay, or for some other child welfare reason' (Doob, 2001). These data are shown in Table 7.10.

Quebec judges are significantly less likely to indicate that youths were being detained largely for social welfare reasons. This is almost certainly a function of the fact that in Quebec obvious child welfare cases are more likely to be diverted out of the youth justice system into the welfare system.

The YCJA makes a number of changes in the laws governing pretrial detention. First, it *requires* that the judge enquire as the availability of a responsible person with whom the youth might reside. Under Section 31(2), 'if a young person would, in the absence of a responsible person, be detained in custody, the youth justice court or the justice shall inquire as to the availability of a responsible person and whether the young person is willing to be placed in that person's care.'

In other words, situations such as those described above where the issue of a 'responsible person' never arose in court should no longer happen. Judges are required to ask about the possibility of finding such a person. Aside from anything else, this may help alert defence counsel to the need to try to find such a person.

Second, youths are not be detained in custody prior to being sentenced 'as a substitute for appropriate child protection, mental health or other social measures' (Section 29(1)).

Third, if the court is considering the secondary ground for detention (substantial likelihood that the youth would commit another offence or interfere with the administration of justice), 'a youth justice court or a justice shall presume that the detention is not necessary under that paragraph if the young person could not, on being found guilty, be committed to custody on [one of the three grounds set out in the act for imposing a custodial sentence: that it is a violent offence, that the youth has repeatedly not complied with non-custodial sanctions, or that it is a serious offence and the youth has a long criminal record]' (Section 29(2)).

In effect, if the youth is seen as a likely candidate to show up for court (the first ground for detention), the youth should not be detained just because of concerns of re-offending if he or she could not be *sentenced* to custody on the basis of the behaviour that the youth is alleged to have committed.

The Use of Pretrial Detention

The YCJA presumes that pretrial detention is to be avoided if at all possible, just as it tries to give priority to more informal methods of dealing with young persons who offend. Nevertheless, a youth may be apprehended for an offence, and brought to the police station but not released by the officer in charge. When this occurs, the youth is then brought before a judge or a justice of the peace for a hearing to determine if he or she is to be released. Some of these youths are released at the bail hearing. In Varma's (2000) study of pretrial detention of youths in Toronto, Crown attorneys argued against release of a youth charged with an offence only 41 per cent of the time. Said differently, in 59 per cent of the cases, Crown Attorneys consented to release. One wonders why it was necessary to hold these youths in the first place.

Even though many youths are released at their bail hearings, remands represent the bulk of young offender admissions to custody. In 1998–9 there were 24,061 remand admissions in Canada, which accounts for 60 per cent of total admissions of youth to custody (Saskatchewan was unable to report remand admissions). Expressed as a rate, in 1998–9 there were ninety-eight youth admissions to remand per 10,000 youth in the population. This rate varied enormously among provinces, with the highest rate of remand reported by Manitoba (168 per 10,000), followed by Ontario (150 per 10,000) and the lowest rates reported by Prince Edward Island (twenty-nine per 10,000), Newfoundland, and Quebec (both forty-three per 10,000) (data from Moldon & Kukec, 2000).

When one looks at the average number of youths who were in custody on a given day, the picture is somewhat different. Many of the youths who are remanded in custody awaiting trial are there for a very short period of time. As a proportion of the overall youth custody population, remanded youths constitute only about 18 per cent of youths in custody at any given time. (These data exclude Quebec, Manitoba, and Nunavut, which were not able to provide average daily counts of youths in custody or detention.) In no jurisdiction where data were available did remand constitute more than 28 per cent of the incarcerated youths (Hendrick, 2001).

The apparent contradiction between these two findings – remands account for more admissions than do sentenced admissions, on the one hand, and remands account for a small portion of youths in custody – is easy to reconcile. In those jurisdictions where data were available, 52 per cent of the youths admitted to custody on remand were released within a week, and an additional 31 per cent spent between a week and a month in detention on remand. Only 1 per cent of youths on remand spent six months or more in detention (ibid.).

Who Is Detained?

Given that the majority of both adult and youth crime is committed by males, perhaps it is not surprising that the majority of youth admissions to remand are for young men. Of all admissions to remand in 1998–9 79 per cent were male (Moldon & Kukec, 2000). That property crimes account for a large proportion of youth crime is also reflected in the admissions to remand – within most jurisdictions, property offences accounted for the largest part of admissions.

Aboriginal youth are over-represented in remand, comprising roughly 37 per cent of all youth admitted to detention in 1998–9, in those provinces that recorded Aboriginal status but making up only 7 per cent of all youth aged 12 to 17 in the general population in those provinces. There was huge variation in the disproportionate representation across provinces. In Manitoba, 69 per cent of admissions to remand were Aboriginal youth, although they represent 16 per cent of the general youth population. In the Atlantic provinces (Newfoundland, Prince Edward Island and Nova Scotia) 4 per cent of youth admitted to remand are Aboriginal; they represent 2 per cent of the general youth population in those provinces (Moldon & Kukec, 2000).

Why Are Young People Held in Pretrial Detention?

One might expect that the primary grounds for detention under the Criminal Code – concerns about the likelihood that the accused would appear in court – would predominate justifications for detaining youth in custody. Research indicates, however, that there are often extra-legal reasons that children are held in detention, including the following: the child lacks adequate parental supervision, a judge is unavailable on nights or weekends, or even to teach a kid a lesson (del Carmen, Parker, & Reddington, 1998).

In a sample of seventy-six transcripts of bail hearings where youths were remanded in custody, Gandy (1992) found that in only about 24 per cent of the cases did judges detain the youth on the primary ground (that the youth might not appear for trial). Gandy found that when the onus was on the accused to demonstrate why he or she should be released, judges often (about 40 per cent of the time) ignored the primary ground and went to the secondary ground for remand (that the youth might commit another offence). One factor that appeared to Gandy to be very important to the decision to detain a youth in custody while awaiting trial was whether the youth was 'out of control.' Evidence of being out of control might be a previous failure to comply with rules of his or her home or other residence or of failure to comply with a previous court order. As we have already noted, about 30 per cent of youth court judges indicated, in a survey, that at least half the youths they detained ended up in pretrial detention for welfare, rather than criminal, reasons.

In an observational study of 118 bail hearings in Toronto youth courts, Varma (2002) reports that a youth's criminal past and the current offence are related to the decision on the part of the justice of the peace or judge to release a youth. In addition, however, variables which appear to relate to ties in the community, such as school attendance and whether or not a youth lives with her or his parents, have some impact on the fate of the youth.

It would appear that judges, when faced with a troubled youth, are often responding to the perceived needs of the youth. The YCJA has an explicit provision (Section 35) allowing the judge to refer the case to child welfare authorities at any stage of the proceedings for assessment. At the detention stage, such a reference might be particularly useful, because it might provide a way of assessing and/or addressing an apparent social welfare problem.

It is understandable that judges when faced with a compelling human problem will tend to try to find a solution to that problem, at least in the short term. Acting in what in the short term might appear to be in 'the best interests of the child' is hard to resist. Still, in his or her search for a humane solution, the judge must rely on the very limited array of tools provided by the law.

Unfortunately, judges do not control the environment that the youth moves into after the youth leaves the court or goes back into his or her community. If youths are detained because they are estranged from their parents, have nowhere to go, and are improperly clothed for a cold winter night, there is of course, no assurance that the situation the next morning, or the next week, will be any better. The main difference is that after the youth leaves court, the decision to send the ill-equipped youth out into the cold will be made by someone else in a less public setting than the courtroom. Short stays in detention are not necessarily neutral. They come with their own risks, risks that may or may not have an impact on the life of a young person.

The Impact of Holding a Young Person in Pretrial Detention

As Gandy (1992, p. 19) has noted, the denial of bail for a young person is 'one of the most intrusive measures provided for in the *Young Offenders Act.*' As with adults, we have to keep in mind that the young person has not yet been found guilty. Therefore, being held is, in the words of the Criminal Code, 'preventive detention' – detention justified not in terms of what the young person has been shown to have done, but on the basis of a prediction of what he or she might do in the future.

Detention facilities are short-term holding facilities for young offenders and generally, therefore, have a minimum of educational programming and services for youth. This, coupled with the generally short-term nature of detention, means that there is little therapeutic or rehabilitative value to holding a young person.

Remand is a highly stressful time for most detainees, but especially for youth because of the uncertainties of charge, conviction, sentence, and family contact (Liebling, 1999). Youths, who are especially dependent on structure, activity, family support, and staff interaction, may be especially prone to boredom, bullying, a high rate of infractions, and at the extreme – suicide (ibid.). There is some evidence to suggest that the experiences of being held on remand and the stress associated with it may exert a negative effect on self-esteem (Power & Beveridge, 1990).

There is a growing body of literature that suggests that the further into the criminal justice system a youth is brought, the more likely there will be a negative impact on that youth. For example, a paper by Stewart, Simons, Conger, and Scaramella (2002) suggests that legal sanctions disrupt the quality of family life in various ways (e.g., by embarrassing the parents), thus increasing conflict and subsequent stress levels in the family. The study looked at youths at three different points in time (average age: 13.5, 14.5, and 15.5 years) and found, not surprisingly, that poor parenting at age 13.5 was associated with increased delinquency at age 15.5.

More relevant in this context was the finding that about half of this effect was the result of the impact of legal sanctions occurring between these two ages. Not surprisingly, those youths who were most involved in delinquency and most subject to poor parenting practices at age 13.5 were most likely to receive legal sanctions. However, the impact of poor parenting practices at age 13.5 was largely mediated by the occurrence of legal sanctions.

Similarly, poor parenting at age 15.5 was associated with higher levels of delinquency at age 13.5. This effect was almost completely due to the impact of legal sanctions that took place between age 13.5 and age 14.5. Simply put, 'poor parenting behaviours led to increases in delinquency and earlier delinquency led to an increase in poor parenting' (Stewart et al., 2002, p. 52). Legal sanctions were a result of delinquency and poor parenting at age 13.5: 'Legal sanctions, in turn, predicted further increases in delinquency and decreases in parenting quality a year later at [age 15.5]' (ibid.).

There are obvious negative effects of increased contact with the criminal justice system. Contact with the youth justice system appears to make it more difficult for parents to act appropriately with their children. Consequently, laws that minimize this impact (e.g., by reducing formal entry into the court, probation, or custodial systems) may ultimately end up reducing recidivism.

In addition to the possible negative psychological outcomes that detention may have on a youth, pretrial detention is likely to have a negative impact on the outcome of the case in court. Several studies suggest that pretrial detention exhibits an independent effect on a young person's eventual disposition – those detained are more likely to plead guilty, to be convicted if tried, and to receive a prison sentence (Fagan & Guggenheim, 1996).

Finally, from a public policy perspective, one might want to consider the financial costs to society of holding a youth in pretrial detention when there are no compelling social benefits from doing so. Detention is expensive. A youth who is facing (but has not yet been found guilty of) a minor charge is going to cost the taxpayer a minimum of about $1,000 a week and perhaps as much as $2,000 a week to detain him or her. Given that there are few benefits to society from short-term detention prior to trial – especially if the youth if convicted will not be incarcerated, pretrial detention would appear to represent a rather poor investment of resources.

Conclusion

We have attempted to demonstrate that diverting the large majority of minor young offenders from the formal criminal justice system probably makes a great deal of sense. Such a practice is seen as sensible both by the public and by the judges who otherwise would see the cases in their courts. The Youth Criminal Justice Act, through mechanisms such as extrajudicial measures, makes that goal seem feasible. The Youth Criminal Justice Act does not, however, require the police to divert cases. Evidence of the effectiveness of the new act would be shown if, in fact, fewer young people were brought before the courts for minor offences where community approaches (extrajudicial measures) would be adequate to hold a youth accountable for his or her actions.

The success of such programs will depend, in part, on members of the community being willing to participate. It appears that there is a willingness from members of the public to be part of such processes. For example, it is interesting to note that many members of the public express an interest in being involved in youth committees or panels, as a means by which to deal with youthful offenders outside the justice system. In a survey of Ontario residents (Doob et al., 1998) more than half of the respondents said they would be interested in becoming involved in ways of holding young people accountable for their offences outside of the court system or in meetings involving young offenders and their victims where compensation and ways of holding the offender are discussed.

CHAPTER EIGHT

Transfers to Adult Court: Treating Children as Adults

Given the number of cases involving youths that are 'transferred' to adult court, a separate chapter on 'transfers' does not seem warranted. As we will see, fewer than one-tenth of 1 per cent of youth court cases in Canada end up in adult court. There are, however, two reasons for looking carefully at this topic. First, as Fagan and Zimring (2000, pp. 1–2) point out in their study of the American juvenile justice scene, a study of this issue 'should force observers to confront fundamental questions about the functions and limits of the juvenile courts ... The view from the backdoor of American juvenile justice must provide a clear picture of the rationale of juvenile justice if waiver [transfer to adult court] policy itself is to be rational and appropriately invoked.' In other words, understanding the issues surrounding these few cases may give us better insight into the youth justice system as a whole.

Second, policy surrounding how decisions are made concerning which cases end up in adult and youth court has been controversial for at least 15 years and is likely to remain so. The *Youth Criminal Justice Act* makes a fundamental change in the way in which transfers take place in Canada. Although this change could be described as a procedural matter, it is, in fact, a fundamental shift in the manner in which youths are defined for the purpose of criminal justice.

Until very recently (from 1908 to 2003), youths age 14 and older were in jeopardy of being transferred out of the youth justice system into the adult system. The most simple way of thinking about transfers is as a kind of safety valve for the youth justice system. The theory is that some cases simply do not fit in the youth justice system. Typically it is thought that these are serious violent cases where the crime does not appear to be consistent with the status of the offender as a youth.

The problem is that one of the purposes of having a separate youth justice system is that there is an understanding that youths, though they know the difference between right and wrong, lack the maturity to be treated as full-fledged adults. As Zimring and Fagan (2000, p. 423) note, 'transferring a fourteen-year-old defendant from one court to another does not add to his or her age or maturity. There is no evidence that the commission of terrible crimes is an indicator that the offender is more mature or sophisticated than his or her age peers.'

As we pointed out in Chapter 2, the major justification for having a separate youth justice system is that youths, on the whole, are different from adults. Why, then, does the allegation that a youth might have committed a criminal offence – or, in particular, a serious violent offence – make that youth a candidate for instant transformation into adulthood?

If youths are not being transferred to the adult criminal court system because they are more 'mature,' then why are they being transferred? The answer is found more in politics than in theory or data. Regarding the United States, Zimring and Fagan (2000, p. 408) point out:

> Transfer of juveniles to criminal court is a fascinating and complex process that has produced almost no principled debate and sustained analysis ... Transfer of persons under maximum age for delinquency has been an important issue for a century, yet there has been almost no thoughtful analysis of the transfer problem during this time. We suspect the reason for this is that all parties to the issue come with strong result preferences that have discouraged them from any interest in the principles that might inform transfer decisions.

Transfer Tests under the JDA and YOA

The transfer to adult court under the JDA and YOA took place in the youth court after the first appearance in that court. A youth could be transferred for all but the most trivial of offences. From 1908 until 1984, the test for transfer was fairly simple sounding: if the court is of the opinion 'that the good of the child and the interest of the community demanded it' that youth could be transferred to adult court (Section 9(1)). Courts obviously 'sharpened' this test somewhat by focusing more on community interests. It remained clear, however, that transfers were meant to be rare. When the Crown would bring an application to transfer, the court would hear evidence from both sides and make its decision. If the decision of the court were to transfer the case to adult criminal court, then the youth, thereafter, would be treated as an adult for all criminal law purposes in this case.

The consequences of being transferred in Canada are serious. First of all, for most purposes under the criminal law, a 14-year-old who is transferred to adult court is deemed to be a full adult. This means that he or she has the rights of an adult (e.g., a choice of a jury trial), but could also be sentenced as an adult. In the case of murder, for example, this meant, between 1977 and 1992, that a youth over age 14 could, if transferred and subsequently found guilty of murder, be sentenced to imprisonment for life, without eligibility for parole for twenty-five years. Prior to 1977, a youth found guilty in adult court of capital murder was automatically sentenced to hang.

For more mundane cases, the consequences were also important: When a case is transferred to the adult court, the youth can be named publicly by the media as soon as the transfer is 'complete' (i.e., all appeals have been disposed of). This means that the special protections afforded by the youth justice system are no longer available to the transferred youth, notwithstanding the obvious fact that he or she has not yet been found guilty. Normally youths are not in jeopardy of being identified in the media at any stage of youth court proceedings or after conviction.

As one might expect, with the shift towards a more legal orientation, the initial test for transfer in the post-1984 (YOA) period became more explicit. It was still possible to transfer almost any youth over age 14 who was charged with almost anything other than the most trivial of offences. In deciding whether a case should stay in the youth court or be transferred to the adult court, a judge had to consider the seriousness of the offence and the age, maturity, and criminal record of the youth. Then the judge had to consider which system – the youth system or the adult system (including the correctional facilities of the two systems) – 'in the interest of society and having regard to the needs of the young person' (Section 16(1)) – could best 'meet the circumstances of the case' (YOA, Section 16(2)(c)). Judges found this a challenging task, in part because they were making decisions about which of two systems could best deal with a case before any of the facts of the case had been established. The notion that the judges were to 'balance' the interests of society and those of the young person was consistent with the rest of the act. When judges were confronted with a fork in the road to justice, the YOA instructed them to take it.

Figure 8.1. Transfers of youths to adult court, Canada, 1991–2000

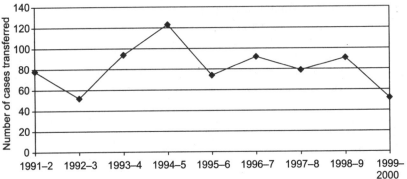

Source: Canadian Centre for Justice Statistics, 1991–2000.

From a political perspective, the law on the transfer of cases to the adult court was clearly vulnerable. In 1992, after a period when people believed that there had been an increase in youth crime, the test for transferring a youth to adult court changed in such a way that priority was given to 'protection' of society:

> The youth court shall consider the interest of society, which includes the objectives of affording protection to the public and rehabilitation of the young person and determine whether those objectives can be reconciled by the youth remaining under the jurisdiction of the youth court, and if the court is of the opinion that those objectives cannot be so reconciled, protection of the public shall be paramount and the court shall order that the young person be [transferred to adult court]. (Section 16(1.1))

The goal was either to make it easier – or to make it be perceived to be easier – to transfer youths charged with an offence to an adult court. However, when examining trends in the use of transfers over the years, there appears to be no evidence of an increase.

Figure 8.1 shows the total number of transfers in Canada each year since 1991, when national data were first available. The data show that there are fluctuations each year in the number of cases transferred to adult court, but there appears to be no meaningful increase. This suggests that although legislation was enacted in 1992 (and again in 1996, as described below) with the apparent intent of making it easier to transfer youths to adult court, no overall increase occurred in the number of children transferred to the adult system. Figure 8.1 also reminds us of another fact: very few cases have ever been transferred into the adult system.

In 1996, the law on the transfer of cases to adult court was again changed. For 16- and 17-year-olds charged with any of four very serious violent offences (murder, manslaughter, attempted murder, and aggravated sexual assault), the youth would be 'presumptively' transferred to adult court unless he or she successfully argued that the transfer should not take place. Interestingly, however, the 'test' as to whether a transfer should take place was the same as it had been. Not surprisingly, there seems to be no evidence that the change in the law had any impact. Data for 16- and 17-year-olds alone (without including the 12- to 15-year-olds) are not easily available. Overall, youth under 16 (and therefore not presumptively transferred) account for only 14 per cent of all cases transferred (CCJS, 1991–2000). Thus, looking at all of the cases coming to court for one of these four 'presumptive offences' during the 1990s, it is clear that there was not much change in practice. It seems that during the 1990s, Canada transferred at most 10 to 19 per cent of the 65 to 94 very serious violent cases involving 16- and 17-year-old accused youths that came to court each year. The data in Table 8.1 do not appear to support the notion that presumptive transfers to adult court (fully in effect from 1997–8 onward) had any impact.

Although there has been a good deal of pressure in both Canada and the United States to modify in some way the age at which a young person can be transformed into an adult as a result of the transfer decision, there has been much less pressure on the lower age limit. As we noted above, the youngest at which a youth can be transferred has remained at age 14 since 1908. This age limit appears to be much less vulnerable to politically motivated changes than most other features of the laws that govern youth justice.

It would be simple to suggest that developmental psychology might help inform the legal ages of vulnerability to being treated like an adult for criminal justice purposes. However, Zimring and Fagan (2000) note that there are three reasons that developmental psychology and data about adolescent maturity will not determine policy on transfers to adult court. First, they note that although there are many developmental justifications for excluding very young children from full criminal liability, there is, in fact, little pressure to transfer very young children (i.e., those under 14) to adult court. As they put it, 'Americans

Table 8.1   All cases, presumptive[a] cases involving those age 16 and 17, and all presumptive cases[b] transferred from youth court to adult court, Canada, 1991–2000

		Presumptive cases		
Year	All cases	16- & 17-year-olds only	Transfers	Percentage transferred (all ages)
1991–2	116,397	65	8	12
1992–3	115,187	83	11	13
1993–4	115,949	74	14	19
1994–5	109,743	91	14	15
1995–6	111,027	87	9	10
1996–7	110,065	80	12	15
1997–8	110,883	89	13	15
1998–9	106,665	69	12	17
1999–2000	102,061	94	13	14

Source: Canadian Centre for Justice Statistics, 1991–2000.
[a] Presumptive offences include murder, manslaughter, attempted murder and aggravated sexual assault.
[b] No figures are available for 16- and 17-year-olds actually transferred. Therefore, actual transfers reported here include all those transferred, regardless of their ages. These figures, and, therefore, the proportion transferred are likely to be slightly inflated.

still know young children when they see them' (ibid., p. 419). It is the older children (i.e., those 14 and over) who are candidates for instant adulthood. Second, most developmental changes during this period are gradual and show high variance on when they occur. Each of these characteristics makes policy decisions based on developmental issues rather unlikely, because of the difficulty of linking a high-variance gradual change to a yes or no decision. Third, assessments of responsibility are, in the final analysis, moral judgments that do not follow in any simple fashion from empirical data. Moral judgments are easily transformed into political ones. In the end, it is politics more than empirical social science that determines when a youth can be transformed into an adult in criminal court.

Transfers in the United States

It is worthwhile looking, at this point, at what was happening in the United States, in large part because the focus on 'turning youths into adults' became an obsession in that country in the latter part of the twentieth century. Although politicians in both the United States and Canada had political concerns about youth crime, the situation in the United States during the final decades of the twentieth century was quite different from that in Canada. Canada's laws on transfer might have become slightly 'tougher,' but the impact of these changes was minimal, and the number of cases transferred was always small. This was not matched in the United States.

During the last quarter of the twentieth century, the jurisdiction of the youth courts changed dramatically in the United States. When a young offender, Willie Bosket, killed two New York City subway passengers shortly after being released from a maximum security youth facility in 1978, the public focus was not on why the state had failed to deal effectively with a young person who had spent only 18 months out of state agency placements between age 9 and age 15. Instead, the focus was on the fact that the law, as it was at that time, allowed him to be incarcerated for 'only' five and a half years – until his twenty-first birthday. Willie Bosket was the unambiguous cause of the introduction, two weeks after he was sentenced, of a change in New York's law deeming children 13 years old or older to be dealt with *automatically* as adults if they were charged with murder. Those 14 years old or older charged with a range of offences, including robbery and certain forms of burglary and assault, are also *automatically* dealt with as adult offenders (Klein, 1998). Since that time, state legislatures in virtually every state have made it easier – or automatic – to try certain juveniles as adults.

The United States, with its fifty-one criminal justice jurisdictions, allows for 'natural variation' in criminal justice policies. Hence there is experience with different forms of transfer. The method we are most familiar with in Canada, 'judicial waiver,' is the most common in U.S. legislation (as of 1998, it existed in 46 of the 51 U.S. jurisdictions; Szymanski, June 1998), but it is quickly becoming less important in terms of its overall impact. 'Presumptive transfers' (similar to Canada's law for 16- and 17-year-olds charged with very serious offences) are becoming more popular and, at least in some locations in the United States, result in dramatically more hearings and dramatically more transfers.

Much more common in recent years has been the 'statutory exclusion': by the end of 1997, 29 of the 50 states automatically make children into adults for criminal justice processing if they are charged with certain serious offences or if they have particular types of youth court records (Szymanski, May 1998). Thirty one states (Szymanski, July

1998) have laws requiring a youth to be considered an adult forever if once convicted in adult court (the so-called once an adult, always an adult laws).

The most recent approach, popular particularly with prosecutors, is the 'direct file' or 'prosecutorial waiver,' where the prosecutor has sole (and usually not reviewable) discretion to prosecute the case either in the juvenile court or the adult court. Prosecutors like it for obvious reasons: it avoids the 'red tape associated with these [transfer] hearings' as the Alabama attorney general put it (Klein, 1998, p. 395). By the end of 2001, fifteen states and Washington, DC, had laws allowing prosecutors to decide if a youth was really an adult (Szymanski, April 2002) by filing charges directly into adult court if they wished to do so.

Snyder and Sickmund (1999) estimate that in 1996 there were about ten thousand youths who were transferred to adult criminal court as a result of a judicial decision. This constitutes about 1 per cent of all formally processed youth court cases in the United States. It will be recalled that in Canada, approximately one-tenth of 1 per cent of cases are transferred to adult court. However, judicial waivers to adult court in the United States constitute a small portion of the cases in which youthful offenders are considered to be adults. Sprott and Snyder (1999) estimate that in the mid-1990s there were approximately 176,000 cases of youths being dealt with in adult court as a result of prosecutorial or statutory exclusions. As they point out, this means that the overall rate of treating youths as adults in the United States is at least 200 times the Canadian transfer rate.

Provincial Variation in Transfers in Canada

There are two obvious lessons to learn from the changes in the law that have taken place over the past few years in the United States. First, the decision to change the law in a given state is politically rather than empirically driven. Second, there is substantial variation across jurisdictions in the manner in which these political decisions are made.

In Canada, obviously, there is only one law related to the transfer of youths to adult court. Nevertheless, since the impetus for a transfer typically comes from the Crown attorney (or in the case of presumptive transfers the Crown attorney can waive the attempt to transfer a youth), the numbers of transfers might well be expected to vary across jurisdictions.

Figure 8.2 shows the rate of transferring cases in the four largest

Figure 8.2. Rate of transferring young offender cases to adult court in four
Canadian provinces, 1991–2000

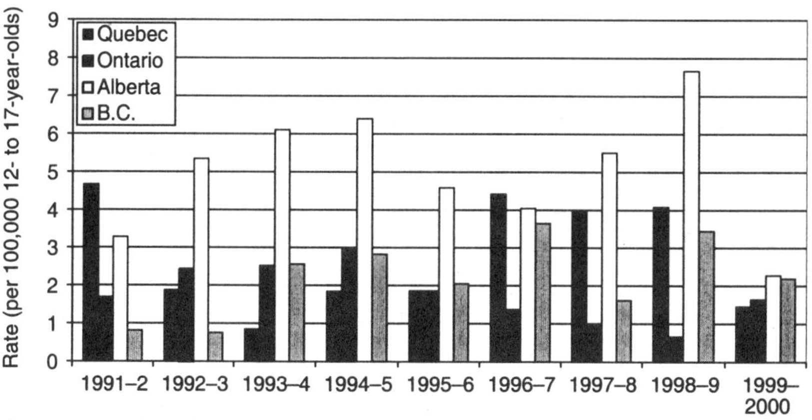

Source: Canadian Centre for Justice Statistics, 2001b.

provinces in Canada over the past decade. The denominator in these
figures is the population of youths in the province. Because provinces
bring cases into court at very different rates (see Chapter 7), we decided
that 'cases in court that are eligible for transfer' in a province was a less
useful denominator.[1] Clearly the rate of transferring youths to adult
court varies across provinces and over time. There is considerable volatility in the rates of transfers. However, transfers, until recently,
appeared to be more likely to occur in some provinces (e.g., Quebec
and Alberta) than in others (e.g., Ontario and British Columbia).

The Quebec–Ontario comparison is particularly interesting, because
Quebec is typically seen as being more 'child-oriented' in its policies
towards youth. Looking at the past decade, it would appear that in

---

1 We have expressed these 'transfers to adult court' rate figures in terms of rates per
  100,000 youths in the province rather than per 1,000 cases to court. The reason for this
  is simple: if some provinces, such as Quebec, bring few cases to court, it would make
  sense that they would transfer a higher portion of these cases to adult court than a
  province like Alberta or Ontario that has large numbers of very minor cases coming to
  court. Expressing 'transfers' as a function of the number of youths in the province,
  then, is a measure of how eager or reluctant a province is to exclude its most difficult
  youths from the youth court process.

Figure 8.3. A comparison of the rate of transfers of young offenders to adult court in Quebec and Ontario, 1991–2000

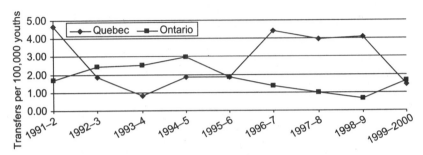

Source: Canadian Centre for Justice Statistics, 2001b.

recent years, Quebec transferred a higher proportion of its youth (per hundred thousand youths in the province) than did Ontario. In the early 1990s, however, the transfer rate in Ontario was somewhat higher. These figures (from Figure 8.2) are shown more clearly in Figure 8.3.

Although national data exist on the number of youths who are actually transferred to adult court, no data exist on the number of times transfer applications are brought to the court. Youth court judges in early 2001 were asked how many transfer hearings they had heard in the previous five years (51 per cent of the judges had heard no transfer hearings) and how many were successful. From these very rough estimates, it appeared that about 60 per cent of the transfer applications were successful. Hence, even if every application were successful, there would be few youths transferred to adult court.

What is interesting about the cases that actually do get transferred is that they are not, invariably, the most serious cases that come into youth courts. In Table 8.2 the details of the cases that were transferred in two recent years are summarized.

Transfers to adult courts, in Canada, are rare events. Even for the most serious offences – those involving youths charged with murder – fewer than one-third of the cases are transferred. The more serious the offence, the more likely it is that the case would end up in adult court. Nevertheless, this table shows two aspects of the transfer decision quite clearly. First, most of the serious cases are dealt with in youth court. Second, many cases that are transferred to adult court do not involve very serious offences.

Table 8.2   Breakdown of cases transferred to adult court and (in parentheses) all cases in youth court for that offence, Canada, 1998–9 and 1999–2000

Most significant charge	1998–9	1999–2000
Murder	7 (25)	12 (44)
Attempted murder	5 (47)	1 (49)
Sexual assault II	1 (50)	1 (43)
Sexual assault I	2 (1,293)	4 (1,198)
Rape / indecent assault[a]	3 (39)	–
Assault III	7 (381)	–
Assault II	8 (3,962)	2 (3,897)
Assault I	3 (10,383)	2 (9,988)
Assault police officer	1 (459)	–
Robbery	15 (3,056)	7 (2,887)
Possession of a weapon	1 (1,590)	–
Kidnapping	–	1 (43)
Extortion	1 (139)	–
Other sexual offences	–	1 (293)
Violent (total)	54 (22,284)	31 (21,518)
Breaking and entering	10 (11,613)	8 (9,779)
Arson	–	1 (382)
Taking vehicle without consent	2 (1,804)	–
Theft	8 (18,065)	–
Other fraudulent transactions	1 (438)	1 (401)
Possession of stolen property	1 (6,114)	1 (5,626)
Mischief / damage to property	5 (5,636)	1 (5,354)
Property (total)	27 (45,636)	12 (40,920)
Escape custody	1 (960)	–
Unlawfully at large	2 (734)	–
Failure to appear	4 (11,701)	2 (11,208)
Other administration of justice	–	1 (1,066)
Disorderly conduct, nuisances	1 (976)	–
Public morals	–	1 (11)
Offences against person, reputation	1 (1,669)	1 (2,061)
Drugs	1 (4,569)	1 (5,389)
Failure to comply with disposition	–	3 (14,150)
Total	91 (106,665)	52 (102,061)

Source: Canadian Centre for Justice Statistics, 1998–2000.
Note: Offences where no youth was transferred in either year are not shown.
[a] Rape and indecent assault have not been offences since 1983. These are, therefore, prosecutions of offences that took place before that time. The accused clearly were youths at the time of the incidents, but adults at the time of the prosecutions. Dash indicates no transfers of this type in that year.

Table 8.3   Breakdown of youth cases in adult
court by type of offence, Canada and United
States (%)

Type of offence	Canada	United States
Violence	59	43
Property	27	37
Drugs	1	14
Other	12	6
Total	100	100

Source: U.S. data, Snyder and Sickmund, 1999,
pp. 170–1; Canadian data for 1998–9 and 1999–
2000, in CCJS 1998–2000.

In gross terms, these percentages are quite similar to data from the
United States relating to a sample of youths from various states who
were transferred to adult court. As shown in Table 8.3, roughly half of
cases dealt with in adult courts in both countries are violent offences.
The largest difference, perhaps not surprisingly, is in the proportion of
youths in adult court for drug offences. Very few Canadian cases
transferred to adult court involve drugs, but one of seven U.S. cases
involving a youth in adult court is a drug case.

The Impact of Transfers

As Zimring and Fagan (2000, p. 409) note, the main premise of proposals to transfer larger numbers of youths to adult court 'is that more
severe punishments for serious juvenile crimes are a good thing, and
the minor premise is that transfer to criminal courts will achieve these
harsher punishments. Rather than producing a set of principles for
when transfer is justified, the proposal assumes that an increase in
transfers will be a policy benefit; the more the merrier.'

   Looking first at what Zimring and Fagan (2000) refer to as the minor
premise, it is not at all clear that youths who are transferred to adult
court are punished more harshly. As Jones and Krisberg (1990) note,
'The evidence reveals that transfers of juveniles to adult court do not
result in harsher penalties than would be expected had the same cases
been tried in juvenile court.'

   When thinking about the relative punitiveness of the adult versus

Table 8.4   Comparison of proportions of youth dismissed and held in custody when retained in juvenile court and when transferred to adult court, three U.S. states (%)

	Juvenile court		Adult court	
State	Dismissed	Custody[a]	Dismissed	Custody[a]
South Carolina	16	35	25	66
Utah	4	68	4	76
Pennsylvania	27	36	34	39

Source: Snyder et al., 2000.
[a] Custody percentages are of the total caseload (including cases dismissed).

the youth justice system, it is important to remember that when a young person was sentenced to custody in the youth justice system under the YOA, he or she would serve the whole term – there was no parole, or period of supervision in the community, or 'statutory release' as there is in the adult system. The result is that it is difficult to compare sentence lengths under the YOA with sentence lengths under the adult system, since an adult sentence of a given length can mean anything from one-sixth of that time being spent in custody to the full term of the sentence being spent in custody. For a youth under the YOA, a sentence was what it sounded like. Under the YCJA, however, the youth will generally serve a predictable two-thirds of his or her sentence.

A detailed study of transfers to criminal court in the 1990s in three U.S. states (Snyder, Sickmund, & Poe-Yamagata, 2000) shows that youths who are transferred to adult court are not, of course, invariably found guilty. Second, a substantial portion of those who are transferred do not, in the end, receive custodial sentences. Not surprisingly, however, as compared with those cases where the process was initiated to transfer the case, but the case was, nevertheless, kept in juvenile court, transferred cases were more likely to result in imprisonment. This almost certainly had to do with the relative seriousness of the offences, a factor which obviously differentiated those cases transferred from those kept in juvenile court. The data from the three U.S. states are summarized in Table 8.4.

Snyder et al. (2000) point out that these comparisons do not tell the whole story. In Pennsylvania, for example, juvenile sentences are indeterminate in length. They note that 'assuming that the juvenile court held serious offenders in a juvenile facility for at least 12 months, no more than 13 per cent of all excluded [transferred] youth received longer sentences in the criminal justice system than they would have received in the juvenile justice system. In addition, the juvenile court placement would have begun 3.5 months earlier than the criminal court incarceration' (ibid., p. 38).

We do not, unfortunately, have any systematic data on the fate of those few Canadian youths who end up in the adult criminal justice system. There are, however, occasional peculiarities of the transfer system which give a glimpse of the relative harshness of the two systems. In 1994–5, there were 123 cases in Canada transferred to adult court – a high for the decade. Fifty-eight of these cases (47 per cent of all the transfers) were from Manitoba. Manitoba accounts for 7.2 per cent of the youth court cases in all of Canada. Hence, it would appear that transfers were dramatically over-represented in Manitoba. Were it not for one critical fact, one might have thought that the Manitoba youth justice system was particularly harsh on youths. These transfers were largely at the request of older youths. As the Statistics Canada 'Youth Court Statistics' *Juristat* for that year delicately put it, 'In Manitoba, youths are choosing to transfer to adult court to avoid the discipline and structure of a sentence to a youth custody facility' (Doherty & de Souza, 1996, p. 7). Informally, these youth-initiated transfers were referred to as 'smoking transfers.' Smoking had, at that time, apparently been prohibited in youth facilities in the province, but had not yet been prohibited in adult facilities.

Whatever the reality might be of the relative punitiveness of the two systems, it is clear that the decision on the part of the Crown to seek to transfer a youth to adult court can have symbolic importance. It is a chance for a provincial attorney general or his or her agent to demonstrate that he or she believes that a youth will get 'adult time' for an 'adult crime.' Whether all of the charges summarized in Table 8.2 constitute 'adult crime' is, of course, another matter. And, of course, the experience in the United States suggests that treatment will not necessarily be more harsh in adult court.

The utilitarian goals of the transfer decision centre around the belief that youths who are transferred will learn from this experience and stop offending – special or individual deterrence. In addition, it is assumed that if youths are routinely dealt with in the adult system, the threat of 'adult punishment' will act as a deterrent for youths generally – general deterrence.

There are a number of studies that demonstrate quite convincingly that youths punished in the adult system are *not* more likely to be deterred from further criminality than youths handled in the juvenile system. Fagan (cited in Bishop & Frazier, 2000) compared robbery and burglary youthful offenders in New York and New Jersey. In New York, the 15- and 16-year-olds were prosecuted in the criminal courts; in New Jersey they were still considered youths. There appeared to be no effect of the court system for burglary offenders, but for robbery offenders transfer to adult court tended to be associated with *increased* subsequent offending.

A similar study (Bishop & Frazier, 2000) took advantage of the fact that in Florida there is a good deal of variation in the manner in which youthful offenders are prosecuted. The study followed 2,738 youths who were transferred into the adult system and carefully matched these youths on seven relevant factors (e.g., offence, past record, age, race) with youths who were prosecuted as youths. Bishop and Frazier's results showed *increased* recidivism for the transferred youths in the short term (roughly two years) on every measure that was examined and similar findings for almost all measures in the long term (up to seven years).

The general deterrence findings are quite similar. Singer and McDowell (1998) examined the impact of legal changes in New York which sent thousands of youths to adult court. In that instance, there were nearly ideal conditions for a general deterrence effect, given that there was a lot of publicity and the law was fairly aggressively implemented. The legal change had no impact. Similarly, in Idaho (where youths 14 years old and older charged with a number of mostly serious offences were automatically prosecuted in adult court) the legal change had no effect on crime rates (Jensen and Metsger, 1994).

Bishop and Frazier (2000, p. 262) draw the following quite reasonable conclusions: 'From the studies that compared rates of recidivism among youths transferred to criminal court and youths retained in the juvenile system ... [it appears that transfer of youths to adult court is] counterproductive: transferred youths are more likely to reoffend, and to reoffend more quickly and more often, than those retained in the juvenile system.' They suggest that one possible reason for the 'transfer' effects on kids is that

The juvenile system [may] communicate messages of caring ... to young people whose backgrounds are often replete with alienation from and rejection by conventional adults. Time and again in our interviews with young offenders we were made aware of their sensitivity to signs of interest and concern from judges, detention workers, and juvenile program staff ... For many of these youths, such messages [of individual worth and potential] had rarely been communicated in the primary spheres of home and school (ibid.).

Nearly all of them – including those who had been transferred – described the juvenile courts in favourable terms ... Most believed that judges were trying to help them. Even those who indicated that the judge's intent was to punish them generally perceived that the punishment was well intended ... Unlike what they had experienced in juvenile court, it appeared to most of [the transferred youths believed] that the [adult] criminal court judges had little interest in them or their problems. (ibid., p. 250)

In addition, research suggests that youths in adult prisons appear to be more likely than their counterparts in youth facilities to be victims of violence (including sexual assaults) from other inmates and staff (Bishop, 2000).

The End of Transfers to Adult Court: The Youth Criminal Justice Act and Adult Sentences

What, then, do we know about transfers to adult court in Canada. First, we know it happens rarely and is not used exclusively for very serious offences. Second, we know that even for the most serious violent offences, a minority of cases are transferred to adult court. Transfers do not, invariably, appear to be 'necessary' for very many cases in Canada. Third, we know that transfers will not reduce crime. Whatever the purpose might be of transferring youths to the adult criminal justice system, we know we cannot justify it in terms of crime control.

What is left, then? Perhaps the easiest way to see a possible justification for having some link with the adult justice system is to look back to debates surrounding the implementation of the Young Offenders Act in the early 1980s. It will be recalled that the maximum sentence *for any offence* (including murder) in the YOA was, initially, three years in custody. The argument for this limit was twofold. First, it was pointed out that three years for a youth is, in fact, a long time. Furthermore, if one believes in the reduced culpability of a youth for his or her actions, punishments for youths must be shorter than punishments given to adults for similar offences. But the argument was made – and continues to be made – that for the most serious offences, for youths who are, for all practical purposes, adults, the sentence in the most serious cases should be more 'adult like.' Transfers to adult court were seen as a way of accomplishing this goal.

For the most part, the Youth Criminal Justice Act maintains the maximum sentence for a youth at three years. Over the years, as we noted in Chapter 1, the maximum sentences available for those youths found guilty of murder have increased. But the maximum sentence for all other offences has remained at three years. If the possibility of transferring a youth to adult court is a 'safety valve' for very serious instances of the most serious offences, then perhaps this safety valve is an important component of the package which includes a relatively modest maximum sentence for most offences in youth court.

The procedure by which youths are transferred has been a source of criticism for some time (Beaulieu, 1994; Standing Committee on Justice and Legal Affairs, 1997). In effect, under the JDA and the YOA, the test required the judge to consider what would be the best way to deal with the youthful offender if the allegations against him or her were found to be true. That may sound simple, but what if the judge had doubts, for example, whether the youth was the ringleader of a group of violent youths and might wish to sentence the youth differently if the youth was fully responsible for the offence than if he or she was a minor participant. Under the YOA, the transfer decision was made before the youth was tried. Hence, to the extent that there are harmful or punishing effects of the transfer (e.g., the ability of the press to publish the name of a youthful suspect), the harm to the youth occurred before the finding of guilt.

The YCJA, instead of having transfers to adult court, changes that procedure in a dramatic way. All cases are tried in youth court. A youth is a youth throughout the trial process. However, for serious offences (where proper notice had been given to the youth by the Crown) the prosecutor can ask, at the sentencing hearing, for an adult sentence. The test as to whether an adult sentence should be given is fairly simple: if a youth sentence 'imposed in accordance with the purpose and principles [of sentencing in the YCJA] would have *sufficient length* to hold the young person accountable for his or her offending behaviour' (emphasis added) the youth shall be sentenced as a youth (Section 72(1)(a)). If not, the youth shall be sentenced as an adult. As we will see in Chapter 9, sentences under the YCJA are to be handed down such that their severity is proportionate to the harm that was done and the youth's responsibility for that harm.

In other words, the test is whether a proportionate sentence can be given in the youth system within the maximum sentences laid out in the act (two or three years of custody and supervision for all offences other than murder). If a youth is sentenced as an adult, the judge then decides whether it is appropriate for the youth to start serving the sentence in a youth or an adult facility. The name of the youth who is sentenced as an adult can be published. Normally, the identify of accused (or convicted) youths cannot be published.[2]

There is, however, one other clearly political wrinkle. It will be recalled that from 1995 onwards youths who were 16 or older and charged with one of four serious violent offences (murder, manslaughter, attempted murder, or aggravated sexual assault) were to be 'presumptively' transferred to adult court. As noted earlier in this chapter (see Table 8.1), this change in the law did not have much impact on what actually happened to youths. Nevertheless, the YCJA indicates that youths age 14 and above found guilty of one of these four offences would presumptively receive an adult sentence. Put simply, the act reduces the age of presumptive adulthood for these offenders from 16 to 14.

In addition, the YCJA creates another class of presumptive adults. Those who have been previously found, on two separate occasions, to have committed 'serious violent offences' and are being sentenced for their third 'serious violent offence' are also to receive, presumptively, an adult sentence. The designation of something as a 'serious violent offence' is a judicial responsibility at sentencing. It is not known, therefore, how many youths would qualify as serious violent offenders with this pattern of previous findings. Given that when violent offenders reoffend, they tend to commit non-violent offences (see Chapter 5), one would not expect many youths to qualify for this presumption. In any case, even though a youth might presumptively receive an adult sentence, there are two sets of reasons to believe it will be a rare event.

---

2 One exception is in the case of a youth charged with a very serious violent offence (one of the 'presumptive offences') but who is given a youth sentence rather than an adult sentence, a judge *may* allow the identify of the convicted youth to be published 'if the court considers it appropriate in the circumstances, taking into account the importance of rehabilitating the young person and the public interest' (Section 75(3)).

First, if a youth is in jeopardy of receiving an adult sentence, that youth is also eligible for a preliminary hearing and a jury trial (in youth court). Crown attorneys may be less than enthusiastic about this prospect and may waive the right to ask for an adult sentence at the end of the court process, knowing that the likelihood of being able to justify more than a three-year sentence is remote. Second, as we have seen from the U.S. data, by the time the facts of a case are brought out fully in court, it may be clear that the maximum sentence available in youth court is fully sufficient.

As we have already pointed out, the decision to seek a youth sentence, under the YCJA, is quite separate from the decision on which correctional system a youth might serve that sentence in. If the youth is over 18, the judge can decide whether the sentence is to be served in a facility for youths or in an adult facility.

The change from 'transfers' to 'adult sentences' is more than procedural, however. With the exception of the fact that those receiving adult sentences can have their identities publicized by the media, the 'adult sentence' provisions provide, in effect, little more than a safety valve at sentencing for those cases where, somehow, the maximum sentences available in youth court do not 'fit' the crime. In other words, rather than considering a youth to be an adult because he or she was charged with a relatively serious offence (as was the case under the Young Offenders Act), the Youth Criminal Justice Act provides only a special 'extended sentence' for very serious offenders. Judges under the YCJA cannot turn a youth into an adult for criminal justice purposes.

It is impossible to know for certain whether many adult sentences will be imposed on youths under the YCJA adult sentencing provisions. In 1999–2000, however, there were only eighteen custodial sentences handed down in youth court that exceeded twenty-four months, out of 23,215 custodial sentences imposed. Even if all of these were, instead, given adult sentences and all of those transferred received adult sentences, one would expect only about seventy or so adult sentences to have been awarded that year.

CHAPTER NINE

Sentencing of Youths

The Juvenile Delinquents Act and the Young Offenders Act: From Punishment without Process to Process without Principles

One could easily characterize youth justice systems by the principles by which sanctions or treatments are imposed on youths who have offended. One recurrent theme of this book is that youth crime and youth justice systems are best thought of as separate phenomena: youth crime has its origins in society itself. The youth justice system, on the other hand, responds to youth crime, but is not, itself, a cause of it or a solution to the problems it creates.

The implicit relationship between youth crime and youth justice has played out in the different ways Canada's three pieces of youth justice legislation have dealt with sentencing. The history of the youth justice system in Canada could be told by looking at the way in which sentencing has taken place over the past century or so.

The Juvenile Delinquents Act

As discussed in Chapter 1, those who favoured the passing of the Juvenile Delinquents Act in the early years of the twentieth century did so, in part, to ensure that delinquent youths were treated in a manner different from that in which offending adults were treated. The seed for this idea began before the turn of century, as a result of reformers' views of children and childhood – that children, even if they 'offended,' should be treated in a caring, and less punitive manner than had been the case (Carrigan, 1998). 'Treatment' of youth meant treating their underlying problems by way of therapeutic sentencing. Sentencing, it followed, would help deal with the problem of youth crime.

One way to ensure special treatment for youths was, of course, to have a separate court for them. Hence, even before the advent of the Juvenile Delinquents Act, a separate court had been established in Toronto in 1894, a few years before the celebrated 'first' North American juvenile court was established in Chicago (Leon, 1977). The juvenile court system was part of a general movement directed toward removing adolescents from the criminal law process and toward special programs (Platt, 1977). Even before separate courts and a separate system were established, however, society's changing views on how to punish young people had established that children and youths should no longer be held or housed with adults. Well before the enactment of the Juvenile Delinquents Act, institutions had been set up that differentiated youths from adults, but also made distinctions among youths. Industrial schools were the preferred option for coping with delinquent youth, while probation and foster care were seen as the option for neglected or less 'hardened' youths.

Although different names are often attached to juvenile institutions, the use of custody, industrial schools, reform schools, training schools, or prisons for youths (or whatever else one might wish to call them) necessitated some kind of legal framework so that youths could be 'placed' involuntarily in such institutions. Concern that such institutions might not be the most appropriate place for delinquent youths has been a central part of Canadian concern for more than a century. Hence it is important to look carefully at the sentencing of youths and the principles that have been used to guide these decisions.

The word that we have used – sentencing – is not a neutral word in youth justice. The Juvenile Delinquents Act did not use the word, even though, it acknowledged that a youth being sentenced under the act would have committed 'an offence to be known as a delinquency' (Section 3(1)). In Section 13, the Juvenile Delinquents Act referred to jails and imprisonment in the context of adults, but referred to youths being 'detained at a detention home or a shelter.' When referring to what could happen to a 'child adjudged to be a juvenile delinquent,' the court was offered various 'courses of actions' which it could take 'as may in its judgement deem proper in the circumstances of the case' (Section 20(1)). Later in that section the options available to the judge to 'commit' the child to the charge of a children's aid society, or to 'commit' the child to an industrial school were listed. These words are, of course, consistent with the legislated guide to interpretation of the act: that 'every juvenile delinquent shall be treated, not as a criminal, but as a misdirected and misguided child, and one needing aid, encouragement, help and assistance' (Section 38). The term 'sentence' entered the act only to contrast the treatment of a juvenile with that of an adult: 'No juvenile delinquent shall, under any circumstances, upon or after conviction, be sentenced to or incarcerated in any penitentiary, or county or other gaol, or police station, or any other place in which adults are or may be imprisoned.' (Section 26(1)). This, of course, did not apply to youths who were transferred into the adult system.

Youths were not to be sentenced as criminals. It is unlikely, however, that youths invariably saw it that way. Youths 'escaped' from juvenile institutions, and fought hard to stay out of them. The framers of the Juvenile Delinquents Act, of course, would point out that children sometimes attempt to avoid painful medical or dental treatment. Hence, it might be argued that the perceptions of the child that he or she was being punished did not necessarily mean that society should view it in that way.

Children are not normally allowed formal appeals from decisions of their parents to impose medical treatment on them. Similarly, it would be argued that it makes sense that they would not have an automatic right of appeal from decisions of judges made in the context of their need for 'aid, encouragement, help and assistance' (Section 38). The state does not need to provide automatic rights to appeal decisions that are for the 'child's own good *and* the best interest of the community' (Section 20(5)). Only by way of 'special leave' (under Section 37) where the superior court judge believed that 'in the particular circumstances of the case it is essential in the public interest or for the due administration of justice that such leave be granted' was the accused youth able to appeal a decision. Sentences, then, were not to be seen as punishments; they were treatments.

The Young Offenders Act

If the sentencing provisions of the Juvenile Delinquents Act can be caricatured as punishment without process, the Young Offenders Act might be caricatured as being process without principles. Once again, the language is important. Under the Young Offenders Act, there were, again, no 'sentences.' Instead, there were 'dispositions.' The list of dispositions was relatively long, at least as compared with the Juvenile Delinquents Act, and ran from an absolute discharge, through fines, restitution, and community service, to probation and custody (Section 20(1)). Custody was subsequently broken down into 'open' and 'secure' facilities (Section 24.1(1)).

The more important change, however, was that there were embry-
onic sentencing principles. Some of these are contained in the Declara-
tion of Principle (Section 3(1)):

(a.1) while young persons should not in all instances be held accountable
in the same manner or suffer the same consequences for their behaviour as
adults, young persons who commit offences should nonetheless bear
responsibility for their contraventions;
(b) society must, although it has the responsibility to take reasonable measures to prevent criminal conduct by young persons, be afforded the necessary protections from illegal behaviour;
(c) young persons who commit offences require supervision, discipline
and control, but, because of their state of dependency and level of development and maturity, they also have special needs and require guidance
and assistance;
(c.1) the protection of society ... is best served by rehabilitation, wherever
possible, of young persons who commit offences, and rehabilitation is best
achieved by addressing the needs and circumstances of a young person
that are relevant to the young person's offending behaviour; ...
(f) in the application of this Act, the rights and freedoms of young persons
include a right to the least possible interference with freedom that is consistent with the protection of society, having regard to the needs of young
persons and the interests of their families; ...
(h) parents have responsibility for the care and supervision of their children, and, for that reason, young persons should be removed from parental supervision either partly or entirely only when measures that provide
for continuing parental supervision are inappropriate.

Section 24 of the Young Offenders Act dealt with the conditions for
custody:

(1) The youth court shall not commit a young person to custody ... unless
the court considers a committal to custody to be necessary for the protection of society having regard to the seriousness of the offence and the circumstances in which it was committed and having regard to the needs
and circumstances of the young person.
(1.1)(a) ... an order of custody shall not be used as a substitute for appropriate child protection, health, and other social measures;
(b) ... a young person who commits an offence that does not involve serious personal injury should be held accountable to the victim and to society
through non-custodial dispositions whenever appropriate;

(c) ... custody shall only be imposed when all available alternatives to custody that are reasonable in the circumstances have been considered.

The Juvenile Delinquents Act had been the subject of criticism because it was seen as too welfare oriented. The Young Offenders Act, however, attempted to be two things: 'legal' in its orientation, but clearly retaining welfare provisions. Without any clear concept of how the two fit together, however, the principles often seemed more confusing than enlightening. This is not a unique problem in statements about how to deal with young offenders.

For example, the United Nations Standard Minimum Rules for the Administration of Juvenile Justice ('The Beijing Rules') which were adopted by the UN General Assembly in 1985 state the following:

5. 1) The juvenile justice system shall emphasize the well-being of the juvenile and shall ensure that any reaction to juvenile offenders shall always be in proportion to the circumstances of both the offenders and the offence.

Later, the rules use similar language when talking about dispositions for young offenders:

17.1) The disposition of the competent authority shall be guided by the following principles:
(a) The reaction taken shall always be in proportion not only to the circumstances and the gravity of the offence but also to the circumstances and the needs of the juvenile as well as to the needs of the society;

The difficulty in applying such a principle is obvious. The disposition, or sentence, is to be proportional to the offence *and* the needs of the juvenile *and* the needs of society. It is hard to see what is left out of this equation.

Lode Walgrave (2003), a Belgian expert on youth justice matters, noted recently that the UN Standard minimum rules

do not go beyond fundamental ambivalence. It is easy to state that the judicial reaction 'should be in proportion to both the offender and the offence (Article 5.1) but it is far from evident that it is actually possible to combine both proportionalities [in an actual case] ... These rules in fact appear to be some kind of what has been called in French a 'mystification of language' ... a rhetoric which does sound good, but which in fact hides its lack of feasibility in practice.

Similarly, there are difficulties in applying the principles that govern sentencing under the YOA to individual cases. The YOA had sections the underlying message of which is that custody should be used with restraint. However, with the exception of the rule against using custody for child protection purposes, there were few 'definite' rules that could be seen to apply to specific cases. The 'least possible interference' rule (Section 3(1)(f)), for example, must be interpreted with the protection of society (presumably from crime). The statement that, in cases not involving serious personal injury, youths should be held accountable with non-custodial dispositions (Section 24(1.1)(b)) is qualified with an important limitation: this is to be done only 'whenever appropriate.' Given that it is the judge doing the sentencing who decides what is appropriate, it seems fair to assume that being appropriate is not much of a challenge: what judge would do something that is not appropriate in his or her eyes?

Similarly, the requirement that custody should be imposed only when all other alternatives have been considered has an important limitation: these alternatives must be 'reasonable in the circumstances.' Judges, once again, decide what is reasonable in the circumstances.

The question raised by these principles is whether they offer serious guidance to the sentencing judge. Serious guidance would mean that the principles make it clear that certain courses of action are excluded. Thus one measure of whether these principles of sentencing had teeth is whether there are sentences that would clearly not be acceptable under these general provisions. Our view is that a wide range of very different sentences could be justified. It is for this reason that we would characterize sentencing under the YOA to be a case of 'process without principles.'

The next section looks in detail at the way in which sentencing took place under the Young Offenders Act. It tells the story, we think, of what happens when the principles that are supposed to guide decisions in the justice system are not laid out in enough detail that certain courses of action would be prohibited by the rules. The picture we will see reflects the vagueness of the YOA. It includes, among other features, the following findings:

- Judges invoked different purposes of sentencing even though they might have be on dealing with similar cases.
- Similar cases got different sentences for no apparent reasons.
- Local (provincial) expectations built up, which led to different practices in different provinces.

- Custody – the most severe of dispositions – was used frequently for minor offences.

It would be wrong to blame judges for these problems. Judges cannot be expected to follow principles which do not exist.

Sentencing under the YOA

As we have pointed out, a rather obvious problem with the YOA is that if the principles of sentencing are not clear, then many quite different sentences can be justified for any case. Some years ago, the YOA was criticized for being ambiguous in its sentencing principles and objectives (Trépanier, 1989). Principles of sentencing are not a mere academic exercise. Unless we can decide what principles should guide youth court dispositions, it is very difficult to know whether they 'make sense.' Thus, for example, if the major principle that the judge is supposed to follow is that the disposition should be proportional to the seriousness of the offence, it would mean that those found guilty of the most serious offences would invariably receive the most severe dispositions (i.e., custody) and those found guilty of the least serious offences would get the least onerous dispositions. However, if the judge were to follow the principle that the disposition should be that which would most likely to reduce the likelihood of future offending, the pattern of dispositions might be quite different.

Imagine a situation where the rationale for dispositions was based solely on lowering future offending. If it could be shown that the best outcome for a young person who had committed a very serious violent offence was a program that existed only in a community setting, a sentence of probation with participation in the program would be the most appropriate sentence under this rationale. If the dominant principle was that the sentence should be proportionate to the seriousness of the offence, then this case would appear to warrant a custodial sentence, even though it might not necessarily be the most rehabilitative.

There was enormous variation in the sentences imposed on similar young people found to have committed similar offences in similar circumstances. In one study (Doob & Beaulieu, 1992), forty-three judges were given the same detailed cases to read and were asked to indicate what they thought was the most appropriate sentence for the young offender. Two important findings in this study are relevant to understanding youth court sentences. First, when judges were asked what goals they were trying to meet in deciding on the sentence, they varied

Table 9.1   Selection of traditional purposes of sentencing, by judge, for youth offences (%)

Purpose	Shoplifter		Assault causing bodily harm	
	First time, age 17	With record, age 15	No real record, age 16	Relevant record, age 15
Punishment	12	10	19	17
Rehabilitation	43	50	33	32
General deterrence	7	5	–	5
Individual deterrence	38	36	48	44
Incapacitation	–	–	–	2
Total:	100	100	100	100

Source: Doob and Beaulieu, 1992.

dramatically in terms of the primary goal. The most important goal that the judges listed for the sentence for each case is indicated in Table 9.1.

Thus, when deciding on a disposition for the young first-time offender, 12 per cent indicated that punishment was most important, 43 per cent thought that rehabilitation was the most important, 38 per cent listed individual deterrence as the primary purpose, and only 7 per cent gave highest priority to general deterrence.

There was enormous variation in what judges were attempting to accomplish when faced with the identical cases. Although rehabilitation and individual deterrence were most often mentioned for all four of the young offenders, judges were more or less evenly split between these two. Judges were fairly consistent across cases: a judge who listed a particular goal as being most important for one young offender tended to list the same goal as being most important for other young offenders. In other words, judges did appear to apply their own theory of dispositions. They had, however, quite different theories.

Ambiguity in the Young Offenders Act

As Trépanier (1989) has noted, ambiguity about what should be guiding dispositions was written into the act. Thus, it would be unfair to criticize judges for not having a single coherent theory of dispositions. Neither the Young Offenders Act nor the courts of appeal provided judges with such a theory. Young (1989, p. 104) notes that: 'The appellate courts have not successfully developed sentencing principles that promote a unique identity for juvenile justice. The special needs of young people are constantly alluded to but the courts appear uncertain as to what exactly these special needs are and how it is that these special needs can be translated into a distinct penal philosophy.'

In a study in 2001, judges in all parts of Canada except Quebec appeared to agree with Young (Doob, 2001). When asked how helpful Court of Appeal decisions are in guiding sentencing decisions, at least one-third of the judges in every jurisdiction outside of Quebec indicated that their Court of Appeal was rarely or never helpful. Though only 20.8 per cent of Quebec judges indicated that their court of appeal was 'rarely or never helpful,' 53 per cent of the youth court judges in the rest of Canada held this view. If the Courts of Appeal are supposed to be 'fine tuning' the interpretation of the legislation, they did not appear to be succeeding, in the eyes of many youth court judges. Only 6.5 per cent of the respondents across Canada indicated that their Court of Appeal was 'very helpful' in the sentencing process. Even Quebec judges were not overwhelmingly enthusiastic about their Court of Appeal's role in sentencing: only 12.5 per cent of Quebec judges indicated that their Court of Appeal was 'very helpful' in giving guidance on sentencing.

It should not be surprising, given that different judges have different philosophies about what a disposition of the court is supposed to accomplish, that the actual dispositions handed down for young offenders vary enormously, depending in large part on the judge who presides over the case.

In the simulation study described above, the judges indicated what they thought the sentence for the four young offenders should be. These data are shown in Table 9.2. As can be seen in this table, sentences varied widely.

It should be pointed out that the judges gave quite detailed and thoughtful explanations on why they believed each disposition was appropriate. The variation did not come from carelessness. The variation came from the fact that the judges had been very thoughtful in the manner in which they crafted dispositions. The sentences, it seemed, were their best (but quite varied) attempt to accomplish a range of different purposes.

Proportionality in Sentencing

The simulation data presented in Table 9.2 certainly imply one important characteristic of the sentencing of youths. Whatever principles

Table 9.2   Proportion of judges giving dispositions of each type to four accused youth in simulation experiment (%)

Most serious component of sentence	Shoplifter		Assault causing bodily harm	
	First time, age 17	With record, age 15	No real record, age 16	Relevant record, age 15
Secure custody	–	–	5	8
Open custody	–	11	37	57
Community service	54	68	40	16
Fine	19	11	3	3
Probation	22	8	16	16
Discharge	5	3	–	–
Total	100	100	100	100

Source: Doob and Beaulieu, 1992.

judges may be thinking of in the sentencing of youths, it appears that, at least in the comparison of these two cases, proportionality plays a role. Very few judges indicated they would use custody for the shoplifting (none for the first offender, 11 per cent for the other offender). For the assault causing bodily harm, however, many more would place the youth in custody (45 per cent for the first offender and 65 per cent for the other offender). Presumably, the seriousness of the offence was a deciding factor in determining this quite different treatment.

Much of the knowledge about sentencing patterns focuses on the use of custodial (prison) sentences and looks at whether a youth is placed in custody or not. There are two reasons for this. First, for various technical reasons, it is the use of custodial decisions that is most readily available to researchers in data that come from Statistics Canada's Canadian Centre for Justice Statistics. Second, because a custodial sentence is generally the most severe and most intrusive sanction available to the court, there is more concern about this sanction than any other.

Looking at actual sentences handed down in Canada, the data in Table 9.3 suggest that the use of custody is determined, to some extent, by the severity of the offence. Table 9.3 shows the proportion of each type of case that resulted in custody.

Within the category of non-sexual offences against persons (such as assault, etc.), more serious offences (aggravated assault and the homicide offences) are considerably more likely to result in a custodial sentence than are less serious offences (common assault, or assault causing bodily harm). The same holds for sexual assaults and, to some extent,

Table 9.3   Frequency of custody for youths found guilty of selected offences. Canada, 1999–2000 (percentage and number that percentage is based on)

Most significant charge	Percentage receiving custody
Common assault	24 (6,462)
Assault causing bodily harm / with weapon	31 (2,447)
Aggravated assault	66 (184)
Homicide offences (including attempts)	78 (32)
Sexual assault	29 (616)
Sexual assault, bodily harm / with weapon and aggravated sexual assault	67 (18)
Theft under $5,000	22 (8,921)
Theft over $5,000	50 (991)
Break and enter	39 (7,342)

Source: CCJS (1999–2000).

property offences. Serious thefts are much more likely to result in a custodial sentence than are minor thefts. These relationships are, obviously, simple ones that do not control for any other relevant factors (e.g., record of offending or age). Using offence categories as a measure of the seriousness of offences is, of course, problematic in that there can be a great range in the details of cases within categories. We have not listed 'robbery' in Table 9.3, for example, because robberies involve a wide range of different behaviours that vary considerably in apparent seriousness. Forty-nine per cent of robbery cases resulted in custodial sentences. It is difficult to know whether – in comparison with 'theft over $5,000' or some other violent offences – this would be seen as supporting a proportionality explanation for sentencing. It would probably be safe, however, to assume that a fair amount of the variability in the severity of sentences is accounted for by the seriousness of the offences.

The YOA, in its language, was clearly more offence oriented than was its predecessor, the JDA. There are references to the seriousness of the offence, and protecting society. A study of dispositions in Toronto youth courts (Doob & Meen, 1993) showed that dispositions were only slightly related to the seriousness of the offence in the final days of the JDA (1982–4). The first couple of years of the YOA (1984–6), however, showed a stronger relationship between the type of offence and the disposition. By 1989–90, the relationship was even stronger. Neverthe-

Table 9.4   Percentage of guilty cases sentenced to custody for selected offences, Canada and the four largest provinces, 1999–2000

	All offences	Assault bodily harm	Minor assault	Break and enter	Theft over $5,000	Theft under $5,000
Canada	34.0	30.4	23.2	38.6	49.1	22.2
Quebec	27.4	24.2	18.6	31.9	35.0	20.1
Ontario	39.8	35.9	27.9	41.7	51.0	25.8
Alberta	28.1	18.9	17.3	38.1	51.7	17.9
B.C.	33.7	29.9	15.3	38.7	47.9	19.5

Source: Data derived from provincial/territorial tables purchased from Canadian Centre for Justice Statistics for, 1999–2000.

less, the offence alone did not account for the majority of the variation in sentences.

Provincial Variation in the Use of Custody

We have already noted in Chapter 7 that there is substantial variation across Canada in the rate at which cases are brought into the youth courts. Provincial variation also exists in the rate at which cases are sent to custody. Some examples (for Canada's most populous provinces) are shown in Table 9.4.

There are two broad conclusions that one might draw from the data in Table 9.4. First, there is variation across provinces in the overall use of custody. Quebec, which brings relatively few cases into its youth courts, might be expected to bring, on average, more serious cases. Its use of custody, however, is considerably lower than the custody rate for Ontario. A youth before an Ontario youth court is much more likely to end up in custody than is a youth appearing in Quebec.

Second, it is clear that there are more subtle differences reflecting, perhaps, different traditions in the manner in which different offences are seen in different parts of Canada. Youths convicted of breaking and entering in Ontario, Alberta, and British Columbia have, roughly speaking, about the same likelihood of ending up with a custodial sentence. The patterns for assault causing bodily harm and minor assault, however, vary considerably across these three provinces.

Part of the interprovincial variation in sentencing *may* relate to the availability of an appropriate range of sanctions. Certainly, one of the traditional concerns of judges and others is the availability of a range of sanctions for sentencing youths. One of the ironies of the youth justice system is that judges can, quite easily, sentence youths to custody. However, for almost any other sanction, there is a need for some other factor to come into play. There is no point in imposing a fine on a youth who has no money and no means to earn it. Ordering community service accomplishes nothing unless there is a reasonable way of ensuring that the youth has an opportunity to do the service. In addition, there was a requirement in the YOA that the person or organization receiving the service (or the provincial official in charge of a program) approved the arrangement whereby the youth did community service. If a probation officer believed that community service was inappropriate for a youth or that community work could not be found for a given youth, that youth was unlikely to be ordered to do community service.

A probation term involving participation in some community program necessitates the existence of that program and the youth's acceptance into it. Hence, although in theory there are no limits on the creativity that can go into a sentence, in reality judges are often presented with relatively few options on how to sentence a youth. Custody, however, is always an option, and provinces must always provide custodial beds, even though they do not have to provide for any other type of disposition.

Table 9.5 presents data from a survey of youth court judges (Doob, 2001) suggesting that Quebec judges – who use custody relatively infrequently – were considerably more likely to believe that they had an adequate range of sanctions available.[1]

The Impact of a Criminal Record

Although the offence may be more important in determining the sentence under the YOA than it had been under the JDA, it is also clear that the seriousness of the offence is insufficient to explain the overall pattern of sentences imposed on youths. As Carrington and Moyer

---

1 Judges who heard youth court cases in more than one community were asked about their largest and smallest community. The pattern was the same when looking at the smallest community: 63 per cent of Quebec judges but only 13 per cent of judges from the rest of Canada indicated that there were definitely an adequate range of sanctions available in the smallest community in which they sat.

Table 9.5 Adequate choice of sanctions available in largest (or only) community (percentage, and in parentheses number)

| Region | Adequate range of sanctions available? | | | |
	Definitely yes	Probably yes	Probably or definitely not	Total
Atlantic	23.3	53.3	23.3	100 (30)
Quebec	62.5	37.5	–	100 (24)
Ontario	23.9	46.3	29.9	100 (67)
Prairies	21.8	38.2	40.0	100 (55)
B.C.	28.3	41.5	30.2	100 (53)
Territories	50.0	–	50.0	100 (4)
Total	28.8	42.5	28.8	100 (233)

Source: Doob, 2001.

(1995) noted, it is, in particular, the administration of justice offences (e.g., escape, or unlawfully at large) that challenge the notion that offence seriousness is an overwhelmingly important factor in determining sentences. Carrington and Moyer (1995, p. 154) conclude:

Although some 'offence orientation' was evident [in their analyses of sentencing data], the primary factor in deciding between custodial and non-custodial dispositions ... appeared to be the offender's criminal record. First offenders were rarely given custodial dispositions, even when convicted of serious offences; offenders who had already received a custodial disposition in the past were likely to receive another one, unless the current offence was very minor. The seriousness of the current offence did play some role in determining dispositions, but it was decisive in only a few types of cases.

The size of the impact of previous convictions is impressive. Kowalski and Caputo (1999) report that in 1995–6 (across Canada), only 12 per cent of first-time offenders were given custodial dispositions. One prior finding of guilt raised the custody rate to 32 per cent; 47 per cent of youths with two prior convictions got custodial sentences. Almost two-thirds (65 per cent) of youths with three or more previous findings of guilt received sentences involving custody. Interestingly, although only 38 per cent of the custodial dispositions for first-time offenders involved secure (as opposed to 'open') custody, 62 per cent of the custodial dispositions handed down to those with three or more previous findings of guilt involved secure custody. This general relationship – custody rates increasing with longer criminal records – held across types of offences (property , violent, drug) and across age groups.

In trying to understand the increased use of custody during the YOA period, Carrington and Moyer (1995, p. 155) suggest that:

> It is implausible that any increase in custodial dispositions under the YOA has been due to 'offence orientation.' If there has indeed been an increase in the use of custody, it is more likely that it reflects an escalation in control measures in response to increased recorded recidivism. This recidivism could have any number of causes: actual youth crime, police charging practices, screening practices, youth court processes leading up to adjudication ... or simply, better record-keeping.

The Use of Custody in Canada for Some of the Less Serious Cases

When the government of Canada released its white paper in the spring of 1998 outlining its plans for youth justice legislation, it noted that Canada not only used youth custody for many very minor offences but also that Canada incarcerates youth at a higher rate than do most western nations. Using the most recent data available, it appears that the concern of the Minister of Justice was well founded.

Table 9.6 shows that eight offences (or groupings of offences) account for the majority of custodial sentences. In Canada, in 1999–2000, there were 23,215 cases that resulted in a custodial sentence.

Theft of goods valued at less than $5,000 accounts for roughly 9 per cent of all cases going to custody in Canada. If we add three other relatively minor offences – possession of stolen property, failure to appear in youth court, and failure to comply with a disposition – we find that these four offences account for roughly 48 per cent of all cases in which an offender is sentenced to custody in Canada. There is a tendency to think that only the most serious cases result in custodial sentences. These data demonstrate that many of the custodial sentences are, in fact, for relatively minor cases.

This proportion varies a bit from province to province and from year to year. But it is safe to suggest that somewhere between one-third and one-half of the cases that end up in custody in any province in any year have as their most serious charge one of these four offences.

When we add in other thefts, mischief and/or damage to property, breaking and entering, and minor assaults, (i.e. common assault, or assault where there was no bodily harm) we find that these eight sets of offences account for approximately three-quarters of all cases that end up with custodial sentences in Canada. Thus, even though more serious offences are, generally, dealt with more harshly by the system, there are large numbers of less serious offences with custodial dispositions.

The practice of imposing custody for relatively minor cases is widespread across Canada. We have presented, in Table 9.6, the pattern for the country as a whole and Canada's two largest provinces, as well as (Saskatchewan), a relatively small province that incarcerates large numbers of youth.

In each province that we have looked at, three of which are contained in Table 9.6, a substantial proportion of custody dispositions are accounted for by relatively minor offences. These data would appear to support Carrington and Moyer's (1995) contention that it is not seriousness of the offence alone that accounts for the widespread use of custody for young offenders.

As noted in Chapter 7, Quebec brings far fewer cases to court, per capita, than do the other provinces and territories and, as we can see in Table 9.6 (bottom row) places far fewer youths in custody, per capita, than the other two provinces. Hence it makes sense that those cases that do end up in custody tend to be somewhat more serious. But even in Quebec, with its relatively low rate of use of court, a substantial number of youths are placed in custody for relatively minor offences: 60.5 per cent of the cases that went to custody in Quebec had, as the most significant charge, one of these eight types of offences. Given that custody is used in Quebec, as elsewhere, for child welfare purposes (contrary to Section 24(1.1)(a)), it is not surprising to find that many not very serious offences often result in custody. When asked about the use of custody, 37 per cent of youth court judges indicated that 'the youth's home (and/or parents) or living conditions were such that there was a need to get him or her into a more stable environment' was a relevant factor in half or more of the cases that they sent to custody (Doob, 2001).

Variation across Provinces in the Impact of Criminal Record on the Sentencing

We have already seen that the youth's record of offending has a dramatic impact on the likelihood of a custodial sentence being imposed.

Table 9.6   Cases to custody: Canada, Quebec, Ontario, and Saskatchewan, 1999–2000

Most significant charge	Canada		Quebec		Ontario		Saskatchewan	
	N	%*	N	%*	N	%	N	%
Theft under $5,000	2,005	9	242	10.1	647	7.0	185	9.2
Possession of stolen property	1,411	6	37	1.5	628	6.8	163	8.1
Failure to appear	2,579	11	123	5.1	1,116	12.0	276	13.7
Failure to comply with a disposition	5,234	23	418	17.4	1,951	21.0	321	15.9
Subtotal	11,229	48	820	34.2	4342	46.7	945	46.9
Other thefts	1,011	4	82	3.4	388	4.2	122	6.1
Mischief/damage	726	3	40	1.7	265	2.8	87	4.3
Break and enter	2,853	12	377	15.7	983	10.6	283	14.1
Minor assault	1,521	7	134	5.6	808	8.7	98	4.9
Total: 8 offences	17,340	75	1,453	60.5	6,786	72.9	1535	76.3
Total: all offences	23,215	100	2400	100	9,303	100	2013	100
Cases to custody per 1,000 youths in the jurisdiction	9.48		4.4		10.2		20.5	

Source: Canadian Centre for Justice Statistics, 1999–2000.
Note: Percentages do not always add to 100 because of rounding.
* Percentage of all custodial sentences which involved this offence.

Table 9.7 Percentage (and number) of offenders receiving custody as a function of the number of previous findings of guilt, selected offences, four largest provinces, 1996–7

Offence / Province	Previous findings of guilt			
	None	1	2	3+
Common assault				
Quebec	7.9 (392)	20.7 (92)	52.8 (36)	78.6 (14)
Ontario	11.8 (2196)	38.7 (506)	62.0 (216)	70.6 (180)
Alberta	3.3 (423)	13.7 (168)	26.5 (83)	38.6 (88)
British Columbia	6.3 (457)	23.1 (104)	44.6 (56)	75.0 (32)
Assault with a weapon				
Quebec	13.3 (263)	28.3 (46)	57.9 (19)	64.7 (17)
Ontario	26.0 (500)	51.9 (129)	75.9 (58)	82.5 (57)
Alberta	14.1 (135)	37.2 (43)	42.1 (19)	67.9 (28)
British Columbia	15.6 (109)	46.7 (30)	75.0 (16)	81.3 (16)
Theft under $5,000				
Quebec	7.2 (595)	16.0 (213)	26.5 (98)	50.0 (58)
Ontario	8.1 (1822)	26.2 (619)	51.6 (225)	64.1 (192)
Alberta	3.5 (898)	9.0 (378)	19.8 (167)	38.7 (181)
British Columbia	3.6 (661)	13.4 (232)	24.7 (77)	47.5 (61)
Break and enter				
Quebec	16.0 (844)	32.6 (307)	53.0 (134)	66.7 (87)
Ontario	23.1 (1491)	62.2 (455)	75.9 (220)	89.3 (253)
Alberta	9.0 (443)	33.1 (175)	53.0 (117)	72.4 (163)
British Columbia	11.8 (389)	30.3 (152)	61.5 (52)	85.9 (64)

Source: Data derived from 1996–7 youth court data purchased from the Canadian Centre for Justice Statistics.

Table 9.7 shows the effect of criminal record on two violent offences (minor assault and assault causing bodily harm) and for two property offences (minor thefts and breaking and entering) for the four largest Canadian provinces. There are three quite separate conclusions that might be drawn from these data:

1 It would appear that seriousness of the offence does make some difference. Comparing the sentences given for a common assault versus an assault with a weapon or causing bodily harm, it would appear that the more serious offence is more likely to result in a sentence of imprisonment. This same general relationship holds for

minor thefts and breaking and entering: the latter offence is, at any given level of criminal record, more likely to result in a custodial sentence. This is, of course, consistent with the data presented in Table 9.4 (which did not control for criminal record).

2 There is a very large effect of criminal record for every offence and within each of these provinces.

3 There are large interprovincial differences in the likelihood of going to prison for a given offence with a given criminal record.

Putting the first two of these conclusions together leads to interesting results: a youth with a criminal record who is found guilty of a minor offence often has a considerably higher likelihood of receiving a custodial sentence than does a youth without a record who is found guilty of more serious offence. In Ontario, for example, 38.7 per cent of minor (or 'common') assaults with one previous conviction receive a custodial disposition, while 26 per cent of assaults causing bodily harm with no previous convictions receive a custodial disposition. A youth with two previous findings of guilt has a .516 probability of receiving a custodial sentence for a theft under $5,000. A first-time burglar in Ontario, on the other hand, is only half as likely ($P = 0.231$) to go to prison for the burglary.

These data, again, support Carrington and Moyer's (1995) contention that it is record of the offender more than the offence that is crucial in understanding the use of custody in the YOA (Table 9.7).

The Impact of Previous Custodial Sentences

It is not, however, simply the criminal record that makes a difference in terms of what happened to a youth at sentencing. Matarazzo, Carrington, and Hiscott (2001) explored the independent impact of the nature of the previous *sentences* on the sentence handed down for repeat offenders. Judges sometimes appear to believe that a sentence must be more severe than the previous sentence imposed on a youth, quite independent of what that sentence was for. The implicit theory of this sentencing practice appears to be individual deterrence: if the youth was not deterred by the previous sentence, a more severe sentence needs to be imposed. The results of the study by Matarazzo et al. (2001) suggest that the most recent prior disposition and the second most recent disposition were each important in determining the sentence handed down. In other words, it is not just that the youth has a record; it is also what the previous sentence was. For example, if a youth received secure custody on his or her most recent as well as the second most recent dispositions, his or her probability of being given secure custody for the current offence was .65. If, however, the most recent disposition was secure custody, but the second most recent disposition was probation, the probability of being handed down secure custody at this time was only .45. Clearly, remote dispositions appear to have an influence on the current sanction.

Not surprisingly, the most recent disposition also has an influence. For instance, one can look at the sentences given to youths whose second most recent previous disposition was open custody. For these youths, the probability of being handed down secure custody for the current offence after having received secure custody as the most recent previous disposition was .48. In contrast, the probability of being given secure custody for the current offence if the most recent previous disposition was open custody was .28. Further, in those cases where the most recent previous disposition was probation, the probability of receiving secure custody dropped to only .13. Statistical analyses demonstrated that these effects were independent of the current offence.

Thus, the disposition handed down to a young person in Canada's youth court is 'strongly influenced by prior dispositions, rather than being entirely guided by the nature of the current offence' (Matarazzo et al., 2001, p. 195). 'Prior dispositions are "sticky" labels which tend to last indefinitely' (ibid.). 'The nature of the most recent prior offence and the age and gender of the offender had only a weak association with the current disposition when relevant case characteristics were controlled ... The finding that the effect of a prior offence is mediated by the disposition awarded for that offence has the intriguing implication that it is the dispositional history rather than the history of offending that is salient in later dispositions ... Thus a criminal history is a history of judicial reactions to past behaviour, rather than the behaviour itself' (ibid., p. 196). 'For young offenders with prior records, it will be difficult for [them] to receive less severe court responses that match any possible reduction in the seriousness of the reoffending' (ibid., p. 197).

Taking these two sets of findings together we see that sentences have been affected to a large degree by two factors that are quite independent of the current offence. First, the record of offending is very important. Second, the decision by a previous judge in dealing with a youth has an independent impact above and beyond what the youth did.

It seems likely that most Canadians would, implicitly, endorse a proportionality model: More serious offences should result in harsher sentences. However, these other two factors – a previous record, and previous dispositions – can easily distort the proportionality principle. Two shoplifters may have committed exactly the same offence and have equal responsibility for it. However, the one that has a previous record is much more likely to be treated harshly this time. If two offenders have exactly the same record of offending, but one had the misfortune in a previous case to have been sentenced to custody, then that previous custodial experience would increase the likelihood of a custodial sentence in the subsequent sentencing. This is particularly problematic in the case of custodial sentences for 'failure to comply with a disposition.' In 1999–2000 more than 5,000 youths were given custodial sentences where the most serious offence they were found guilty of was a failure to comply with a disposition. Forty-seven per cent of those sentenced for this 'administration of justice' offence were given custodial sentences. A few days in custody for non-compliance with a curfew order may not appear very serious. This study shows, however, that the next time such a youth appeared before a youth court judge, the likelihood of custody would increase dramatically.

Canada–United States Comparisons on the Use of Custody

Not only does Canada tend to use custodial sentences for relatively minor offences, but compared with other countries, Canada appears to sentence a relatively high rate of youth to custody. For example, Canada has a similar or slightly higher rate than the United States in use of custody for violence and property offences (Sprott & Snyder, 1999). These data are shown in Figures 9.1 to 9.3.[2]

Clearly, for violent offences the rate of imposing custody is more or less the same in the two countries. For property offences the rate of custody in the two countries was similar at the beginning of the decade, but by the end of the decade, Canada was placing youths in custody at a rate higher than the United States was. For drug offences, on the other hand, the United States incarcerates youths at a rate that is higher than Canada's.

Canada tends to see itself as being less punitive than the United States. Yet, when looking at the use of custody this does not seem to be the case, at least for certain types of offences.

---

2 These data were updated by Jane Sprott (from Sprott and Snyder, 1999) and, very kindly, made available to us.

Figure 9.1. Percentage of youth convicted for violent offences who received custody, Canada and the United States, 1991–8

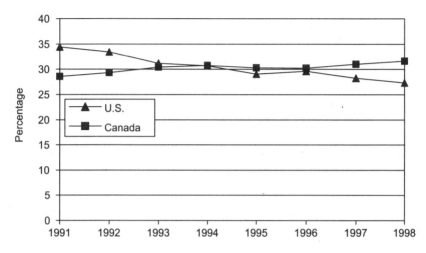

Source: Sprott and Snyder, 1999; data updated by Jane Sprott.

Figure 9.2. Percentage of youth convicted for property offences who received custody, Canada and the United States, 1991–8

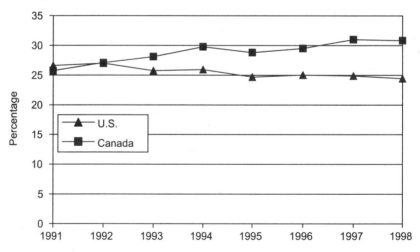

Source: Sprott and Snyder, 1999; data updated by Jane Sprott.

Figure 9.3. Percentage of youth convicted for drug offences who received custody, Canada and the United States, 1991–8

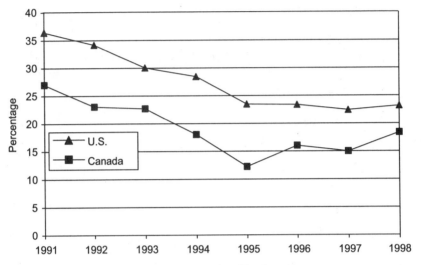

Source: Sprott and Snyder, 1999; data updated by Jane Sprott.

Short Custodial Sentences

In Canada, however, the majority of custodial sentences are relatively short.[3] For example, as shown in Table 9.8, in 1999–2000, 33.8 per cent of custodial sentences in Canada were for less than one month and another 43.5 per cent of custodial sentences were for one to three months. Thus, more than three- quarters of the custodial sentences in Canada are for three months or less. What accounts, if anything, for this practice in youth court sentencing in Canada? Marinos (1998, pp. 363–5) suggests that:

> For certain kinds of offences – violent, sexual, or serious property – denunciation is an important purpose in sentencing a young offender. For the less serious instances of these offences (e.g., where the role of the particular offender was minor or where the particular offence was relatively minor), denunciation may still be seen as being important, but a custodial

---

3 We were not able to find comparable data for the United States.

Table 9.8   Distribution of lengths for
custodial sentences (secure and open),
Canada, 1999–2000

Sentence length (months)	N	%
<1	7,857	33.8
1–3	10,102	43.5
4–6	3,808	16.4
7–12	1,211	5.2
13–24	219	0.9
>24	18	0.08
Total	23,215	100

Source: Canadian Centre for Justice Statistics, 2001b.

sentence may be seen as inappropriately harsh. One way to resolve this conflict is to impose a very short custodial sentence (e.g., a total sentence of thirty days or less) and combine it with the 'appropriate' intermediate sanction (e.g., a community service order).

Her findings support this explanation. Intermediate sanctions (e.g., community service orders or fines) tended to be combined with short sentences in the more serious kinds of offences (robberies, sexual assaults, breaking and entering, serious assaults). For less serious offences receiving custody, however, short sentences did not have intermediate sanctions attached to them. It would appear that judges may not feel that intermediate sanctions, on their own, had sufficient denunciatory power. As a result, they would achieve denunciation by imposing a short custodial sentence. Such combinations of short custodial sentences with an intermediate sanction such as community service are not necessary, and hence not often given, when the case did not 'require' denunciation. Hence for minor thefts or possession of stolen property, these combinations of sanctions were much less likely to occur.

Short sentences as a way of dealing with youthful offenders were not as prevalent in the early years of the YOA as they are now. It will be recalled that the maximum age of jurisdiction of the youth courts varied from the sixteenth birthday to the eighteenth birthday prior to 1985. Doob (1992) looked at the escalation in the use of short sentences

Table 9.9   Percentage of young offender cases receiving custody

	Newfoundland	Quebec	Manitoba	Saskatchewan	Alberta	British Columbia
1984–5	14	30	14	25	10	11
1986–7	24	30	25	23	20	21
1988–9	21	31	28	25	18	22

Source: Data adapted from Doob, 1992.
Note: Data include only cases where the age of the offender was within the jurisdiction of the JDA in each province.

for those youths who had been subject to the JDA.[4] Two separate phenomena were evident.

First, the use of custody for these youths increased in a number of provinces during the first few years of the YOA. As shown in Table 9.9, the proportion of youths receiving custody doubled during this time period in Manitoba and British Columbia and increased considerably in Newfoundland and Alberta.

What is equally interesting is that the increase in the use of custody occurred largely in the use of short sentences. The number, and proportion, of long sentences decreased in most of the six provinces that were examined (Table 9.10). The size of the increase in the use of short sentences was dramatic over this time period. In each of these six provinces the increased use of short sentence was notable. In Alberta, for example, 25 per cent of the custodial sentences were for three months or less in 1984–5. Four years later this had increased to 66 per cent.

What is equally true is that the proportion, and in many cases the *number*, of long sentences also decreased dramatically. Long sentences of custody were not, even in the first days of the YOA, a frequent occurrence. Nevertheless, there appeared to be a general decrease in the use of long custodial sentences. As we have already pointed out, by the end of the century, custodial sentences of more than a year constituted only about 1 per cent of all custodial sentences.

One of the concerns that was expressed about the YOA was that it

4 Data were not available from all jurisdictions until about 1991. In this paper, only a subset of jurisdictions could be examined.

Table 9.10   Length of custodial sentences in the first few years of the Young Offenders Act, selected provinces

	≤3 months		4–12 months		≥13 months		Total	
	%	N	%	N	%	N	%	N
Newfoundland								
1984–5	58	103	34	61	8	15	100	179
1986–7	63	259	34	139	3	14	100	412
1988–9	71	202	28	81	1	3	100	286
Quebec								
1984–5	29	491	54	919	17	290	100	1,700
1986–7	44	902	50	1,032	5	110	100	2,044
1988–9	51	985	45	861	4	74	100	1,920
Manitoba								
1984–5	16	82	62	311	22	110	100	503
1986–7	44	396	51	463	6	50	100	909
1988–9	42	418	53	523	5	45	100	986
Saskatchewan								
1984–5	45	97	50	107	5	10	100	214
1986–7	55	210	43	164	2	6	100	380
1988–9	68	332	29	144	3	14	100	490
Alberta								
1984–5	25	130	68	355	8	40	100	525
1986–7	65	621	34	319	1	10	100	950
1988–9	66	620	32	302	1	13	100	935
British Columbia								
1984–5	44	237	46	249	9	50	100	536
1986–7	61	722	36	425	3	35	100	1,182
1988–9	71	821	26	306	3	29	100	1,156

Source: Data adapted from Doob, 1992.
Note: Data include only those ages that were previously under the jurisdiction of the JDA in each province.

appeared to be responsible for increased use of custody (Markwart & Corrado, 1989). It would appear that at least some provinces were increasing the number of youths going to custody, but decreasing, on average, the amount of time that they spent there.

In a 2001 survey, youth court judges were asked for their reasons for imposing short custodial sentences. Each judge was asked to indicate

Table 9.11   Importance of various factors (%) in the decision to hand down a short (60 days or less) custodial disposition (*N* = 238)

Factor	Not important	Middle	Important	Total
The seriousness of the offence required a custodial sentence	12	10	79	100
Failure of non-custodial dispositions handed down to this youth to stop offending	13	19	68	100
Youth would be deterred from offending in the future by 'short sharp shocks'	17	20	63	100
Longer time in custody would interfere with productive activities (e.g., school)	16	28	56	100
Youth had spent substantial time in pretrial detention	24	15	60	100
Probation says non-custody is not appropriate	39	31	31	100
A short custodial sentence might deter others	54	23	23	100
Social conditions in youth's life made it sensible to get the youth into a new environment	49	28	23	100
No community sanctions were available	71	13	15	100

Source: Doob, 2001.

on a 5-point scale the importance of each of nine different reasons. Their responses are reproduced in Table 9.11.[5]

A number of points can be made from these findings. First, for each of these reasons for handing down short sentences, there were judges who indicated that the reason was 'very important' as well as judges who indicated that it was 'not at all important' as an explanation for short sentences. Judges, it would seem, have different reasons for giving out short sentences. Second, the argument that short sentences

---

5 The responses are 'collapsed' such that 1 ('Not at all important') and 2 (unlabelled) are combined as 'not important,' and 5 ('very important') is combined with 4 (unlabelled).

were being used because community sanctions were not available was *not* seen by very many judges as an important factor.

Apparently judges are imposing short custodial sentences for two quite different sets of reasons. First, congruent with Marinos's (1998) explanation for very short sentences, from the judge's perspective some offences simply 'required' a custodial sentence because of the relative seriousness of the offence. In other words, judges indicated that they had to respond to particular offences with custody because, somehow, custody – albeit a short custodial sentence – was 'necessary.' Second, many judges believed that a short custodial sentence would be good for the youth or that a youth who had continued to offend after serving a non-custodial sentence might stop if placed in custody for a few days. There is, however, no evidence that short sharp shocks act as an effective deterrent among those who are subjected to them.

Probation

Probation is the most frequently used disposition for youths in Canada, in part because it is often used in conjunction with other dispositions (e.g., community service orders, fines, conditional discharges, and custody). Probation was ordered – alone or in combination with one or more other dispositions – in 75 per cent of the cases without custody in 1999–2000.

Although probation is frequently used in all provinces, its length varies somewhat from province to province. Generally speaking, however, probation terms tend to be fairly long – typically more than six months and often more than one year. The variation in the length of probation terms for selected provinces is shown in Table 9.12.

The variation across provinces is most evident if one looks at the proportion of probation terms of over one year. Compared with the other provinces, Newfoundland and Ontario tend to have a higher portion of these relatively long probation terms, while Quebec tends to have fewer. The length of a probation term is important for a number of reasons, including the fact that breaking a condition of probation (e.g., not abiding by a curfew or violating an order not to associate with certain other youths) constitutes a common reason (see Chapter 7) for returning a youth to youth court with a new charge of failure to comply with a disposition. In addition, as shown in Table 9.6, this is frequently the basis of a new custodial sentence.

Given that a custodial sentence under the YOA does not automati-

Table 9.12   Distribution of lengths of probation without custody (%)

| | Months | | | | | | |
	<1	1–3	4–6	7–12	13–24	>24	Total (N)
NF	–	2	15	53	30	–	100 (869)
NS	<1	2	19	53	26	<1	100 (1,122)
QC	<1	2	25	67	6	<1	100 (4,964)
ON	<1	1	12	57	29	<1	100 (11,083)
SK	<1	6	26	50	19	–	100 (3,185)
AB	<1	4	27	55	13	<1	100 (4,732)
BC	<1	5	22	53	19	<1	100 (4,662)

Source: CCJS, 1998–9, Table 6 for each jurisdiction.

Table 9.13   Custodial sentences also getting a probation order as a function of total sentence length, 1994–5 (percentage, with number in parentheses)

| | Sentence length (days) | | |
Type of custody sentence	1–30	31–180	≥ 181
Secure custody only	35.5 (5,078)	45.8 (3,839)	58.3 (1,183)
Open custody only	44.4 (6,143)	64.0 (6,293)	66.4 (1,161)
Secure followed by open custody	45.9 (205)	62.4 (756)	73.3 (555)

Source: Data purchased from Canadian Centre for Justice Statistics.

cally require a period of reintegration into society (as is the case under the YCJA's 'custody and supervision order,' where a third of the custody and supervision order is normally served in the community), it would not be surprising to see a probation order almost invariably imposed after a custody order. In fact, however, this is not the case. In 1994–5, it was found that in only about a half (51 per cent) of the cases was a custody order followed by a probation order. As shown in Table 9.13, probation tended to be associated with longer terms in custody than with short terms. These data suggest that large numbers of youths are released without supervision from fairly long custodial sentences, but obviously the proportion of those receiving probation after custody increases substantially as the length of the sentence increases.

A survey of adults in Ontario (Doob et al., 1998) found that most members of the public (78 per cent) wanted *all* youths to receive a period of supervision and support after a period in custody. This is

Table 9.14   View of youth court sentences by province (percentage, with number in parentheses)

| Province | View of sentences | | Total |
	Too severe or about right	Not severe enough	
Newfoundland	13.6 (3)	86.4 (19)	100 (22)
Nova Scotia	15.8 (6)	84.2 (32)	100 (38)
New Brunswick	19.4 (6)	80.6 (25)	100 (31)
P.E.I.	–	100.0 (5)	100 (5)
Quebec	34.1 (95)	65.9 (184)	100 (279)
Ontario	15.9 (68)	84.1 (359)	100 (427)
Manitoba	8.9 (4)	91.1 (41)	100 (45)
Saskatchewan	12.5 (5)	87.5 (35)	100 (40)
Alberta	11.9 (13)	88.1 (96)	100 (109)
B.C.	14.9 (22)	85.1 (126)	100 (148)
Total	19.4 (222)	80.6 (922)	100 (1,144)

Source: Macdonald, 2001.

consistent with the changes brought in by the YCJA where, typically, one-third of a youth's custodial sentence involves supervision in the community. An additional 19 per cent of survey respondents wanted supervision and support only if ordered by the judge, the situation that exists under the YOA.

Public Concern about Youth Court Sentencing

It is well established that members of the public are not content with youth court sentences. In Ontario, 86 per cent of those surveyed in 1997 (Doob et al., 1998) thought that youth court sentences were too lenient. This is higher than the proportion who thought that adult sentences were not severe enough. In a national survey in 1999 (Macdonald, 2001), similar findings emerged. More interesting, however, is the fact that residents of Quebec, a province which uses youth court less frequently, and whose government in recent decades has generally resisted taking a 'tough on youth crime' stance, are *less* likely than residents of any other province to view sentences as being too lenient (Table 9.14).

In 1999, Statistics Canada, as part of its General Social Survey program, asked Canadians to indicate whether they would recommend a prison sentence for young offenders found guilty in four different cases (CCJS, 2000). The results are shown in Table 9.15.

Table 9.15   Preference for prison sentences for four different cases, Quebec vs rest of Canada (%)

| | Region | Preferred sentence | | |
		Prison	Non-prison	Total
First offence				
Breaking and entering	Quebec	15.1	89.4	100
	Rest of Canada	25.5	74.5	100
Assault with minor injuries	Quebec	16.5	83.5	100
	Rest of Canada	21.5	78.5	100
Second offence				
Breaking and entering	Quebec	31.8	68.2	100
	Rest of Canada	52.9	47.1	100
Assault with minor injuries	Quebec	36.9	63.1	100
	Rest of Canada	51.9	48.1	100

Source: Canadian Centre for Justice Statistics, 2000.

As this table demonstrates, residents of Quebec were less likely overall to prefer prison for young offenders found guilty of any of four different offences than were residents of almost any other region. The exception was for the first time offender found guilty of assault. In this case, residents of the Atlantic provinces were more or less the same as residents of Quebec: only 16.9 per cent of Atlantic Canadians preferred a prison sentence for this case.

Part of the difficulty for the public with non-custodial sentences is that people do not appear to believe that non-custodial sentences are actually carried out. For example, about one-quarter of Ontario residents think that community service orders are 'rarely or almost never' carried out by young offenders. An additional 38 per cent think that community service orders are carried out only about half of the time. Not surprisingly, the pessimism about community service orders is particularly acute for those who believe that sentences are not harsh enough. As shown in Table 9.16, of those who thought that sentences were too severe or about right, 12.9 per cent thought that CSOs were completed rarely. Among the majority of Ontario residents who thought that sentences were not severe enough, however, 27.4 per cent thought that CSOs were rarely completed.

Table 9.16   Relationship between assessment of youth court sentences and belief in the likelihood that a youth would complete a community service order (percentage, and in parentheses number)

View of youth court sentences	Youth likely to complete a CSO				
	Always	Most of the time	About half the time	Rarely	Total
Too severe / about right	3.2 (2)	53.2 (33)	30.6 (19)	12.9 (8)	100 (62)
Not severe enough	7.3 (28)	25.6 (98)	39.7 (152)	27.4 (105)	100 (383)
Total	6.7 (30)	29.4 (131)	38.4 (171)	25.4 (113)	100 (445)

Source: Doob et al., 1998.
Note: Percentages do not all total 100 because of rounding.

Judges and Public Opinion

Many youth court judges report that they take public opinion into account. In a 2001 survey (Doob, 2001), 49.3 per cent of youth court judges indicated that they frequently or occasionally 'consider the impact that a decision (e.g., a sentencing decision) might have on public opinion.' More interesting is the fact that taking public opinion into account and taking into account the prevalence of youth crime in the community are linked. These data are shown in Table 9.17. Judges who take prevalence of youth crime in the neighbourhood into account are more likely to be affected by public opinion. 'Taking the prevalence of youth crime in the neighbourhood' into account is, of course, an interesting problem itself. The judge typically has little information about this other than the frequency with which certain types of cases are brought into youth court. Others who might provide assertions about crime levels in communities – prosecutors and police, for example – typically have little direct systematic information about crime in a particular neighbourhood that is independent of enforcement and apprehension. (See Chapter 4 for a discussion of the difficulties of assessing youth crime.) 'Taking prevalence of a crime into account' probably means that the judge, implicitly, believes that there is a connection between the level of crime in a community and sentence severity. This issue is discussed in more detail in Chapter 11. All that need be said at this point, however, is that the evidence does not support assertions that harsher sentences will deter crime.

Table 9.17 Relationship between whether a judge considers prevalence of crime and whether the judge considers the impact of a decision on public opinion (percentage and, in parentheses, number)

| | Considers impact of decision on public opinion | | |
| | | | |
Considers prevalence of crime	Frequently or occasionally	Rarely never	Total
Always, usually	67.5 (54)	32.5 (26)	100.0 (80)
Occasionally	44.3 (54)	55.7 (68)	100.0 (122)
Almost never, never	29.0 (9)	71.0 (22)	100.0 (31)
Total	50.2 (117)	49.8 (116)	100.0 (233)

Source: Doob, 2001.

As Table 9.17 suggests, then, public opinion is, for about half of the judges, quite relevant in their sentencing decisions especially when there are concerns about the prevalence of crime. Public opinion is considerably more important to judges who take 'prevalence of crime' into account.

Where Are We Now in the Sentencing of Youths?

The findings that we have summarized in this chapter appear to give a fairly coherent picture of a somewhat complex process of sentencing youths under the YOA:

- Judges differ dramatically in their choices of what purposes of sentencing should dominate a sentencing decision in a given case. Given that judges approach the same case attempting to serve different purposes, it is not surprising that they end up with quite different sentences for identical cases.
- There is some evidence of 'proportionality' in sentencing of youths, though the role of the seriousness of the offence may not be as important as the rather dramatic impact of a youth's previous record of offending on the sentence. The impact of a youth's record varies somewhat across provinces.
- Previous sentences appear to have an effect on the sentence being handed down, so that youths who received more severe sentences in

the past are most likely to be dealt with severely, even controlling for the seriousness of the current offence.

- There is a good deal of variation across provinces in the use of custody.
- Part of the variation in the use of custody across provinces may relate to the availability (or at least the perceived availability) of other sanctions for youths found guilty of offences. Quebec judges, who tend to use custody less often than it is used in many other provinces, were most likely to believe that they had adequate choices of sanctions available to them.
- Close to half of the custodial sentences handed down across the country involve cases where the most serious offence was relatively minor (minor theft or possession of stolen property, or failure to appear or failure to comply with a disposition). Quebec stands out as being *somewhat* less likely to be using its custodial sentences for relatively minor offences.
- Canada tends to use custody as much as, or more, than it is used in the United States for property and violence cases, but not for drug offences.
- Custodial sentences tend to be very short in Canada. Short sentences appear to be handed down for two reasons: judges appear to believe that a custodial sentence is necessary in particular types of offences, and judges believe in their own ability to stop crime through individual deterrence.
- Probation, the most often imposed sanction in the youth justice system, is awarded for dramatically different time periods across provinces.
- The public – particularly people outside of Quebec – tends to believe that youth court sentences are too lenient. The belief that sentences are too short is particularly likely to be heard from those who believe that crime in their neighbourhood is increasing. Many judges take their beliefs about the prevalence of crime into account at sentencing. Those who do so are the most likely also to indicate that they consider their decisions in light not only of what is happening in the court in front of them, but also in the court of public opinion.

We have suggested that many of these findings can be understood in the context of the failure, until recently, of Parliament to specify clearly what it wanted judges to do in sentencing youths. Some of these problems – in particular, the overuse of custodial sentences for minor offences – were identified by the government in various statements justifying the YCJA. For example, in its booklet describing the YCJA to the public, the Department of Justice Canada (2002) noted that 'significant problems in the youth justice system include' among other things:

- Incarceration is overused.
- Sentencing decisions by the courts have resulted in disparities and unfairness in youth sentencing.
- The YOA does not ensure effective reintegration of a young person after being released from custody.
- The system does not make a clear distinction between serious violent offences and less serious offences.

The Youth Criminal Justice Act, then, represents an explicit attempt to address problems such as those described above.

Sentencing in the Youth Criminal Justice Act

Unlike its predecessor, the Youth Criminal Justice Act has a fairly explicit set of statements defining the purpose and principles of sentencing.

When a youth has been found guilty, judges are told that 'the purpose of sentencing ... is to hold a young person accountable for an offence through the imposition of just sanctions that have meaningful consequences for the young person and that promote his or her rehabilitation and reintegration into society, thereby contributing to the long-term protection of the public' (Section 38(1)).

There are two notable aspects of this statement about purpose. The first is that 'protection of the public' is the consequence of just sanctions which promote rehabilitation and reintegration. Second, the focus is on long-term protection rather than short-term protection (e.g., through incapacitation).

The single most important provision of the sentencing sections of the YCJA, however, is the proportionality requirement. Section 38(2)(c) states that 'The sentence must be proportionate to the seriousness of the offence and the degree of responsibility of the young person for that offence.' Proportionality is not a goal; it is a *requirement* of every youth court sentence.

Subject to the proportionality requirement, the sentence must be the least restrictive sentence that is capable of holding the youth accountable and must be 'the one that is most likely to rehabilitate the young person and reintegrate him or her into society' (Section 38(2)).

Hence, the proportionality principle sets the rules by which the relative severity of sentences is determined. The actual sentence (within the limits set by proportionality) must be the one most likely to rehabilitate or reintegrate. As various commentators (e.g., von Hirsch, 1976) have pointed out, a proportionality principle on its own defines the *relative* severity of punishments. It does not, however, define, on its own, the level of punishments that should be given. Nor does it indicate what sanctions should actually be handed down. Perfect proportionality, therefore, could be achieved by giving all young persons custodial sentences if their length were proportional to the seriousness of the offence. It is necessary, therefore, to set at least some standards within the framework of proportionality. The YCJA chose to focus on the decision of whether a youth receives a custodial sentence.

Custodial sentences can only be imposed if one or more of four conditions are met:

- It is a violent offence.
- The youth has previously failed to comply with non-custodial sentences (i.e., more than one sentence).
- The youth has been found guilty of a moderately serious offence and has a history that indicates a pattern of findings of guilt (i.e., more than one and possibly more than two).
- 'In exceptional cases where the young person has committed an ... offence, such that the imposition of a non-custodial sentence would be inconsistent with the purpose and principles [of sentencing]' (Section 39(1)).

Judges are also told that non-custodial sanctions can be used repeatedly on a given offender. Section 39(3)(b) indicates that the court shall consider submissions related to 'the likelihood that the young person will comply with a non-custodial sentence, taking into account his or her compliance with previous non-custodial sentences.' Section 39(4) states that 'the previous imposition of a particular non-custodial sentence on a young person does not preclude a youth justice court from imposing the same or any other non-custodial sentence for another offence.'

In other words, if a youth complied in the past with a given sanction, that is evidence that would support the use of that same sanction again. Previous compliance with a non-custodial sanction is, therefore, evidence of a successfully imposed sentence (the youth complied) rather than evidence of its failure (the youth re-offended). And, there is no requirement that sentences 'step up' from one type of sentence to another as they did under the YOA.

Furthermore, in cases where custody is imposed, the judge is specifically required by Section 39(9) 'to state the reasons why it has determined that a non-custodial sentence is not adequate to achieve the purpose [of sentencing] including, if applicable, the reasons why the case is an exceptional case' (i.e., those cases where the youth was sentenced to custody on the basis of the 'exceptional case' criterion in Section 39(1)(d)). The point of these, and other similar requirements is clear: judges are forced to think about whether custody is really necessary.

In 1996, the traditional purposes of sentencing (individual and general deterrence, incapacitation, denunciation, rehabilitation and denunciation) were added as explicit 'objectives' of the sentencing laws for adults (Criminal Code of Canada, Section 718). The judge, when sentencing an adult, is supposed to impose 'just sanctions that have one or more of [these] objectives' but is to do so within the principle that 'A sentence must be proportionate to the gravity of the offence and the degree of responsibility of the offender' (Section 718.1). Generally speaking, these sections have been criticized as being too vague and contradictory (Roberts & von Hirsch, 1999). There is no evidence that we are aware of that codifying these sections had any impact on sentencing above and beyond what had been common practice before these changes (Doob, 2000; Roberts & von Hirsch, 1999).

There are two notable differences between the YCJA sentencing provisions and the adult criminal code provisions. First the YCJA provisions are clear in their intent. They are designed to limit the use of custody. The most obvious mechanism to limit the use of custody is that one or more of four explicit criteria must be met before a youth can be placed in custody. Explanations for the decision must be given.

The second important difference between the sentencing of adults under the Criminal Code and youths under the YCJA is that the YCJA contains no references to general or specific deterrence or to incapacitation in the context of sentencing. Canadian judges have tended to interpret 'protection of society' as being accomplished in part through deterrence and incapacitation. In the YCJA, however, 'protection' in the context of sentencing is to be accomplished by 'holding a youth accountable ... through the imposition of just sanctions that have meaningful consequences and that promote his or her rehabilitation and reintegration into society' (Section 38(1)). Though there is no section that specifically says that deterrence and incapacitation have no place in the sentencing of youths, there is a section that indicates that, in general, the adult sentencing provisions do not apply (Section 50(1)) except when an adult sentence is being imposed on a youth (Section 74(1)).

When determining the severity of the sentence, proportionality principles are obviously meant to dominate. However, in the choice of the exact sanction that is to be imposed, the judge is required to choose the sentence that is the least restrictive possible, that is most likely to rehabilitate and reintegrate, and which promotes a sense of responsibility and acknowledgement of the harm done (Section 38(2)). But if a custodial order is imposed, there are additional changes. In order to accomplish 'reintegration' a sentence of 'custody' has been transformed into a 'custody and supervision' order whereby a fixed portion (one-third) of the sentence is normally served in the community after the custodial portion. Reviews of dispositions by the court are also still possible, just as they were under the YOA.

Clearly, the YCJA is designed to address three of the problems that we have identified with the Young Offenders Act. First, the YCJA provides a fairly clear statement of the purpose of sentencing. This purpose is limited, in that it does not claim that judges through their sentencing decisions can stop youths from committing crimes. More important, however, is that the principles of sentencing – proportionality in particular – are made explicit. Second, there are explicit restrictions on the use of custody. Third, by providing a uniform statement about principles and purposes, there exists the possibility that there will be more uniformity of approach across jurisdictions.

The YCJA sentencing provisions represent a dramatic shift in the locus of control of the sentencing process from anything Canada has experienced in the past. Judges now implement Parliament's sentencing policy rather than being almost solely responsible for developing and implementing it themselves. Whether the goals of the YCJA – more limited and principled use of custody, for example – will be successful in changing the face of sentencing will not be known for a few years.

CHAPTER TEN

The Impact of Custody

The belief that youths should not be held in custody with adults – a belief, as we have seen, that predates the enactment of the Juvenile Delinquents Act – remains central to views on punishment today. Overall, there is still little support for placing youths in the same facilities as adults. Even those who oppose a separate justice system for youth still believe that youths should not be held in the same facilities as adults (Sprott, 1998). One can speculate that the reasons for this view range from fear of youth being victimized or even 'corrupted' by the values of adult inmates to beliefs regarding the possibility of rehabilitation for youth. These beliefs coupled with the desire to keep young people separate from adult inmates highlight concerns which led to the need for a separate youth justice system.

Custody is almost certainly the most invasive and punitive sanction the modern youth justice system has at its disposal. Because of this, it is often argued that it should be used sparingly, and for very specific purposes, particularly if it has negative impacts on a young person's future prospects. We will discuss in some detail the possible impact the experience of custody may have on the life of a young person later in this chapter.

This chapter will address the following points:

- Youths in custody are, compared with other youths, vulnerable because of a high level of psychiatric problems and difficult family backgrounds.
- There are special risks that youths in custody experience, such as high levels of violent victimization.
- Youth in custodial correctional institutions are inherently vulnerable because of their powerless position.

• Imprisonment, for youths, is a particularly stressful experience.

Why Is Custody Used as a Disposition?

In Chapter 9 we pointed out that custody is heavily used in Canada and that there has been a dramatic increase in the use of short sentences since the enactment of the YOA. But what factors are relevant to a judge's decision to impose custody?

Two traditional utilitarian purposes of sentencing are typically invoked as justifications for placing young offenders in custodial institutions. Incapacitation – making it impossible for people to commit crimes in the community by removing them from that community – is probably the most obvious justification for the use of custody. Certainly the theory that an identifiable and dangerous group of youths poses a special danger to members of the community is an attractive one. All one needs to do is to identify who these youths are, lock them up, and the problem is solved. Such a theory poses two clear challenges. First, one has to identify the offenders. Second, one has to ensure that when they are released from prison, they will have a reduced likelihood of offending.

Typically the operationalization of an incapacitation strategy begins with the goal of identifying high-rate offenders. Incapacitation as a strategy will be more efficient if it correctly identifies serious high-rate offenders. In a study described in detail in Chapter 5, Hagel and Newburn (1994) presented a detailed analysis of what might be considered to be an attempt to identify high-rate offenders. The problem, it will be recalled, is that different definitions of what constituted 'high rate' created different groups of youths who would be considered to be high rate. In addition, youths who, at one point in time, might be considered to be high-rate offenders were not necessarily the same youths who would be identified as such at another point in time.

These results should not be very surprising. We cannot reliably identify who is likely to be a persistent offender in part because behaviour during adolescence is not very predictable. This volatility or unpredictability is, in fact, one of the defining characteristics of adolescence. Definitions can be created and applied, but equally reasonably sounding definitions would identify a different group of offenders. Persistent young offenders, by any definition, may have committed more offences, but the offences that they commit on average are no more serious than the offences committed by others. A special regime such as a long custodial sentence for such offenders may look good as long as one does not look carefully at the effects. Such an approach would, in effect, isolate a rather arbitrarily defined group of youths.

The second justification for prison sentences for youths relates to the notion that these will deter youths generally from committing crime. General deterrence will be discussed in more detail in Chapter 11. At this point all that needs to be said is the idea that harsher sentences (e.g., a custodial sentence in comparison with a non-custodial sentence) will deter crime is not supported by the evidence. A deterrence theory of custody suggests that serving time in custody not only alerts young offenders to the painful consequences of continued offending (individual or special deterrence) but also demonstrates to other young people what may happen to them if they offend (general deterrence). It suggests that specific and general awareness of the 'pains of imprisonment' will cause young people to refrain from crime out of fear of punishment. Among members of the public, deterrence as a purpose of sentencing appears very popular though, interestingly enough, incapacitation is much less popular (Doob et al., 1998).

As discussed in Chapter 9, judges consider both incapacitation and deterrence along with a number of other principles of sentencing when imposing custody as a disposition, but among judges in Canada a great deal of variation exists with regard to the relevance of these different factors (Doob, 2001; Doob & Beaulieu, 1992).

'Short sharp shocks' are interesting in part because it is easy to imagine that one could find alternative sanctions instead of short custodial sentences. As discussed in Chapter 9, one explanation for short custodial sentences is that they are necessary for denunciatory reasons. In addition, however, it appears that judges see them as a tool for deterring crime.

As can be seen in Table 10.1, judges who believe that general deterrence is important in sentencing are more likely to invoke 'deterrence' as a justification for using short periods of custody. Only 24 per cent of judges who saw general deterrence as relatively unimportant invoked deterrence as a justification for short sharp shocks, whereas 41 per cent of those who rated deterrence as being a very important fact in sentencing saw deterrence as a justification for short custodial sentences. Custody, it seems, is associated with deterring youths from crime. Custody and deterrence are, then, linked, at least in judges' minds. Unfortunately, as we have already mentioned, the data on general deterrence (see Chapter 11) do not support this belief.

The other side of the deterrence coin is 'individual deterrence,' the

Table 10.1   Relationship of judges' views of the importance of general deterrence to the invocation of deterrence as a justification for short custodial sentences

Importance of general deterrence in three types of cases	Importance of deterrence as a justification for short sharp shocks			
	Low	Medium	High	Total
Low	51	25	24	100
Medium	37	30	33	100
High	24	35	41	100
Total	38	29	33	100

Source: Doob, 2001.

idea that harsher sentences (in this case, custody) will stop this offender from offending. One study that compared the individual deterrent impact of custodial sentences to a non-custodial equivalent was carried out by Killias, Aebi, and Ribeaud (2000) with adults in Switzerland. Offenders who were assigned sentences which probably could be characterized as short sharp shocks (sentences of fourteen days or less) were, on a random basis, either forced to serve their sentences as imposed by the judge or were given the option of carrying out community work. Those given the option chose, not surprisingly, to avoid prison. The obvious advantage of a study of this sort is that the two groups – those who served the short prison sentence and those who did not – can be considered to be similar, since the assignment to groups was done on a random basis.

The progress of both groups was then monitored for two years. There was no evidence of a difference in the reconviction rate between the two groups, though those who had been given the option of community service were somewhat less likely to be re-arrested. Community sentences were seen by the offenders as being more fair. The argument that custody 'works' to reduce future offending is challenged by these data. Other data on the impact of custodial sentences are similar.

Judges also use custody for rehabilitative purposes. Thirty-seven per cent of Canadian youth court judges who were surveyed (Doob, 2001) indicated that in at least half of the cases before them where custody was imposed, one of the relevant factors was that 'the youth's home and/or parents or living conditions were such that there was a need to get him or her into a more stable environment.' Of the judges, 67 per cent indicated that at in at least half of the cases before them where custody was imposed, a relevant factor was that that the youth was 'out of control' and needed a custodial sentence to break the current cycle of behavior. In 26 per cent of the cases, judges indicated that it was relevant that there was a program that the youth would benefit from that was only available in custody.

The difficulty with these welfare arguments is that judges do not control the environment that the youth moves into after the youth leaves the court. The judge does not control, for example, whether a youth sent to custody because of the existence of a custodial program will actually get that program. Correctional officials may decide that the youth would not benefit from the program. Or they may decide that there are limited resources and there are other incarcerated youths who are more in need of the program. If this is the case, then the youth who is incarcerated for rehabilitative purposes may end up being incarcerated for no purpose at all. Nor does the judge have any control over the environment that the youth returns to after a period of time in custody. The idea that the judge 'needs' to get the youth out of a dysfunctional home may sound good until one considers that in a week or a month (whatever the length of sentence) the youth will return to the same home from which he or she was removed. There is no assurance that the situation the next morning, or the next week will be any better. Good intentions do not, unfortunately, guarantee effective delivery of needed services. As described in the next chapter, there are data that suggest that encounters with the youth justice system may *increase* the likelihood of inadequate parenting.

Given that we seem to be sending a relatively high proportion of young people to custody, and that the desired effect of punishment may not be what we anticipate, what is known about how a young person actually experiences being in custody?

The Experience of Custody

Presumably, the hope that motivates the youth court judge when sentencing a young person to a custodial sentence is that the youth will leave the institution no worse off than when he or she first arrived. There are some data to suggest, however, that this may not be the case. This is not to mean that custodial institutions are not well intentioned.

Instead, it means that intervention by the criminal justice system into the life of a young person is not invariably good or neutral (Petrosino, Turpin-Petrosino, & Finkenauer, 2000).

Custody appears to be a significant event in the life of an adolescent. For young people, custody ranks high among traumatic lifetime stressors, superceded only by the death of a parent or the divorce of parents (Frydenberg, 1997). For many young offenders, incarceration is likely to be the most significant time they have spent away from family and friends (Biggam & Power, 1997). For the youngest offenders this may be their first time away from home. There is some evidence to suggest that most of this time is spent in facilities that are far from home communities (Doob, 1999).

Qualitative interviews give some indication of how youths feel when they first come into custody. The following descriptions have been offered by youths to describe their feelings when faced with custodial dispositions: 'Very ill,' 'Distraught,' 'Totally embarrassed by the strip search,' 'Scared [of] leaving my parents,' 'Anyone that comes into custody is scared,' 'I cried at night,' 'I felt kind of lost' (Ontario Office of the Child and Family Advocacy, 1998, p. 9; O'Malley, Coventry & Walters, 1993, p. 179). One thing that is clear is that placing youth in custody is not inherently neutral because 'it is clear that when young offenders are placed in custody for a period of time they do not emerge from these institutions the same as they went in' (Matthews & Pitts 1998, p. 392).

The implications of locking up increasing numbers of young people are particularly important when one considers which youth are likely to be incarcerated and the traumas that youths may experience while in a custodial facility.

As a group, incarcerated young offenders are characterized by multiple forms of familial, socioemotional, and academic disadvantage. The prevalence of psychiatric disorders in incarcerated youth is known to be high (Ulzen & Hamilton, 1998). The prevalence of behavioral, emotional, personality, and psychophysiological disorders among young offenders is higher than in the general population, perhaps as high as 60 per cent (Hunzeker, 1993; Cocozza & Skowyra, 2000). In addition, research has suggested that up to 75 per cent of incarcerated young offenders may have some sort of learning disability (Henteleff, 1999). Young offenders are also likely to have come in contact with the child welfare system prior to custody (Doob et al., 1995) and there are many significant measures of family adversity that are associated with incarceration status, including physical abuse, family breakup and violence between parents (Bortner & Williams, 1997).

To date, the majority of the criminological literature that exists on youths in custody tends to focus on the 'bullying' or the victimization of inmates by their peers (Mutchnik & Fawcett, 1991; Shields & Simourd, 1991; Beck, 1995; Connell & Farrington, 1976). Perhaps this is not surprising, given evidence that suggests that bullying is a normative event in youth facilities. Between 20 and 45 per cent of prisoners in young offenders institutions report they have been victimized during the course of their current sentence (Adler, 1994; Beck, 1995; O'Donnell & Edgar, 1999).

Based on an analysis of over 900 detention centres in the United States, Parent et al. (1994) calculated the rate of peer-on-peer abuse in detention settings to be 3.6 incidents of violence per 100 youths over thirty days. According to the Howard League Commission of Inquiry Into Violence in Penal Institutions for Teenagers (1995, p. 13) the 'nature of prison life breeds bullying ... Violence and aggression are entrenched as normal behavior ... Those not inclined to violence before entering prison are forced to use it to survive.'

In Canada, there is evidence to suggest that a custodial sentence for a young person comes with its share of risks that are unique to the experience of being in custody. Institutional risks include peer-on-peer violence, physical restraint, and placement in isolation. Peer abuse and inmate-on-inmate violence appear to be frequent features of custodial life for incarcerated youth according to several Canadian reports and reviews[1] – but abuse is not necessarily only at the hands of other youth.

Peer victimization can, of course, occur in schools and local neighborhoods. Peer abuse within custody centres differs significantly from peer abuse in other settings, however, because 'youth who are captive and cannot extricate themselves from the circumstances have little hope of escape or relief from abuse' (Ombudsman of B.C., 1994, p. 4). Peer-on-

---

1 Restoring Dignity: Responding to Child Abuse in Canadian Institutions, 2000; Coroner's Explanation of the Verdict of the Jury at the Inquest into the Death of James Lonnee, 1999; Issues Affecting Youth in Conflict with the Law: A Review of Issues Raised with Saskatchewan Children's Advocate Office, 1999; The Experiences of Phase II Male Young Offenders in the Province of Ontario, 1999; Leschied et al. 1997; Building Respect: A Review of Youth Custody Centres in British Columbia, 1994.

peer violence can occur in the context of intimidation, extortion, stealing, destruction of personal possessions, and/or verbal abuse. The consequences for the victims include not only physical injury but also psychological distress, which manifests itself in an inability to sleep, attempts to escape, and in extreme cases, suicide (Leschied, Cunningham & Mazaheri, 1997). A study by McCorkle (1993) suggests that level of fear is an extremely important predictor of general well-being for prison inmates. As Shields and Simourd (1991, p. 181) suggest, 'the violence which is inherent in predatory relationships poses a threat to safety to the non-predatory population and renders a correctional facility more difficult to manage.'

There is reason to believe that in at least some facilities peer-on-peer violence is condoned or encouraged by staff in custodial facilities for youth. A study (Peterson-Badali & Koegl, 2001) of a sample of relatively older young offenders (those 16–17 years old when they offended) in secure custody facilities in Ontario includes reports of staff involvement in the spreading of rumours which led youth to assault other youth, turning a blind eye to violence, and bribing youth to assault other youths. There is little doubt that at least some of the violence experienced by youth in custodial institutions is the direct result of behavior of those paid to serve the needs of youth and society more generally.

A Law Commission of Canada (2000) report entitled *Restoring Dignity: Responding to Child Abuse in Canadian Institutions* describes a litany of physical and sexual abuse of children who lived in institutions, including custodial facilities, that were funded by governments. Evidence from the commission's report suggests that significant harm has been done to children in institutions that have been created for their benefit. The Law Commission of Canada suggested that key issues which may explain the apparently high rate of abuse of children in Canadian institutions included a significant power imbalance that exists between children and those in charge of institutions. This goes beyond the obvious power imbalance between a child and an adult in a position of authority. Many staff, for example, had the added weight of institutional authority behind them – or the official power of the government. There was little independent monitoring of what goes on inside these institutions. This lack of effective protection of children cannot be attributed to a single, simple cause. In some cases however, the desire to preserve the good name of the institution took precedence over a concern for the welfare of the children.

A study of a sample of incarcerated relatively younger inmates (those 12–15 years old when they offended) in Ontario (Cesaroni & Peterson-Badali, 2003) demonstrated that those young people who entered an institution with a higher number of vulnerabilities (child welfare involvement, difficulties with school, delinquent peers, instability in the home) were more likely to show difficulties with adjustment and psychological well-being. In addition, several institutional risks were related to poor adjustment as measured by internalizing behaviours (such as depression or anxiety): having no friends, experiencing peer conflicts as difficult, and worry about, anticipation of, and lack of peer support during victimization. Three of these variables (peer conflicts, worry about victimization, and perceiving victimization as likely) emerged as significant predictors of poor adjustment even after controlling for pre-existing risks.

Risk factors associated with institutional life appear to have an impact on adjustment above and beyond the pre-existing risk factors with which a youth 'walks into' a facility. One possible explanation for this finding is that current adjustment is closely tied to current concerns (e.g., relationships with peers and issues of safety). It is also possible that participants who enter custody with significant vulnerabilities are more socially isolated and worry more about victimization, as well as reporting more internalizing concerns while in custody. In addition, the study found that institutional measures used to identify youth who were experiencing higher stress and difficulties in coping were not necessarily effective. Youth who 'act out,' who get into fights with other inmates, or 'externalize' offer staff a fairly obvious indicator of lack of adjustment. Youth who in a sense 'internalize' or keep their pain to themselves may outwardly appear to be compliant and well behaved while in custody.

An implication of these findings is that identifying juveniles who have significant internalizing problems (e.g., anxiety, depression) may be difficult in youth justice systems where youths are not systematically screened for mental health difficulties. This difficulty is compounded by the fact that young offenders, like most adolescents, may find it difficult to ask for help when distressed. As Gottlieb (1991, p. 293) argues, there is an 'adolescent code' which makes it problematic for youth to signal their distress.

Young offenders have the added burden of the 'inmate code.' For example, in a recent study of incarcerated young offenders (Peterson-Badali & Koegl, 2001), only 49 per cent suggested that if something bad happened there was an adult, staff member, or professional inside or outside of the institution they could ask for help. Furthermore, of these, almost half (42 per cent) said they would be unwilling to ask for help for fear of being labeled a 'rat.' In sum, the lack of relationship between institutional indicators of adjustment and internalizing problems, compounded by juveniles' reluctance to seek help when distressed, means that staff may have little means of identifying and obtaining help for those youth who are experiencing significant levels of emotional distress.

It could be argued that any psychological distress that a young person experiences while in custody is relatively transient and has no long-term implications for their well-being. Though we still have relatively few data on the long-term psychological consequences of the custodial experience on the life of a young person, there is some evidence of the long-term developmental effects. Sampson and Laub's (1997) reanalysis of the natural histories of 500 delinquents found that the long-term consequences of youth custody independent of adult incarceration had significant negative effects on their job stability at ages 25 to 32.

According to Sampson and Laub (1997, p. 149), 'the structural disadvantages accorded institutionalized adolescents are so great (e.g., through dropping out of high school, record of confinement known to employers) that their influence lingers throughout adult development.' Testing for cumulative effects by examining the duration of custody as an adolescent goes through the transition into adulthood, they found that 'as the total time served in juvenile and adult correctional facilities increased, later job stability decreased (controlling for prior record and unofficial deviance)' (ibid.). As the authors suggest, incarceration appears to cut off opportunities and prospects for employment later in life: 'This "knifing off" has important development implications – job stability and also marital attachment in adulthood are significantly related to changes in adult crime' (ibid., p. 150).

Given the possible short- and long-term implications that custody may have on a young person's future, the reasons for arguing that custody should be imposed only rarely are apparent.

The Importance of Aftercare

Youthful offenders who are placed in confinement eventually return to the community. Altschuler and Armstrong (1991) argue that it is both unfortunate and ironic that one area of juvenile corrections that should receive the greatest emphasis – community-based aftercare – ends up being underfunded at best and ignored or entirely forgotten at worst. According to Armstrong and Altschuler (1994), two of the most troubling deficiencies plaguing most youth justice systems are that secure custody does not adequately prepare youth for return to the community and that lessons learned and skills acquired while in custody are not being sufficiently built upon or reinforced outside the institution following release.

Greenwood and Zimring (1985) suggest that as long as a substantial number of youth continue to reoffend following their release from any type of intensive custodial program, there will be an issue regarding whether they should have remained under supervision longer. The authors note, however, that changes in the length of programs do not appear to have substantial effects on outcomes, and they argue that this is because of the inevitable effects of returning to old patterns and influences that are waiting to ensnare youth when they return to their home communities.

Reintegrative confinement is defined as 'an incarceration experience that includes a major focus on structured transition and a follow-up period of aftercare characterized by both surveillance and service provision in the community' (Altschuler, Armstrong & MacKenzie, 1999, p. 2). Any rehabilitative gains made by youth in corrections quickly evaporate following release, but better outcomes are apparent when a highly structured and enhanced transition from custody into the community is implemented (Altschuler et al., 1999). In boot camps (discussed in Chapter 11), for example, there is some evidence that the highly structured and intensive reintegrative services associated with some boot camp programs may provide the only favourable impact of boot camps on future offending.

Much of the recent experimentation with innovative aftercare has focused on ways to develop more intensive programs. Hence, there has been an examination of caseload size and frequency of contact, classification and assessment procedures, and the respective roles of surveillance and treatment or service-provision activities (Altschuler et al., 1999). Researchers seem to believe that success is related to active, direct intervention in the home community and the offender's social network. But there is evidence to suggest that when the response to an offender's aftercare program is predominately a matter of surveillance and social control (drug and alcohol testing, electronic monitoring, frequent curfew checks) and the service-related components are lacking or inadequate, neither a reduction in recidivism nor an improvement in social, cognitive, and behavioural functioning is likely to occur (ibid.).

As discussed in the previous chapter, under the YOA a high proportion of young people served their custodial sentences and were then released 'cold' back into their home communities, without any kind of probation or community service. Under the YCJA two-thirds of each sentence will be served in custody and the remaining third will be served in the community.

In addition, the YCJA contains provisions that facilitate and encourage reintegration planning. Of particular relevance is Section 90, which mandates the designation of a youth worker to help the youth plan for his or her reintegration at the point of sentencing. Section 91 of the YCJA gives the provincial director the discretion to grant reintegration leaves.

A large number of members of the public say they want to help ex-prisoners (adults and youth) get back into society. More than three-quarters (78 per cent) of Ontario residents thought that some supervision and help in reintegration should be given to both adults and youth following a custody sentence (Doob et al., 1998). Giving help to prisoners may be seen as helping the unfortunate or protecting oneself, but whatever the motive, government programs which do not support reintegration strategies are going against public opinion.

Conclusion

The Youth Criminal Justice Act, by placing explicit restrictions on the use of custody, would appear to endorse the view that the use of custody represents a failure to find some more appropriate sanction to hold a youth accountable for his or her actions. Custodial sanctions do not appear to accomplish the various purposes sometimes attributed to them and can, instead, put youths at additional risk.

CHAPTER ELEVEN

Conclusion: How Do We Best Approach the Problem of Youth Crime?

As illustrated throughout this book, a fair amount of research has been conducted in Canada on the operation of the youth justice system. We have a good idea of how the youth justice system works, and what issues surround its operation. Probably the most interesting finding to come from our review of the issues associated with youth crime is that few researchers suggest that the best way – or even *an* effective one – of reducing the amount of youth crime is to make changes in the youth justice system.

There are, however, a number of ways in which governments have tried to influence crime rates through changes in the justice system. And, because the youth justice system is seen as something whose purpose is to govern youths rather than simply responding to youth crime, it is important to examine how these attempts at controlling youth crime through the justice system have fared.

This chapter will do two things. First, it will focus on three examples of 'quick-fix' approaches to youth crime – harsher sentences, boot camps, and curfews. These are not the only examples of political quick fixes to youth crime, but they are popular approaches which do a good job of illustrating how not to approach the problem of youth crime. What is interesting about these quick-fix approaches is that none of them addresses what is known about the causes of youth crime. We end the chapter, and the book, on a more optimistic, but cautious, note, pointing out that not only do we know what does not work, we also know quite a bit about what kinds of interventions *do* have an impact on youth crime.

Can Youth Crime Be Addressed by Imposing Harsh Penalties?

Probably one of the most popular ways of thinking about the causes of offending is to suppose that young people are controlled by the harshness of the punishments that could be imposed on them if they offend. Many people appear to hold an economic theory of crime: if the penalties for offending are high, people will not offend; if they are low, and the 'value' of offending is sufficiently high, they will offend. This theory is attractive because it suggests that crime control is directly under the control of the youth justice system. This theory suggests that by 'turning up' the penalties, crime can be reduced. By 'turning down' the penalties, crime will increase. It sounds very simple, but two crucial parts of the equation have been ignored. First, calculations about the utility of offending must take into account the *probability of apprehension* as well as the *likely penalty*. Few young people are ever apprehended for the delinquencies they commit, and young people do not often commit offences expecting to get caught. Second, it is not the actual (or legislated maximum) penalty, or even the penalty that is handed down in court that has the potential of changing a youth's behaviour. It is what youths *believe* the penalty would be that has the potential to affect their behaviour. In other words, it is the perceived penalty that might be important (along with the perceived likelihood of apprehension) rather than the actual penalty or the actual probability of being apprehended.

The first assumption of a rational choice model of offending, of course, is that young people or people in general go through a thoughtful process when they 'decide' to offend. In other words, it assumes that they go through a form of 'moral calculus' where, when they are thinking about committing an offence, they first think about what it is that they will be gaining from the offence. The theory would then suggest that they think about what the likelihood is of being apprehended and, if apprehended, what the penalty would be. Next, it assumes that they do a psychological calculation, comparing the value of offending to some combination of the probability of being apprehended and the likely penalty.

Research does not support the view that this process takes place. Cusson (1983) argues that young people do, in fact, make what might be considered to be rational choices. However, the choice to engage in delinquent behaviour is based on opportunities that are available which may be illegitimate, yet meet particular goals of the moment. Making a decision on the basis of the immediate situation is, however, quite different from a careful calculation of a utility function based on long-term consequences.

This is not to say that *no* young people, under any circumstances, behave according to a rational weighing of long- and short-term costs and benefits. A more appropriate way of thinking about how young people come to engage in delinquent behaviour is to acknowledge that, for the most part, their actions are influenced by utilitarianism and hedonism. It must also be remembered that the distinction between 'delinquent' and 'non-delinquent' activities may be rather unimportant for young people.

LeBlanc and Fréchette (1989) suggest that in early adolescence (ages 12 to 15), young people make almost no preparation for an offence and, from an observer's perspective, it is clearly not a calculated or well thought out process. As young people get older, the offences may involve more planning and skill. However, offences are still often committed quite impulsively.

A study by Ladouceur and Biron (1993), based on an examination of twenty-five young burglars, illustrates quite clearly that these young people did not make what adults would consider to be rational choices. When trying to understand how young burglars make decisions *from their points of view*, it was clear that hedonism was most important. 'It was fun' seems to best explain the reasons behind their criminal behaviour. Yet, this is not to suggest that young people invariably make decisions without thought. They may make plans not only about their immediate offences, but also about how to follow through and profit from them. Plans or thoughts about the long-term future do not, for the most part, enter into the decision process.

Thus, it would appear that when thinking about the decision-making process of young people, the distinction must be made between rational choice in the short term – the manner in which they evaluate the immediate situation – and the extent to which they consider long-term consequences. The difficulty, of course, is that they just do not consider the long term. This applies not only to matters of delinquency but to their behaviour generally. For example, they may fail to consider the long-term consequences of not getting an education. School drop-out rates may be high, in part, because young people do not consider the long-term impact of their decisions.

It should be noted, however, that risk taking generally may be linked to developmental concerns. Research suggests that time perspective is developmentally linked, and adolescents seem to discount the future more than adults (Scott, Repucci, & Woolard, 1995). This makes short-term consequences seem more salient to their evaluation of their options in regard to decision making (Scott et al., 1995). In other words, for a young person, participating in antisocial behavior in order to 'fit in' or be 'cool' may be more important in the present than the possibility of any future consequences.

Young people take a variety of risks that older people would not take, in part because they do not consider the consequences of what they are about to do. It is quite well established, for example, that the technical driving skills of young male automobile drivers exceed those of older drivers. And yet, because of the risks they take, they are involved in many more traffic accidents than older drivers.

If young people are going to be deterred by the actions of the criminal justice system, they need, first of all, to be thinking about the consequences of their actions (to themselves and others) rather than thinking about the actions themselves. Impulsive acts are not likely to be deterred. Second, they must consider the possibility of being apprehended. There are problems with the deterrence doctrine at the apprehension stage. For many of the offences that young people are most likely to commit (such as thefts or vandalism) the data are quite clear: for both adults and young people, the probability of being apprehended is small. In one study of vandalism, for example, it was found that about 90 per cent of secondary school students admitted to having committed one or more acts of vandalism in the previous year. The average number of separate acts admitted to was about ten. However, only 3 per cent of these same students indicated that they had *ever* been apprehended for vandalism (Task Force on Vandalism, 1981). When they were asked, it was clear that they knew that the chance of being apprehended was low. Only about 7 per cent of secondary school students thought that they would 'probably' be caught if they committed further acts of vandalism. The objective data also support the conclusion that vandalism is likely to go unpunished, no matter what the legislated punishment might be. In 2000, for example, only about 7.3 per cent of *reported* vandalism was cleared by the police with someone being charged (CCJS, 2001a). Hence, the vast majority of these young people assessed, correctly, that there was only a small probability of there being criminal justice consequences to committing acts of vandalism. The result is that even if young vandals *did* consider the actual consequences of offending, they would realize that they would probably not be caught.

The probability of receiving the reward for an offence – excitement, the product of a theft, respect from peers – on the other hand, is high and immediate. In other words, if young people were to think about the criminal justice consequences of their actions, they would conclude that criminal justice *consequences* are irrelevant, because it is very unlikely that there will be any. Furthermore, in a rational choice model, it is likely that these costs would be outweighed by the certainty and immediacy of the rewards from offending.

This, however, focuses on the objective probability of apprehension. The objective likelihood of being caught is not as relevant as subjective beliefs about the probability of being apprehended. With adults, it appears that it is not that difficult to affect the subjective probability of apprehension for a short time. Publicity about a drinking and driving apprehension program, for example, may increase the perceived likelihood of apprehension. However, if the actual likelihood of apprehension does not increase, then it is likely to be only a matter of time until people re-establish their original view that they will not be caught.

There is research that suggests, not surprisingly, that the *perceived likelihood* of being punished does, in fact, relate to levels of offending. In one American study carried out some time ago, high school students reported their own offending behaviour. In addition, they reported how they saw the risk that they themselves would be apprehended as well as the risk that offenders generally would be apprehended for the offence. The data demonstrated that it was the student's perceived *personal* risk (in contrast with the generalized risk of being punished) that was most strongly related to self-reported offending (Jensen, Erickson, & Gibbs, 1978). Similar findings were reported for vandalism in Ontario (Task Force on Vandalism, 1981).

In a study of the perceptions young offenders and youth court dispositions, 40 per cent of young offenders interviewed indicated that 'they either did not think that what they were doing was serious enough to warrant police intervention or failed to even consider the possibility of getting caught' (Peterson-Badali, Ruck & Koegl, 2001, p. 601). Only half of the respondents felt that their sentence would deter them from future offending and fewer thought that it would deter others.

Youths, in relation to general deterrence, do not appear to be much different from adults. For example, in a study of ordinary repetitive offenders, Tunnell (1996) interviewed sixty prisoners who had been in prison twice or more, at least once for armed robbery or burglary. Respondents were asked to describe their most recent crime, the context in which they made the decision to commit it, and their method of assessing the risk and rewards of committing the crime. All sixty respondents reported that they (and nearly every thief they knew) simply do not think about the possible legal consequences of their criminal actions before committing crimes (Tunnell, 1996).

Deterrence and decision-making theories inform us that 'risk' ideally is conceptualized and evaluated before acting. Again, however, contrary to decision-making theories, those few participants who conceptualized the possible negative consequences of their actions when deciding to commit a crime reported that they did not evaluate them. They managed to put thoughts of negative consequences out of their minds to complete the crime. Their fear was neutralized as they turned away from signs of danger. This finding suggests that the use of fear to influence behaviour through punitive policies for repeat property criminals may be misplaced and may lack empirical support. Even more important, the respondents reported that they rarely thought of the prison environment or their incarceration. Fifty-two of the sixty reported that they simply believed that they would not be caught and refused to think beyond that point.

One exchange between the interviewer and a respondent who specialized in stealing kitchen appliances from newly built apartment complexes illustrates the challenges facing a general deterrence approach to crime control:

'As you did the burglaries, what came first – the crime or thinking about getting caught for the crime?'

'The crime comes first because it's enough to worry about doing the actual crime itself without worry about what's going to happen if you get caught.' (Tunnell, 1996, p. 43)

More generally, the author pointed out:

Many of the offenders had unrealistic or erroneous perceptions of the severity of the punishment for their crimes. Each participant reported that he knew his actions were illegal, and therefore did his best to avoid capture. Yet a surprising number ($N = 32$ [of the 60 interviewed]) did not know the severity of the punishment for their offences before their arrest. Most learned the 'going rate' *after* arrest.' (ibid., p. 44)

> While committing crimes, most of the respondents (N = 51) considered
> themselves immune from arrest and incarceration, although they believed
> that every habitual criminal eventually would be arrested ... Their belief in
> their own immunity disallowed adequate consideration of the likelihood
> of legal consequences. (ibid., p. 47)

This study, of course, talks about the deterrent impact of punishment on repeat offenders. The author points out: 'They [repeat offenders] view themselves as immune from criminal sanction and hence are undeterred. They tend to believe that they simply will not be apprehended for their criminal actions; if they are caught they will be imprisoned for a very short amount of time. Those who actually consider the possibilities of brief imprisonment view prison as a nonthreatening environment' (ibid., p. 48).

It seems rather obvious to point out that if adults are not thinking ahead, and are not seriously considering the impact of apprehension, it is unlikely that youths will be the kinds of rational decision makers that economists would like them to be.

This is illustrated in a study (Thomas & Bishop, 1984) involving 2147 high school students (average age of 15). About 18 per cent had had some contact with police and about one-third had been involved with school authorities. The authors reported that 'delinquency involvement tends to diminish perceptions of risk ... [a result which] is hardly what is predicted by those who contend that sanctions serve the goal of specific deterrence' (ibid., p. 1244).

Most of the public discussion about deterrence focuses on penalties – legislated maximum penalties and the actual penalties given out. Legislated maximum penalties are an attractive focus of public attention for an obvious reason: they can be altered by the decision of a small number of people, the members of the Parliament of Canada. Said differently, those who suggest that it is the maximum sentence which deters youth, hold, in effect, the view that Parliament can turn down the level of youth crime by turning up the maximum penalties.

This is a theory that is worth examining carefully. First of all, in order for this to work, young people have to know the penalties. Information campaigns on penalties in the past (e.g., the information campaign to inform the Canadian public about the change in minimum penalties for drinking and driving in the mid-1980s) have not been very successful (Canadian Sentencing Commission, 1987). Second, young people have to assume that they will be caught. Third, they have to assume that the penalty they get will relate in some way to the maximum. In other words, they have to assume that they will get a heavier penalty than they would have otherwise because the maximum penalty has increased.

Finally, this assumes that the result of the potential offender's calculation is that it would have been worth committing the offence for the earlier, lower, penalty, but it would not be worth doing it for the new higher penalty. Thus, for example, if the maximum penalty for an offence were shifted from two years of custody to three years of custody for reasons of general deterrence, it assumes that 14-year-olds would be willing to commit the offence (e.g., a break and enter) if they knew they would 'only' receive two years in secure custody, but would not commit the offence if they would receive three years.

Logically, however, it should be pointed out that young people cannot possibly know the likely penalty for particular offences, because there is so much variation in the penalties actually imposed. A youth is almost certainly unable to predict whether a charge will result in a conviction, and if it were to result in a conviction, what the actual penalty would be. The data on sentencing reviewed in Chapter 9 show rather dramatic variation across cases in the level of punishment imposed on a youth. A youth who was completely informed about the likely outcome of a case would have little more than a distribution of possible outcomes and an estimate of the probability that each type of penalty would be the result of the case.

Few, if any, would argue, even for the purpose of deterrence, that there should be a single fixed penalty for an offence such as breaking and entering. After all, youths committing this offence can vary in age (from 12 to 17), criminal record (none to serious), as well as in other ways. The role the youth played in the break-in could be central or peripheral. The offence could be very minor (no damage on entry, nothing taken) or very serious (much damage, much gratuitous vandalism, much unrecovered stolen property, or a particularly vulnerable victim). Under our current sentencing system for young offenders, then, it would be impossible to communicate the likely penalty.

The authors of a recent report on the deterrent impact of variation in the harshness of sentences (von Hirsch, Bottoms, Burney, & Wikström, 1999). are not optimistic about the ability of increased sentences to deter crime. After noting that the evidence on the effects of certainty of apprehension on crime is not overwhelmingly strong, they suggest that 'the evidence concerning severity effects is less impressive [than the evidence suggesting that certainty or perceived certainty of apprehension has a deterrent impact]. Present ... research, mirroring earlier studies fails ... to disclose significant and consistent negative associations between severity levels (such as the likelihood or duration of imprisonment) and crime rates' (ibid.). Put in simple language, the review did not support the conclusion that harsh sentences deter.

This conclusion is quite similar to one by Doob and Webster (2003), who reviewed much of the recent research on the deterrent effects of punishment severity, focusing in large part on the research on the impact of 'three-strikes' sentencing laws in the United States. These laws provide a nearly ideal setting for examining the possible impact of sentence severity on crime. Three-strikes laws typically require a somewhat harsher sentence for the second conviction for certain offences and a dramatically harsher sentence for the third conviction. From a deterrence perspective, three-strikes legislation should have an impact, since the changes that were brought in typically were abrupt, large, and accompanied by a substantial amount of publicity. Nevertheless, the evidence even from examinations of the impact of three-strikes sentencing laws did not support the conclusion that harsh sentences deter. Doob and Webster (2003) conclude:

> Strictly speaking, one cannot prove the absence of a phenomenon. It may exist somewhere, but research may not have (yet) identified where this is. Having said this, one can still conclude that no consistent body of literature has developed over the last 25–30 years indicating that harsh sanctions deter. While one must always reserve judgment for the possibility that – in the future – someone may discover persons or situations in which the relative severity of sentences does, in fact, have an impact on crime, it would not seem unreasonable to conclude that at the present time in western populations and with the current methods and measures available, variation in sentence severity does not affect the levels of crime in society. (Doob and Webster, 2003)

The Supreme Court of Canada and General Deterrence for Young Offenders: Faith May Be Stronger Than Facts

The Supreme Court of Canada suggested that for young people deterrence was particularly relevant because they commit offences in groups and, therefore, will know what the likely penalty would be. Specifically, they suggested:

There is reason to believe that *Young Offenders Act* dispositions can have an effective deterrent effect. The crimes committed by the young tend to be a group activity. The group lends support and assistance to the prime offenders. The criminological literature is clear that about 80% of juvenile delinquency is a group activity, whether as part of an organized gang or with an informal group of accomplices [see Cusson, 1983, pp. 138–9; Zimring, 1981, p. 867]. If the activity of the group is criminal then the disposition imposed on an individual member of the group should be such that it would deter other members of the group. For example, the sentence imposed on one member of a 'swarming group' should serve to deter others in the gang.

Having said that, I would underline that general deterrence should not, through undue emphasis, have the same importance in fashioning the disposition for a youthful offender as it would in the case of an adult. One youthful offender should not be obliged to accept the responsibility for all the young offenders of his or her generation. (*R. v M* (J.J.), 1993, pp. 496–7)

It is important to note that although the Supreme Court provided references for the fact that much of 'juvenile delinquency is a group activity' it carefully avoided citing *any* social science evidence on the general deterrent effect of sentences of different levels of severity on offending. Other Canadian courts, having looked at this evidence for adults (e.g., *R. v McGinn*, 1989) have discovered that, within the range of sentences likely to be given in Canada, varying the sentence will not vary the deterrent effect. The judges on the Supreme Court of Canada should be given their due, however, in that they were creative – though undoubtedly wrong – in their attempt to differentiate the deterrent effect of sentences for youth from the deterrent effect of sentences on adults by noting that youths commit offences in groups. Unfortunately, the Supreme Court's theory of deterrence, though plausible in the absence of data, is not supported by empirical evidence.

On the issue of age, the variable that the Supreme Court of Canada used to distinguish this case from deterrence of adult offenders, those people who have studied the data on deterrence rather than simply thinking about it suggest that 'the deterrence doctrine nowhere claims that deterrence is an age-specific process, and we should expect to find it operating (if it does) across samples of differing ages and life events' (Paternoster, Saltzman, Waldo, & Chiricos, 1983, p. 273).

No doubt the most important difficulty with the reasoning of the Supreme Court of Canada is the idea that young people will commit offences thinking that they will be apprehended. In fact, the logic of the court's particular decision would seem to suggest that young people would be deterred from committing a break and enter if they thought that the likely penalty (if they were caught) was two years (the sentence handed down by the youth court and confirmed by the Manitoba Court of Appeal), but would not be deterred if it were one year (the sentence recommended by the one dissenting judge at the appeal level). To be fair to the Supreme Court of Canada, however, their decision to maintain the higher sentence was not based solely on general deterrence: the rather serious social needs of the youth in question contributed to their view that he needed an extra year of punishment.

The Supreme Court of Canada did not have to stray into the criminological literature to have a look at the deterrent impact of sentences. Commenting on this case, Bala (1994, p. 310) pointed out that 'there is a significant amount of empirical research that indicates that longer sentences for young offenders have no deterrent effect on other youths' (p. 310). Bala cites McEachern (C.J.B.C. in *R. v D. (E.L.)*) who noted:

> If I thought for a moment that there was any real possibility that a four year sentence for this youth would deter some other youth from committing the same or any other offence, then I would naturally balance that against the advantages of trying to rehabilitate this offender. I believe sending this youth to prison may possibly deter some other youth from offending, *but none of the scientific material I have read, including various reports of the Canadian Law Reform Commission and the Canadian Sentencing Commission persuade me that a long sentence is any more useful for this purpose than a moderate sentence.* (Cited in Bala, 1994, emphasis added)

Bala's 1994 summary of our state of knowledge is, we believe, still quite reasonable:

> The unfortunate reality is that youths who are committing offences generally have a real lack of judgment and appreciation of any consequences of their actions. Lengthening sentences for other youths who are apprehended is not likely to have any appreciable effect on their behaviour. Improving policing and increasing the chance that a young offender will be apprehended almost certainly has a greater deterrent effect on youthful criminality than lengthening sentences. It is the prospect of being caught that is more likely to deter than an assessment of the consequences of being caught. (ibid., p. 311)

More recently Bala (2003) suggests that 'Increasing the severity of sanctions – that is increasing the consequences of getting caught – appears to have no impact on youth crime. This is not to argue that there should be no consequences for youths who commit criminal offences, but that there should be no expectation that social protection can be increased by imposing more severe punishments on young offenders' (p. 4).

One could argue, perhaps, that there is no obvious reason why one should expect 'deterrence' to be relevant to all forms of delinquency all of the time. For this reason, some researchers have attempted to look for more specific kinds of evidence. Paternoster (1989), for example, differentiated among factors that are relevant to the decision to *begin* offending, factors that relate to *repeating* one's offending pattern, and factors that relate to *desisting* from further offending. He kept in touch with about 2,700 students over a two-year period, looking at the students' perceptions of the certainty and severity of punishment for four common delinquent offences (marijuana use, underage drinking, theft, and vandalism).

Beginning offending was *unrelated* to the perceived severity or certainty of official punishment. Not surprisingly, beginning offending was related to being male, having few inhibitions about offending, lacking parental supervision, and closer relationships with peers.

Decisions to offend appeared to be somewhat unstable; people moved from being offenders and non-offenders in a rather fluid manner. But more importantly, in terms of the deterrence hypothesis, no single factor had a uniform effect across the four offences. In particular, the perceived severity of the punishment, looked at in terms of either the reactions of peers and parents or in terms of the response of the youth justice system, 'had virtually no effect on the decision to offend or to quit offending' (Paternoster, 1989, p. 37). In fact, the 'costs' of punishment seemed to be focused more on the non-legal factors (friends or family) than on the criminal justice consequences. The *likelihood* of apprehension was somewhat more important, but even then, the effects were not consistent. However, even in those instances when the perceived likelihood of apprehension was relevant, it was not as important as whether or not the youth had friends who were either participating in the same activity or whether their friends would approve or disapprove of the behaviour.

One problem that researchers in this area have noted is that it is sometimes assumed that the perceptions of young people (of the likelihood of apprehension and of the likely penalty) will be stable. In a study that looked at the degree of consistency of reports of offending and of deterrence relevant concepts (likelihood of apprehension, perceived penalties), it was concluded that 'for the high school student respondents [in the study], the experience of committing illegal acts and getting away with them is likely to lead them to modify their estimates of the risk of getting caught rather than their estimates of the penalties should they be discovered' (Paternoster et al., 1983, p. 289). Looking at offences that young people are likely to engage in (largely offences where one *might* expect young people to be thinking about possible consequences) – theft, marijuana use, underage drinking, vandalism – there was no consistent support for deterrence notions. In fact, the most consistent variable explaining whether or not a young person committed offences was the respondent's 'moral commitment to the rules' (ibid., p. 295).

There is almost no support for the view that the *strength* of the possible punishment is important in understanding whether or not a young person will commit offences. The data for adults are, as we have already noted, more extensive and similar: harsher sentences do not deter more effectively than less harsh sentences. It is clear, however, that in some situations, the *perceived* risk of formal legal sanctions is important. Young people may choose targets, for example, in terms of the perceived likelihood of apprehension. Furthermore, young people clearly choose the time and place for committing certain offences with an eye to the likelihood of apprehension. It is important, therefore, to differentiate these details of offending from the willingness that a young person has, in general, to commit an offence. The research literature does not typically address itself to when or where a young person will commit a particular offence (such as vandalism or theft) but simply whether he or she has committed it in the past or is likely to commit it in the future.

It should not be surprising that young people feel a variety of concerns about the possibility of being caught. The criminal justice consequences are less predictable than are the social consequences. More importantly, the social consequences may be longer lasting. It is a serious mistake to focus solely on the *criminal justice* consequences of being apprehended for an offence. In fact, it is likely to be more effective to focus on the interpersonal and community consequences of offending and look to ways of reintegrating offenders back into the community.

The conclusion that variation in the harshness of sentences would not affect the likelihood that youths would offend does *not* mean that there is no deterrent impact of criminalizing certain behaviours. In other words, we are not suggesting that the criminal justice system as a whole does not have a deterrent impact. People's behaviour is affected by the existence of the criminal justice system and the fact that certain behaviours are sanctioned under the criminal law. Hence to conclude that plausible changes in the severity of sanctions do not reduce crime is *not* to suggest that the system as a whole, and the presence of penalties, does not have deterrent value.

Boot Camps

The policy of imposing harsher sentences is almost certainly the most popular ineffective quick fix attempt to reduce crime, generally. For youths who offend, the 'boot camp' evolved, during the 1990s, as one of the youth justice system's most politically popular, but ineffective, approaches. Much has been written on the impact of boot camps on youths and young adults. Boot camps are an interesting phenomenon in the justice system, in part because they are based on an analogy that makes little correctional sense. Most analyses of youthful offending suggest that youths are not thinking about the consequences of their behaviour, and are not deciding for themselves what to do. Youths may, instead, be following the urgings of others rather than making careful decisions themselves. In other words, youths who offend may be thoughtless about consequences for themselves or others. We have already noted that youths do, in fact, tend to offend in groups. Thus, they may be focusing on the group – and their relationship to the group – rather than on their own behaviour and the consequences for them and for their victims.

Keeping this in mind, it is interesting to consider the model on which boot camps are typically based:

The basic elements of the modern penal boot camp is a 'reproduction in appearance and tone of military basic training of the type familiar throughout much of the 20th century and known colloquially as 'boot camp.' The new penal boot camps typically include military-style drilling and quartering, ceremonies at entrance and exit, harsh verbal evaluations from correctional officers trained to act like drill sergeants, and summary punishments for disciplinary infractions in the form of physically taxing

exercises. In some places, officers and inmates are dressed in approxima-
tions of military uniforms and use terms derived from boot-camp lore.
(Simon, 1995, p. 26)

Hence, the classic military boot camp focuses on the necessity of
each individual soldier following, and not questioning, orders that are
received. Blind obedience to others rather than thoughtfulness and
individual responsibility for one's actions is emphasized. As Simon
(1995, p. 36) points out, the importation of the military boot camp into
the penal system can best be thought of as an 'exercise in nostalgia.' He
notes that: 'the preeminence of the military metaphor does not necessarily reflect even relative superiority of the military to other bad models for the penal process. Instead it reflects the relative standing of the
military as a rich source of nostalgia for modernity' (ibid., p. 37).

Interestingly enough, the boot camp model of blind obedience and
the deferring of individual needs and outcomes to the good of the
group does not even appear to be a model that is unequivocally
accepted any more in the military or in corporate structures: 'Studies
conducted by the military itself since the 1970s have suggested overwhelmingly that the classic boot camp model is counterproductive for
many of the military's own goals ... The new training model emphasizes such things as health and stress reduction. Thus, the military –
the model for the boot camp – is a remembered military' (ibid., p. 35).

Most importantly, the boot camp model does not make sense as a
model for training youths to live in the world of today:

The bigger picture of labor deployment ... is one quite different from the
military model. In a work force organized for maximum global competi-
tiveness, with an open flow of both capital and labour across borders, loy-
alty is less valued than individual initiative. Rote obedience is denigrated
in favour of flexible authority lines and encouragement of innovation at all
levels of enterprise. Indeed, while the military model might have fit the
classical industrial economy, where corporations promised lifetime
employment and generous benefits, it is about the least viable model
imaginable for the new flexible accumulation / just-in-time-production
model that emphasizes constant change and individual responsibility.

Critics have noted ruefully that it seems peculiar to take a device
intended for the introductory transition into a more prolonged experience
of military duty and to use it on a population destined only for return to
the same communities where they operated as criminals ... The penal boot

camp is lacking in any real-world referents. Indeed, what referents it does have are self-consciously fabricated images of the past that characterize the model of willful nostalgia. (ibid., p. 36)

By the mid-1990s, most American states had boot camps of one kind or another. Some of these appeared, if anything, to increase recidivism. Wright and Mays (1998), for example, investigated recidivism rates among first time offenders ($N = 1,937$) who were placed on probation, in traditional custodial institutions, or in boot camps. The majority of offenders had been convicted of property offences. The results revealed that offenders who were placed in boot camps were if anything *more* likely to recidivate after release than the offenders placed on probation or in a normal prison. During a 2.5-year period, 17 per cent of the offenders placed on probation, and 20 per cent of the offenders in prison re-offended, while 35 per cent of offenders who had been in boot camps re-offended.

The evidence, by the mid-1990s, on the effectiveness of boot camps was quite clear. Some of the early evaluations of the overall *programs* associated with boot camps showed positive impacts of boot camps on recidivism. However, the research suggests that the beneficial impacts of boot camps had nothing to do with the boot camp experience per se. As MacKenzie and Souryal point out, 'after careful examination of the results, there is very little evidence that the [boot camp] experience leads to a reduction in offender recidivism' (1994, p. 394).

Instead, the data supported the conclusion that because many boot camp programs were paired with intensive 'after care' programs for the youths when they returned to their communities, there were positive effects. Good correctional programming in the community appeared to help keep young people from re-offending.

There are, however, some other benefits from boot camps. In the United States, and perhaps elsewhere, enthusiastic staff, new or recently improved facilities, and better internal rehabilitative programs, are more likely to be associated with boot camps than with traditional young offender facilities. Styve, MacKenzie, Gover, and Mitchell (2000) examined the perception of boot camps by juvenile inmates. There is a good deal of research showing that prisons have been found to be places where youth feel afraid and bored. Twenty-two pairs of juvenile institutions were compared: a boot camp and the state facility where the youth would have gone if he had not been sent to the boot camp. Thirteen different 'conditions of confinement' were measured using questionnaires. There are lessons to be learned from the operation of boot camps. In at least three-quarters of the pairs of institutions, inmates of boot camps tended to see their institution as having more therapeutic programs, more planned activities, more structure and control, and to be better preparing them for release than traditional juvenile institutions. Boot camp inmates also felt less at risk from other inmates, and from the correctional environment generally. However, not all boot camps were seen as being better than their 'bootless' counterparts. On some dimensions – danger from staff, quality of life, and freedom – there were significant differences across the pairs of institutions with the boot camp sometimes looking better and sometimes worse than the traditional prison.

One of the advantages of having highly structured environments is that juvenile inmates feel safer and feel that someone cares about what happens to them. These are important dimensions to consider, because an environment which is safe from violence presumably constitutes a minimum standard for incarcerated youth. If boot camps do have 'healthier' atmospheres on some dimensions than traditional prisons for youth, one can ask why they are not more effective in changing behaviour. It may be that, although youths perceive that they are receiving better programming and, as a result, they perceive that the institution cares for them, the programming that they are given in the institution may not be addressing the circumstances responsible for their being in prison in the first place.

One of the people most involved in the evaluations of boot camp summarized the evidence: 'When examined, there are few differences between boot camp graduates and probationers and parolees in terms of antisocial attitudes, positive activities during community supervision, and recidivism. [Such differences as do occur between groups] may be related to the intensive therapeutic activities in boot camp combined with intensive supervision in the community' (MacKenzie & Souryal, 1994).

Thus it was, within the context of American boot camp experience, that on 20 November 1995, the Solicitor General and Minister of Correctional Services for Ontario, announced that he was establishing a committee – the majority of whom had police or military backgrounds – to develop a 'strict discipline program for Ontario young offenders' within the tradition of programs that have 'a highly structured atmosphere of rigorous physical discipline.'

Ontario set up a 'strict discipline' boot camp in 1997 for young offenders aged 16 to 17. When the evaluation of this institution (T3 Associates, 2001) was released, the ministry's press release suggested that the boot camp was responsible for a drop in recidivism from 50 per cent (for a 'comparable sample of youth who were not exposed to the program') to 33 per cent for Ontario's boot camp.

The evaluation compared boot camp graduates and a comparison group on two sets of dimensions: psychological changes between the beginning and the end of their custodial experience and recidivism after they were released. The comparison group was comprised of youths who met the criteria for the boot camp, but did not participate because there was no space at the time. They differed from the boot camp group on several dimensions, although it is difficult to know whether these differences were important.

The recidivism data are easy to summarize. The comparison group (n = 60) was used as a baseline for comparisons with (1) all boot camp participants (n = 59 for the highly advertised comparison) and (2) boot camp completers (n = 51). This last group is problematic for the obvious reason: the 'non-completers' are clearly a troubled group. They have a high rate of recidivism. Their omission from the boot camp group with no attempt being made to eliminate 'failures' from the comparison group is a lethal methodological error for two reasons. First, the two groups are no longer comparable, since the 'worst' youths have been excluded from the boot camp group but not from the other subsample. Second, we are no longer looking at the impact *of the institution* itself: we are looking only at the impact of the institution on a subset of youths.

For almost all recidivism comparisons, no standard statistics were presented in the report. However, they can be calculated from the data that are available. The main comparison that is highlighted by the government (T3 Associates, 2001, p. 47) shows differences which do not even approach normal statistical significance for the contrast of the comparison group and all boot camp participants. Furthermore, when one looks at the 'boot camp completers' versus the comparison group, the difference does not approach statistical significance when the appropriate statistical test is carried out. In other words, there is no reliable effect of the boot camp experience on recidivism.

The report is very thorough in its investigation of differences between subsets of boot camp graduates and the comparison group. There are over thirty sets of comparisons drawn between subsets of boot camp and non-boot-camp youths (for various periods of time). In none of these comparisons was a proper statistically significant difference found between the groups.

The actual findings from Ontario's boot camp are, therefore, easy to describe: a very thorough examination of the data found no significant differences on recidivism between boot camp participants (or boot camp completers) and a comparison group. It did not matter whether one looked at recidivism at six months, one year, or whatever length of time the youth had been in the community. There was also no evidence of any overall beneficial psychological or academic impact of the boot camp experience over a standard correctional institution. As we have already pointed out, the generalized failure of Ontario's boot camp to show statistically significant positive effects on youth is consistent with evaluations elsewhere.

Curfews

One of the obvious disadvantages of recommending boot camps as a quick fix to the problem of youth crime is that one has to set up a boot camp in order to implement it. Legislative changes that do not involve administrative efforts are preferable as quick fixes, since all of the work can be done in the legislature. Curfew laws offer exactly this kind of opportunity. By the mid-1990s, three-quarters of the 200 largest U.S. cities had curfews for young people. Fortunately, these have been studied quite extensively.

The theory behind juvenile curfew laws is simple: control the hours during which youths can be in public; keep youths from getting together in groups; and give parents additional powers to control their kids. There are two general problems with this logic. First, the laws depend on enforcement for their effectiveness. Second, and most important, while curfews generally attempt to control behaviour from late evening to early the next morning, youth crime generally peaks in the afternoon immediately after school finishes and then decreases thereafter. Curfews, therefore, tend to prohibit juvenile mobility at times when youth are least likely to be committing crimes.

McDowell, Loftin, and Wiersema (2000) looked at juvenile arrest data for those aged 17 and younger from 1985 to 1996 in the fifty-seven largest U.S. cities. While arrests are not a perfect measure of youth involvement in crime, claims of effectiveness of simple solutions to youth crime often use these types of measures. In order to look at serious juvenile victimization, homicides involving juveniles as victims were also examined. These crime measures were examined as a function of the presence or absence of new curfew laws. In addition, some jurisdictions modified their laws, providing an opportunity to examine the effects of the change, as well as the publicity that probably accompanied the change. However, some cities were, in fact, counties, and those could be examined separately. The analyses controlled for a number of different factors: total population size, per capita income, and a correlate of the poverty level (the infant mortality rate).

The results are simple to describe. Ten different offence (arrest) rates were examined, ranging in seriousness from homicide and rape to theft and vandalism. In no case did the passing of new curfew laws create a consistent significant drop in any of these crimes. What support could be found for an effect of curfews was so inconsistent that the effects were most likely the result of other factors. When enforcement activities (curfew arrests) were examined, they, too, appeared unrelated to arrests for other crimes.

Another study of curfews (Reynolds, Seydlitz, & Jenkins, 2000) examined the effects of the curfew in New Orleans, Louisiana, which had the most restrictive juvenile curfew of all U.S. cities. Youths under 17 were prohibited from being in public places, unless accompanied by an adult, after 8 p.m. on weekdays and 11 p.m. on weekends during the school year. During the summer, youths could stay out until 9 p.m. The twist in the New Orleans law is that the youth's legal guardian can be fined, ordered to take counselling or do parenting courses, or ordered to do community service. Business operators can be fined or imprisoned for letting a youth set foot in their premises during curfew hours.

The study examined victim reports and juvenile arrests for the year before and the year after the law was enacted on 1 June 1994. The findings were clear. 'The implementation of the curfew law did not significantly reduce victimizations, juvenile victimizations nor juvenile arrests during curfew hours' (ibid., p. 212). This study confirms the findings of other studies of curfews:

> Juvenile curfew laws are ineffective for reducing crime because they do not include many of the perpetrators of crime, namely older adolescents and young adults; they do not include the hours when juveniles are most likely to commit offences; they are based on the incorrect assumption that police crackdowns reduce crime; and they do not fully utilize the theories and research concerning juvenile delinquency. Finally they do not alter substantially the major correlates of delinquency: exposure to delinquent

peers, schools, and the family. Delinquent behaviour does not happen in isolation, but in a social context consisting of an individual's peers, school, and family. (ibid., p. 226)

Delinquency will not be reduced by forcing children into negative family situations marked by rejection, negative community patterns, excessively lax or severe supervision and discipline, criminal family members, and abuse. Yet curfew laws force all youths to be at home ... without ascertaining whether the home is a safe and positive place for these juveniles. (ibid., p. 225)

Quick Fixes and the Causes of Youthful Offending

As we have noted throughout this chapter, the major hurdle of the quick fix approaches to youthful offending is that these methods appear to be developed completely independently of what is known about youthful offending. Whether one is considering harsher sentences, boot camps, curfews, or other simplistic approaches such as making parents financially responsible for the costs of damage done by their misbehaving children, the most notable aspect of these approaches is their failure to take into account what is known about the cases of youthful offending.

This book does not focus on the causes of youth crime. However, almost all assessments of youth crime would look elsewhere than the youth justice system for places to intervene. Interventions could take place early in a child's life, in the family, in schools, or in communities.

Focusing on Long-Term Prevention

It turns out that we have a lot of information about how to reduce youth crime. Almost invariably, those who have studied interventions designed to reduce youth crime focus on early childhood. Yoshikawa (1994, p. 28) suggests that the focus of intervention programs should be on 'chronic delinquency, rather than delinquency in general' for a number of reasons, including the fact that a disproportionate number of serious offences are committed by chronic delinquents. But equally important is that chronic delinquency is associated with other social and psychological problems. There is a stability of 'troublesomeness' within this group from early childhood (ages 8–10) through adulthood.

Although it is the case that chronic offenders cannot be perfectly and reliably identified early in their lives, there is enough information to identify a group who might be considered to be severely at risk. As Yoshikawa (1994, p. 31) notes, however, one does not have to take the view that 'predictors of chronic juvenile delinquency be used to single out those children most likely to become delinquent and mandate an intervention for them' Children who seem to be particularly at risk for both childhood psychopathology and delinquency appeared to be those who had a number of risk factors. And, it turns out that adding on additional risks increases dramatically the likelihood that young person will engage in antisocial behaviour.

Risks begin early. Some studies have shown that factors such as low birth weight are related to subsequent social problems. Similarly, the data are quite clear that low cognitive abilities and poor school achievement predispose young people to engage in delinquency. Low cognitive abilities at age 6, for example, have been shown to predict conduct problems more than ten years later. In a similar vein, a variety of factors relating to parental behaviour – lack of supervision, rejection of children, lack of involvement with children – were highly related to delinquency. A range of other similar factors having to do with the experiences and the school and home environment of the young person also appear to be important in understanding delinquency (Loeber & Farrington, 1998).

In a paper descriptively titled 'Never Too Early, Never Too Late,' Loeber and Farrington (1998) suggested that are a number of known risk factors that make a young person likely to engage in serious or violent offending, but these may not be evident at the young person's first court appearance. Hence, they suggested that 'public health approaches' which target youths in 'at risk' (disadvantaged) neighbourhoods are likely to be the most effective. The challenge for communities (and for the various levels of government that have an interest in the reduction of crime) is to integrate services across agencies such as the youth justice system, schools, and social and child protection services, as well as the health system. It is probably not too much of an oversimplification to suggest that programs that lead to healthy children are likely to be effective in addressing many of the precursors to delinquency.

When considering 'late' intervention, the study found that interventions aimed at those youth who already had become serious and/or violent offenders were also possible, though 'interventions for serious and/or violent offenders often have to be multi-modal in order to address problems, including law breaking, substance use and abuse, and academic problems. The administration of multimodal programs requires integration of services of the juvenile justice system, mental health, schools, and child welfare agencies. Aftercare programs are essential' (Loeber & Farrington, 1998).

One example of a very early intervention into a child's life comes from a study of the impact of home visits by a nurse. It is well established that factors such as low birth weight (especially when combined with a disadvantaged childhood), harsh parenting styles (or practices of rejection), and association with deviant peers will increase the likelihood of offending in adolescence and adulthood. The policy question which needs to be addressed is a simple one: how can communities intervene, in positive ways, to decrease the likelihood of later offending?

Olds et al. (1998) used the 'gold standard' of research designs for attributing causality – the randomized trial – to determine the effects of broad-based intervention in a child's life. Specifically, they investigated the impact of home visits by a nurse before and after the birth of a child on offending behaviour during adolescence. Mothers in their first completed pregnancy who were 'at risk' (i.e., young, single and/or of low socioeconomic status) participated in the experiment. These women were assigned to different groups on a randomized basis. As such, the groups can be considered to be equivalent for all practical purposes. For some of the mothers (the control groups), the program simply provided assessment and referrals for treatment. For one 'experimental' group, they received this same assessment and referrals, but a nurse also visited them an average of nine times during pregnancy. The nurse promoted positive health-related behaviours during pregnancy and the early years of the child as well as general help to the mother (e.g., family planning, getting a job) during these visits. For the second experimental group, this monthly support visitation program continued until the child was 2 years old.

Approaches such as the one used in this study are attractive for a number of reasons. First, they address a number of actual basic needs. In this case, the visiting nurse was able to help pregnant women and new mothers in a number of different areas (e.g., nutrition and child-rearing techniques) that have nothing directly to do with crime. The immediate benefits of the intervention are obvious. Furthermore, there are few risks of stigmatizing a youth or a family.

The results of the study are simple to summarize. The nurse visitation program, especially when the monthly visits continued until the child's second birthday, reduced the incidence of involvement with the police, arrests, and contact with the child welfare system as a 'person in need of supervision' during the child's early adolescent years, up to age

15 (Olds et al., 1998, p. 1242). In summary, 'Adolescents born to nurse-visited women who were unmarried and from low-SES families had fewer episodes of running away from home, arrests, convictions and violations of probation than did their counterparts in the comparison group. They also had fewer sexual partners and engaged in cigarette smoking and alcohol consumption less frequently' (ibid., pp. 1241–2).

It would appear that programs designed to promote healthy children can reduce crime. If a community wants to be tough on crime and simultaneously promote good health in children, it can do so by providing public health services to mothers during their pregnancy and to mothers and children in their first few years of life.

Communities can do other things in addition to programs such as home visitation programs. For example, training programs for parents, school-based programs, and programs that integrate these two appear to be successful (Graham, 1998).

Another form of intensive intervention is to work with the problem child in school. Walker et al. (1998) examined a school-based program, 'First Step to Success,' which focuses on 'at risk' children in kindergarten, but involves teachers, peers, and parents or caregivers, as well as the child. It starts with a formal screening of kindergarten children to identify problem children. The school intervention has thirty formal days of programming, though since a child must 'pass' each day, it may take more than thirty days to complete. Typically it takes about forty days. The first five days involve a 'consultant,' who need not be a formal professional. On each of these days, there are two 20- to 30-minute sessions in school. Essentially, it is a program where the child earns negotiated school and home privileges for appropriate behaviour. The details of how the privileges are earned change over time. What is important, however, is that it is a fairly rigid program designed to effect change at home and at school.

The study involved comparing a group of children with a randomly assigned 'waiting list control' group of children. Quite large (and statistically significant) changes were found in the treatment group that were not found in the waiting list control group. Although the experiment was carried out when the children were in kindergarten, one group was followed through Grade 2. The improvements in the children's behaviour continued. The results are

consistent with existing literature on the case for early intervention with at-risk children ... That is, comprehensive early interventions, especially those involving parents, appear to (a) teach relationships between choices and their resulting consequences, (b) develop the social-behavioural and academically related competencies that allow children to cope effectively with the demands of friendship-making ... and (c) reduce the long-term probability that at-risk children will adopt a delinquent lifestyle in adolescence. (Walker et al., 1998, p. 74)

By the standards used in other fields, [the program] is a relatively brief and inexpensive intervention. (ibid., p. 76)

This intervention into the lives of at risk children appears to have been successful in reducing antisocial behaviour. Furthermore, it would appear to be a program that parents and teachers approve of and which can be implemented with rather minimal cost. Although it is hard to estimate the actual cost of the program, it would appear that the cost of 'treating' a single child would be less than the dollar cost of charging a single child with a common assault and having that child go through the court system and receive an absolute discharge at the end. This cost estimate, of course, ignores the other beneficial effects of the program and the harmful impact of contact with the criminal justice system.

Child psychologist Lawrence Steinberg suggests that interventions designed to improve the state of the family can have direct beneficial impacts on families and also reduce levels of violence of children growing up in these households. Hence, public health approaches, which would help reduce the stresses experienced by all families, are much more likely to have a substantial impact on youth violence than programs that target individual violent children: 'Any attempt to reduce youth violence ... must include a systematic effort to improve the home environments of ... children and adolescents and, in particular, to engage ... parents in the business of parenting ... We can do this by improving prenatal care, expanding parent education, and promoting family friendly policies that reduce poverty, prevent and treat mental health and substance abuse problems, and enhance parental effectiveness' (Steinberg, 2000, p.38).

Finding programs that attempt to treat delinquent youths is not difficult. Finding programs that are effective is somewhat more difficult. And finding the 'best' way to invest money in reducing crime is even more difficult. Aos, Barnoski, and Lieb (1998) examined programs for youth where there was sound research to examine their costs and outcomes. Programs do exist, but their impact on youth is often 'modest.' They certainly will not guarantee success. 'The best interventions for juvenile offenders lower the chance of re-offending by about 40%' (Aos et al., 1998, p. 7). Typically, the programs reduce rates of recidivism by about 20 to 30 per cent. This is important to keep in mind, because it means that the graduates from the best known programs will often re-offend. It is also relevant when one hears claims in the media about 'quick fix' interventions. But these modest impacts, for example, a reduction of reconviction rates from 45 per cent to 27 per cent (a 40 per cent reduction) for probationers in some locations, may still be worthwhile.

The question, from a public policy perspective is simple: If a program is likely to reduce recidivism by only modest amounts (20 to 30 per cent), is it still worth it? The answer is 'yes' – sometimes. First, one has to ask whether one is interested only in public costs – typically those of the criminal justice system. Some programs do not show a savings on criminal justice costs alone, but do show savings if the costs to victims of crimes are included. Also, for some programs (e.g., early intervention programs directed at health or education issues), other benefits of the program to society can be measured.

But for many of the sixteen programs that were examined by Aos et al. (1998), there are criminal justice savings that can be shown within a year or two. For example, in a 'program for first time minor offenders on diversion where youth appear before a community accountability board shortly after committing an offence,' there is a 29 per cent reduction in offending, with a savings to the criminal justice system of about $2,700 per participant after one year. In large part, this saving may come from the fact that its costs to taxpayers are low ($136 per participant). Other intensive programs funded solely with public money take longer to show criminal justice savings.

There are, however, some expensive, and thoroughly evaluated, programs that will never show any kind of benefit when one looks at a measure like 'felony reconvictions by age 25.' Juvenile boot camps are one notable example.

Aos et al. (1998) suggest that although cost effective programs exist for reducing recidivism of juvenile offenders and to prevent delinquency, these programs are not necessarily cheap to implement. When considered as investments, however, they are sensible. Some of the intensive supervision programs, for example, cost $4,500 to $6,000 per participant and take a few years to show criminal justice savings. A program for chronic juvenile offenders including a home placement with trained foster parents and other treatment and probation services was quite expensive, but showed benefits to victims and for criminal justice budgets. Evaluated solely in terms of changes in recidivism rates, however, these programs might be seen as having only modest benefits. Nevertheless, as investments to achieve victim and criminal justice savings, they were very effective. To put a $5,000 cost in perspective, a thirty-day custodial sentence for a 15-year-old in Ontario could easily cost more than that.

The solutions to delinquency problems are not likely to be easy ones. Yoshikawa (1994) notes that successful programs appear to have some elements in common:

- They focus on multiple risks (rather than seeing delinquency as being a result of a single problem).
- The interventions are broadly based – dealing with matters within the family, school, and other areas of the young person's life (e.g., the young person's relations with peers). In fact, Yoshikawa suggests that 'the combination of family support and early educational models of intervention may have been crucial to obtaining effects on multiple risks for chronic delinquency.' The *Head Start* program in the United States, for example, was originally conceived of as 'combining comprehensive family support services with its preschool education program ... [H]owever, the family support component is not up to par with Head Start performance standards' (ibid., p. 45). Nevertheless, these programs have shown impressive long-term impacts.
- They focus on urban, low-income families. Interestingly, some of the most successful programs did *not* have prevention of delinquency as their primary goal. The focus was on providing help to disadvantaged groups. One evaluation found, however, that families which are traditionally not at risk of having children with problems also benefited from the various educational and support programs.
- The interventions were relatively long lasting – two to five years. There are, it seems, no quick fixes. More importantly, for a program to be effective, there has to be a long-term commitment on the part of society to improve the life chances of its most vulnerable children. It must be remembered that crime prevention was not the only, and seldom the primary, goal of any of these programs.
- Intervention should come early, typically in the first five years of life.

Other researchers, coming at the problem of delinquency from a somewhat different direction, have come to remarkably similar conclusions. Farrington (1994) has been directing a longitudinal study of 411 South London (England) males from age 8 onwards far into adulthood. The advantages of a longitudinal study are clear: one can examine the impact of certain kinds of early experiences on behaviour that occurs years or decades later. One can examine, for those who become serious delinquent youths or young adults, what differences exist that might have been amenable to intervention. Farrington concludes:

> The main practical implication of the Cambridge Study is that, in order to reduce delinquency and antisocial behaviour, early prevention experiments are needed. These should target four important predictors of delinquency that may be both causal and modifiable: poverty, low educational attainment, poor parental child-rearing behaviour and impulsivity.
>
> In this survey, as in many others, the worst offenders were drawn from the poorest families in the worst housing. Of all the factors measured at age 8–10, low family income was the best predictor of general social dysfunction at age 32. These results suggest that more economic resources should be targeted selectively on the poorest families, to try to improve their economic circumstances in comparison with other families.
>
> Again, low attainment has been shown to be an important predictor and correlate of delinquency in numerous surveys. There are indicators from the United States that the pre-school intellectual enrichment programs of the 1960s led to significant decreases in school failure and later offending. (1994, p. 38)
>
> Because of the link between delinquency and numerous other social problems, any measure that succeeds in reducing crime will probably have benefits that go far beyond this. (ibid., p. 40)
>
> It is clear from our research that antisocial children tend to grow up into antisocial adults, and that antisocial adults tend to produce antisocial children. Sooner or later, serious efforts, firmly grounded on empirical research results ... must be made to break this cycle. (ibid., p. 40)

We should, however, be cautious about believing that any intervention outside of the justice system would be good. Joan McCord (1978, 2002), reports some disturbing findings of a long-term follow-up of a program started in 1939. For approximately 5.5 years, youths in congested urban areas of Cambridge and Somerville, Massachusetts, were interviewed and each was matched with another similar young person. As a result of a flip of a coin, one of these individuals was assigned to a control group in which normal social services in the community were provided. In contrast, the other youth was given intensive interventions including guidance, after-school activities, social support, tutoring, and medical and psychiatric attention. By the end of the program in 1945, the boys in the treatment group had generally received a variety of services and help, from tutoring to medical intervention, being sent to summer camp, or assistance in finding a job. Many of them showed dramatic improvements and suggested in a formal follow-up study conducted twenty years later that the program had been beneficial to them. Based simply of these findings, one could not help but consider this program to have been a success.

The results are not, however, as simple as one may have initially thought. Indeed, the improvements in the treatment group have to be compared with those in the control group before any confident conclusions regarding the success of the program may be drawn. In fact, it was found that almost equal numbers of youths in both groups showed unexpected improvement. Similarly, the involvement of the two groups in the criminal justice system was nearly identical. However, when these individuals were re-examined in a follow-up study between 1975 and 1981 (the participants were middle aged by this time), disturbing differences emerged. More specifically, those in the *treatment* group were more likely to have been convicted of serious crimes, to have died early, to have serious problems with mental illness, and to be alcoholics than those in the control group. In fact, the deleterious effects of treatment appeared to occur most often with those youths who had cooperated most with the youth study staff. Indeed, the more frequently that they received treatment, the worse off they were. These harmful effects of the program were only evident because an equivalent control group was used. Without the control group, a program that appeared to have had harmful effects would have been seen as a success.

Unfortunately, this is not the only study that has demonstrated adverse effects of treatment. Other counselling programs (e.g., a court counselling program in the United States, a social skills program, and a peer counselling program) have also been shown to have similar negative impacts.

The lesson from interventions such as the 1939–45 Cambridge–Somerville initiative for youth is that programs which sound good can still have negative impacts. Said differently, we cannot automatically assume that these interventions will have beneficial effects or at worst will have no effects. While the reasons for the adverse impacts are not clear, the lesson from this study is that social interventions into the lives of youths need to be assessed carefully before they can be presumed to be safe, let alone helpful.

Addressing Youth Crime and the Youth Justice System

As we have stated throughout this book, addressing the problem of youth crime and determining what might be a sensible youth justice system are two quite different things. In the first part of this chapter, we described a number of different types of approaches to youth crime. Interventions into the lives of young people can have positive impacts.

Elsewhere, we described both what youth crime looks like and how the youth justice system responds to it. It is easy to identify what the goal of a 'youth crime reduction' program would be: less youth crime. It is not so easy to describe – and there is probably less consensus on – what the goal should be for a youth justice system. Nevertheless, Parliament has determined, in a manner that is more explicit than in the past, what these goals should be in the Youth Criminal Justice Act. If the goal of a youth justice system is to respond in a measured fashion to youth crime and to hold youths appropriately accountable, the question that this answer obviously begs is a simple one, 'How should it do this?'

We have pointed out that much of youth crime is minor. The challenge is to find an appropriate way of dealing with specific offences so that the process has an integrative effect on the young person and is, at the same time, just, acceptable to the victim, and acceptable to the community. The problem with most criminal justice or court-based 'dispositions' of cases is that they have none of these goals as main purposes. Reintegrating the young offender into the community is neither addressed nor is it an explicit goal of most dispositions. Coming to a resolution which is seen as appropriate by the victim (and the victim's community) is, at best, a chance by-product of the justice system. Programs that now label themselves as falling within the category of 'Restorative justice' often have as their intention a resolution that is satisfactory to the victim, the offender, and the community.

Modern interest in restorative justice began with the wider use of restitution, community service and reparative sanctions in the 1970s (Bazemore & Umbreit, 1995; Bazemore & Schiff, 2001). Restorative justice practices grew primarily out of victim–offender mediation approaches which became popular in the 1980s. These would later become prevalent in several western jurisdictions throughout the 1990s including Australia, New Zealand, Canada, the United States, and the United Kingdom, in the form of victim–offender mediation, family group conferencing, and circle sentencing (Bazemore and Schiff, 2001).

Bazemore and Umbreit (1995, p. 302) provide a fairly clear definition of the philosophy behind restorative justice sanctions: 'Restorative justice emphasizes the need for the active involvement of the victims, the community, and the offenders in a process focused on denunciation of the offence, offender responsibility (accountability) and reparation, followed by resolution of conflict resulting from the criminal act and offender reintegration.'

It has been suggested that the 'success' of restorative justice approaches should best be measured not necessarily in terms of recidivism but by (1) victim satisfaction and involvement in the process, (2) the offender gaining an understanding of the consequences of crime to victims, prompt repayment or other reparative requirements, and (3) the community feeling that justice has been served and that the offender has been held accountable.

Although restorative justice programs are still, for the most part, in their infancy, there are sufficient data to comment on its ability to deliver on its intended outcomes.

The 'family group conference' is based on the idea of 'shaming of criminal *acts* and [providing for the] subsequent reintegration of deviant *actors* once suitable redress and apology have been made' (Braithwaite & Mugford, 1994). Braithwaite and Mugford describe the approach in the following way:

> The approach ... involves assembling in a room the offender and supporters of the offender (usually the nuclear family, often [relatives], sometimes neighbours, counsellors, even a teacher or a football coach) along with the victim of the crime (and supporters of the victim, usually from the nuclear family) under the supervision of a coordinator – a police sergeant ... In conferences we observed, the number of people in the room ranged from five to thirty ... The offender plays an important role in describing the nature of the offence. The psychological, social, and economic consequences of the offence – for victims, offenders and others – are elicited in discussions guided by the coordinator. Disapproval, often emotional disapproval, is usually communicated by victims and often by victim supporters and family members of the offender. At the same time, the

professional who coordinates the conference strives to bring out support for and forgiveness toward the offender from the participants in the conference. (ibid., pp. 140–1)

Furthermore, as Braithwaite and Mugford (1994, p. 142) point out, 'courtroom ceremonies tend to degradation rather than reintegration – that is, they remove both event *and* perpetrator from the everyday domain.'

In contrast, the conferences themselves sound quite different from what goes on in court:

> The average conference, with perhaps a dozen people in attendance, runs for a period of between forty minutes and an hour-and-a-half. During that time, a conference follows a basic sequence. The offender gives his/her version of events, followed by the version of events as perceived by the offender's supporters. Then it is the turn of the victim to provide what usually proves to be a startling different version. The victim's supporters also make a contribution here and these too often include surprising revelations. In a number of cases, for instance, evidence of feuds between individuals, families or larger groups have been revealed. An apparently straightforward assault may, in fact, be only one small part of a much larger picture. Differences stretching back to over a decade have been revealed and addressed in the conferences. A long process of reconciliation has then been initiated.
>
> More generally, conferences address problems that the old system ignored, problems such as the anger and resentment of victims and the possibility of compensation. The issue of compensation has proved less problematic than anticipated. In many cases, return of goods and monetary compensation for damage has been readily undertaken. In the event of damage to buildings, supervised repair work as agreed to by both parties has normally been arranged. Interestingly, nearly all young offenders offer to impose tougher demands on themselves than the victims consider appropriate. Offenders, wishing to emphasize their willingness to earn respect, argue the case for a tougher penalty. The group's collective compromise is rarely considered unfair.
>
> Conferences also offer better solutions to those problems which the old system did address; problems such as the need to disapprove of the offence and to discourage further offending. If recidivism rates are reduced by the scheme ... police will have saved themselves and court officials a good deal of future effort. If there is no net change to rates of recid-

ivism ... the scheme will nevertheless have provided a better response to the needs of victims. This hardly constitutes a waste of time. (Moore & O'Connell, undated, pp. 65–6)

The point of raising the program of 'family group conferences' in this context is largely to point out that there are alternatives to dealing with all offenders in court which have certain advantages from both a theoretical and a practical perspective. Since the mid-1990s, there has been a virtual explosion of interest in 'conferences' and in restorative approaches more generally. To a large extent, the focus is less on the hypothesis that such procedures have their impact through 'shaming' or any other special mechanism. Similarly, since the mid-1990s, there is both more enthusiasm on the part of some true believers and more scepticism on the part of others about what their impact actually is.

As described in Chapter 7 (see Table 7.2) public opinion data collected in Ontario in 1997 (Doob et al., 1998) suggest that most members of the public see conferences as a more appropriate way of responding to minor crime by youths (as well as adults) than taking such cases to court. It is not surprising, therefore, that the Youth Criminal Justice Act allows conferences to be convened by almost anyone (Section 19) for the purpose of 'giving advice on appropriate extrajudicial measures, conditions for judicial interim release, sentences, including the review of sentences, and reintegration plans' (Section 19(2)).

It should not be assumed that family group conferences will miraculously reduce the rate of recidivism of those whose offending is addressed in this way. Recent evidence from what is probably the methodologically most sound study of the impact of conferencing on recidivism would appear to suggest that conferencing does not significantly affect recidivism as compared with normal court processing. Sherman (2000) found that the drop in offending from before to after the conference experience did not differ significantly between a group of offenders offered a conference and a group that went through the court system.

If the long-term impact on the youth is no less favourable than a court appearance but victims, offenders, and their communities are more likely to believe that justice was done, then, of course, this may be a more appropriate response to youthful offending than formal court processing. Like other approaches, however, it does not appear that restorative approaches in general or family group conferences in particular, will be effective quick fixes for youth crime.

Conclusion

We began this book by suggesting that there was a need to differentiate three phenomena:

1 Youth crime, as it exists in our community
2 The youth justice system, and how it responds to those youth who are apprehended for offending
3 The causes of youth crime

In this chapter we have attempted to argue that effective programs which tackle the causes of youth crime and youth crime as it exists in our community are likely to reside outside the youth justice system. It appears that worthwhile programs deal effectively with problems by addressing them directly.

For young people who offend and are apprehended there are programs that 'work,' just as there are programs that harm youths. The definition of 'What works?' however, should be extended beyond simple measures of recidivism. A sensible youth justice system may not be able to solve the problem of youth crime any more than can a dysfunctional youth justice system. But youth justice systems can be seen as 'working' if they respond appropriately to youth crime.

In the long run, there appears to be value in both addressing the problems of youth crime in sensible ways and – separately – determining how best to respond to the not-so-serious and occasionally very serious acts which young offenders commit in our communities.

The challenge for youth justice in Canada and for those administering the Youth Criminal Justice Act will be to differentiate between 'youth justice' issues and 'youth crime' problems.

References

Abrahamse, A. (1997). *The coming wave of violence in California*. Santa Monica, CA: Rand Corporation.

Abramovitch, R., Higgins-Biss, K.L., & Biss, S.R. (1993). Young persons' comprehension of waivers in criminal proceedings. *Canadian Journal of Criminology, 35*(3), 309–22.

Adler, J. (1994). The incidence of fear: A survey of prisoners. *Prison Service Journal, 96,* 34–7.

Albrecht, H. (2003). Juvenile criminal justice in the Federal Republic of Germany: A theoretical and empirical account of the history of and trends in juvenile criminal justice. In M. Tonry & A.N. Doob (Eds.), *Comparative youth justice*. Chicago: University of Chicago Press.

Altschuler, D.M., & Armstrong, T.L. (1991). Intensive aftercare for the high-risk parolee: Issues and approaches in reintegration and community supervision. In T.L. Armstrong (Ed.), *Intensive interventions with high risk youth*. New York: Criminal Justice Press.

Altschuler, D.M., Armstrong, T.L., & MacKenzie, D.L. (1999). Reintegration, supervised release, and intensive aftercare. *Juvenile Justice Bulletin* (July), 1–23. NCJ 175715. Washington, DC: U.S. Department of Justice, Office of Justice Programs, Office of Juvenile Justice and Delinquency Programs.

Anand, S., & Robb, J. (2002). The admissibility of young people's statements under the proposed *Youth Criminal Justice Act. Alberta Law Review, 39,* 771–87.

Anderson, A., & Dvorak, B. (1928). Differences between college students and their elders in standards of conduct. *Journal of Abnormal & Social Psychology, 23,* 286–92.

Aos, S., Barnoski, R., & Lieb, R. (1998). Preventive programs for young offenders effective and cost-effective. *Overcrowded Times, 9*(2), 1 & 7–11.

Armstrong, T.L., & Altschuler, D.M. (1994). Recent developments in program-
    ming for high-risk juvenile parolees: Assessment findings and program pro-
    totype development. In R. Roberts (Ed.), *Critical issues in crime and justice* (pp.
    189–213). Thousand Oaks: Sage.

Augimeri, L.K., Goldberg, K., & Koegl, C.J. (1999). *Canadian children under 12
    committing offences: Police protocols.* Ottawa: Department of Justice Canada.

Bala, N. (1994). What's wrong with YOA bashing? What's wrong with the
    YOA? – Recognizing the limits of the law. *Canadian Journal of Criminology,
    36*(3), 247–70.

– (2003). *Youth Criminal Justice Law.* Toronto: Irwin Law.

Bala, N., & Mahoney, D. (1994). *Responding to criminal behaviour of children
    under 12: An analysis of Canadian law and practice.* Canada: Department of
    Justice.

Baumeister, R.F., Boden, J.M., & Smart, L. (1996). Relation of threatened ego-
    tism to violence and aggression: The dark side of high self-esteem. *Psycholog-
    ical Review, 103*(1), 5–33.

Bazemore, G., & Schiff, M. (2001). When and why: Understanding restorative
    justice. In G. Bazemore & M. Schiff (Eds.), *Restorative community justice:
    Repairing harm and transforming communities* (pp. 21–46). Cincinnati: Ander-
    son Publishing.

Bazemore, G., & Umbreit, M. (1995). Rethinking the sanctioning function in
    juvenile court: Retributive or restorative responses to youth crime. *Crime &
    Delinquency, 41*(3), 296–316.

Beaulieu, L. A. (1994). Youth offences: Adult consequences. *Canadian Journal of
    Criminology, 36*(3), 329–42.

Beck, G. (1995). Bullying among young offenders in custody. *Issues in Crimino-
    logical & Legal Psychology, 22,* 54–70.

Besserer, S., & Trainor, C. (2000). Criminal victimization in Canada, 1999.
    Juristat, 20(10). Cat. no. 85-002-XPE. Ottawa: Canadian Centre for Justice Sta-
    tistics, Statistics Canada.

Biggam, F.H., & Power, K.G. (1997). Social support and psychological distress
    in a group of incarcerated young offenders. *International Journal of Offender
    Therapy & Comparative Criminology, 41*(3), 213–30.

Bishop, D.M. (1984). Legal and extralegal barriers to delinquency: A panel
    analysis. *Criminology, 22*(3), 403–19.

– (2000). Juvenile offenders in the adult criminal justice system. In M. Tonry
    (Ed.), *Crime and justice: A review of research,* vol. 27 (pp. 81–167). Chicago:
    University of Chicago Press.

Bishop, D.M., & Frazier, C. (2000). Consequences of transfer. In J. Fagan &
    F.E. Zimring (Eds.), *The changing borders of juvenile justice: Transfer of adoles-*

cents to the criminal court (pp. 227–76). Chicago: University of Chicago Press.

Bortner, M.A., & Williams, L.M. (1997). *Youth in prison: We the people of unit four*. New York: Routledge.

Braithwaite, J., & Mugford, S. (1994). Conditions of successful reintegration ceremonies: Dealing with juvenile offenders. *British Journal of Criminology,* 34(2), 139–71.

Canadian Centre for Justice Statistics. (1983). *Juvenile Delinquents*. Ottawa: Canadian Centre for Justice Statistics, Statistics Canada.

– (1992). *Report on the involvement of children under 12 in criminal conduct.* Ottawa: Canadian Centre for Justice Statistics, Statistics Canada.

– (2000). *The 1999 general social survey, GSS-13.* Ottawa: Canadian Centre for Justice Statistics, Statistics Canada.

– (2001a). *Canadian crime statistics, 2000.* Ottawa: Canadian Centre for Justice Statistics, Statistics Canada.

– (2001b). *Youth court data tables, 1999–2000.* Ottawa: Canadian Centre for Justice Statistics, Statistics Canada.

– *The national longitudinal study of children and youth*. Ottawa: Canadian Centre for Justice Statistics, Statistics Canada.

Canadian Charter of Rights and Freedoms, R.S.C. 1985, En. *Canada Act 1982* (U.K.), c. 11.

Canadian Sentencing Commission. (1987). *Sentencing reform: A Canadian approach*. Ottawa: Supply and Services, Canada.

Carrigan, O.D. (1998). *Juvenile delinquency in Canada: A history*. Concord: Irwin.

Carrington, P.J. (1995). Has violent youth crime increased? Comment on Corrado and Markwart. *Canadian Journal of Criminology,* 37(1), 61–73.

– (1998). Factors affecting police diversion of young offenders: A statistical analysis. Report to the Solicitor General, Canada. http://www.sgc.gc.ca/epub/pol/e199802/e199802.htm

– (1999). Trends in youth crime in Canada, 1977–1996. *Canadian Journal of Criminology,* 41(1), 1–32.

– (2002). Group crime in Canada. *Canadian Journal of Criminology,* 44(3), 277–315.

Carrington, P.J., & Moyer, S. (1994). Trends in youth crime and police response, pre- and post-YOA. *Canadian Journal of Criminology,* 36(1), 1–28.

– (1995). Factors affecting custodial dispositions under the *Young Offenders Act. Canadian Journal of Criminology,* 37(2), 127–62.

Cauffman, E., & Steinberg, L. (2000). Researching adolescents' judgment and culpability. In T. Grisso & R.G. Schwartz (Eds.), *Youth on trial: A developmen-*

tal perspective on juvenile justice (pp. 325–43). Chicago: University of Chicago Press.

Cesaroni, C., & Peterson-Badali, M. (2003). Young offenders in custody: Risk and adjustment. In *Criminal justice and behavior*, in press.

Child and Family Services Act, R.S.O. 2001, c. 13, s. 5.

Cocozza, J.J., & Skowyra, K. (2000). Youth with mental health disorders: Issues and emerging responses. *Juvenile Justice, 7*(1), 3–14.

Conly, D. (1978). *Patterns of delinquency and police action in the major metropolitan areas of Canada during the month of december, 1976.* Ottawa: Solicitor General, Canada.

Connell, A., & Farrington, D. (1996). Bullying among incarcerated young offenders: Developing an interview schedule and some preliminary results. *Journal of Adolescence, 19*, 75–93.

Controlled Drugs and Substances Act, S.C. 1996, c. 19.

Corrado, R.R., & Markwart, A. (1994). The need to reform the YOA in response to violent young offenders: Confusion, reality and myth? *Canadian Journal of Criminology, 36*(3), 343–78.

Cox, E.W. (1870). *The principles of punishment as applied in the administration of criminal law by judges and magistrates.* London: Law Times Office.

Criminal Code, R.S.C. 1985, c. C-46.

Cullen, F.T., Fisher, B.S., & Applegate, B.K. (2000). Public opinion about punishment and corrections. In M. Tonry (Ed.), *Crime and justice: A review of research,* vol. 27 (pp. 1–79). Chicago: University of Chicago Press.

Cusson, M. (1983). *Why delinquency?* Toronto: University of Toronto Press.

del Carmen, R.V., Parker, M., & Reddington, F.P. (1998). *Briefs of leading cases in juvenile justice.* Cincinnati: Anderson Publishing.

Department of Justice Canada. (1998). *A strategy for the renewal of youth justice.* Ottawa: Department of Justice Canada.

– (1999, 11 March). Minister of justice introduces new youth justice law. On-line. http://canada.justice.gc.ca/en/news/nr/1999/yoa.html

– (2001, 5 Feb.). Minister of Justice reintroduces *Youth Criminal Justice Act.* On-line. Available: http://canada.justice.gc.ca/en/news/nr/2001/doc_25946.html

– (2002). Improving the youth justice system. On-line. Available: http//canada.justice.gc.ca/en/ps/yj/repository/2overvw/2010001b.html

Doherty, G., & de Souza, P. (1995). Recidivism in youth courts. *Juristat, 15*(16). Cat, no. 85-002. Ottawa: Canadian Centre for Justice Statistics, Statistics Canada.

– (1996). Youth court statistics, 1994–1995 highlights. *Juristat, 16*(4). Cat, no. 85-002-XPB. Ottawa: Canadian Centre for Justice Statistics, Statistics Canada.

Donohue, E., Schiraldi, V., & Ziedenberg, J. (1999). *School house hype: School shooting and the real risks kids face in America.* Washington, DC: Justice Policy Institute, Centre on Juvenile and Criminal Justice.

Doob, A.N. (1992). Trends in the use of custodial dispositions for young offenders. *Canadian Journal of Criminology, 34*(1), 75–84.

– (1999). *The experiences of phase II male young offenders in secure facilities in the province of Ontario.* Toronto: Canadian Foundation for Children, Youth and the Law.

– (2000). Transforming the punishment environment: Understanding public views of what should be accomplished at sentencing. *Canadian Journal of Criminology, 42*(3), 323–40.

– (2001). *Youth court judges' views of the youth justice system: The results of a survey.* Toronto: Centre of Criminology, University of Toronto.

Doob, A. N., & Beaulieu, L.A. (1992). Variation in the exercise of judicial discretion with young offenders. *Canadian Journal of Criminology, 34*(1), 35–50.

Doob, A.N., & Chan, J.B.L. (1982). Factors affecting police decisions to take juveniles to court. *Canadian Journal of Criminology, 24*(1), 25–37.

Doob, A.N., Marinos, V., & Varma, K.N. (1995). *Youth crime and the youth justice system in Canada.* Toronto: Centre of Criminology, University of Toronto.

Doob, A.N., & Meen, J. (1993). An exploration of changes in dispositions for young offenders in Toronto. *Canadian Journal of Criminology, 35*(1), 19–29.

Doob, A.N. & Robert, J.V. (1988). Public punitiveness and public knowledge of the facts: Some Canadian surveys. In N. Walker & M. Hough (Eds.), *Public attitudes to sentencing: Surveys from five countries.* Aldershot, England: Gower.

Doob, A.N., & Sprott, J.B. (1998). Is the 'quality' of youth violence becoming more serious? *Canadian Journal of Criminology, 40*(2), 185–94.

– (1999). The pitfalls of determining validity by consensus. *Canadian Journal of Criminology, 41,* 535–43.

Doob, A.N., Sprott, J.B., Marinos, V., & Varma, K.N. (1998). *An exploration of Ontario residents' views of crime and the criminal justice system.* Toronto: Centre of Criminology, University of Toronto.

Doob, A.N., and Webster, C.M. (2003) Sentence severity and crime: Accepting the null hypothesis. In M. Tonry (Ed.), *Crime and justice: A review of research,* vol. 30. Chicago: University of Chicago Press.

Ericson, R.V., & Baranek, P.M. (1982). *The ordering of justice: A study of accused persons as defendants in the criminal process.* Toronto: University of Toronto Press.

Esbensen, F., Winfree, Jr, L.T., He, N., & Taylor, T.J. (2001). Youth gangs and definitional issues: When is a gang a gang, and why does it matter? *Crime & Delinquency, 47*(1), 105–30.

Estrada, F. (2001). Juvenile violence as a social problem: Trends, media attention and societal response. *British Journal of Criminology, 41*(4), 639–55.

Fagan, J., & Guggenheim, M. (1996). Preventive detention and the judicial prediction of dangerousness for juveniles: A natural experiment. *Journal of Criminal Law & Criminology, 86*(2), 415–48.

Fagan, J., & Zimring, F.E. (Eds.). (2000). *The changing borders of juvenile justice: Transfer of adolescents to the criminal court.* Chicago: University of Chicago Press.

Farrington, D.P. (1977). The effects of public labelling. *British Journal of Criminology, 17*(2), 112–25.

– (1994). *The nature and origins of delinquency.* Text of the Jack Tizard Memorial Lecture given at the second European Conference of the Association for Child Psychology and Psychiatry. Winchester, England.

Farrington, D.P., Osborn, S.G., & West, D.J. (1978). The persistence of labelling effects. *British Journal of Criminology, 18*(3), 277–84.

Federal-Provincial-Territorial Task Force on Youth Justice. Department of Justice Canada. (1996). *A Review of the Young Offenders Act and the youth justice system in Canada.* Ottawa: Department of Justice Canada.

Fedorowycz, O. (2001). Homicide in Canada, 2000. *Juristat, 21*(9). Cat. no. 85-002-XPE Ottawa: Canadian Centre for Justice Statistics, Statistics Canada.

Feld, B.C. (1999). *Bad kids: Race and the transformation of the juvenile court.* New York and Oxford: Oxford University Press.

– (2000). Juveniles' waiver of legal rights: Confessions, *Miranda*, and the right to counsel. In T. Grisso & R.G. Schwartz (Eds.), *Youth on trial: A developmental perspective on juvenile justice* (pp. 105–38). Chicago: University of Chicago Press.

Fox, J.A. (1996). *Trends in juvenile violence: A report to the United States attorney general on current and future fates of juvenile offending.* Washington, DC: U.S. Department of Justice.

– (2000). Demographics and U.S. homicide. In A. Blumstein and J. Wallman (Eds.), *The crime drop in America* (pp. 218–317). Cambridge: Cambridge University Press.

Freiberg, A. (2001). Affective versus effective justice: Instrumentalism and emotionalism in criminal justice. *Punishment & Society, 3*(2), 265–78.

Frydenberg, E. (1997). *Adolescent coping: Theoretical and research perspectives.* New York: Routledge.

Gabor, T. (1999). Trends in youth crime: Some evidence pointing to increases in the severity and volume of violence on the part of young people. *Canadian Journal of Criminology, 41*(3), 385–92.

Gandy, J. (1992). *Judicial interim release (bail) hearings that resulted in detention prior to trial of youths charged under the Young Offenders Act in three Ontario cities.* Toronto: Policy Research Centre of Children, Youth, and Families.

Gartner, R., & Doob, A.N. (1994). Trends in criminal victimization, 1988–1993. *Juristat 14*(13). Cat. no. 85-002-XPE. Ottawa: Canadian Centre for Justice Statistics, Statistics Canada.

Gordon, R.M. (2000). Criminal business organizations, street gangs and 'wanna-be' groups: A Vancouver perspective. *Canadian Journal of Criminology, 42*(1), 39–60.

Gottlieb, B.H. (1991). Social support in adolescence. In M.E. Colten & S. Gore (Eds.), *Adolescent stresses: Causes and consequences* (pp. 281–306). New York: Aldine de Gruyter.

Government of Canada. (1982). *The criminal law in Canadian society.* Ottawa: Government of Canada.

Government of Ontario. (2001, 18 May). Ontario calls on federal government to put justice into the Youth Criminal Justice Act. On-line. http://www.newswire.ca/government/ontario/english/releases/May2001/18/c6109.html

Graham, J. (1998). What works in preventing criminality. In P. Goldblatt & C. Lewis (Eds.), *Reducing offending: An assessment of research evidence on ways of dealing with offending behaviour* (pp. 7–22). London: Home Office.

Greenwood, P.W., & Zimring, F.E. (1985). *One more chance: The pursuit of promising intervention strategies for chronic juvenile offenders.* Santa Monica, CA: Rand Corporation.

Grisso, T. (2000). What we know about youths' capacities as trial defendants. In T. Grisso & R.G. Schwartz (Eds.), *Youth on trial: A developmental perspective on juvenile justice* (pp. 139–71). Chicago: University of Chicago Press.

Hagel, A., & Newburn, T. (1994). *Persistent young offenders.* London: Policy Studies Institute.

Hamai, K. (1999). *Japanese juveniles are becoming violent: Moral panic or reality?* Presented at the ACS meeting in Toronto. Japan: Research and Training Institute, Ministry of Justice.

Hendrick, D. (2001). Youth custody and community services in Canada, 1999/2000. *Juristat, 21*(12). Cat. no. 85-002-XPE. Ottawa: Canadian Centre for Justice Statistics, Statistics Canada.

Henteleff, Y. (1999, Sept.). *The learning disabled child-at-risk: Why youth service systems have so badly failed them.* Presented at the Working Together for Children: Protection and Prevention Conference in Ottawa.

Howard League for Penal Reform. (1995). *Banged up, beaten up, cutting up: Report of the Howard League Commission of Inquiry into Violence in Penal Institutions for Teenagers under Eighteen.* London: Howard League for Penal Reform.

Howell, J.C. (1997). *Juvenile justice and youth violence.* Thousand Oaks, CA: Sage.

Hunzeker, D. (1993). Mentally disordered juvenile offenders. *State Legislative Report: National Conference of State Legislatures, 18*(3), 1–4.

Jensen, E.L., & Metsger, L.K. (1994) A test of the deterrent effect of legislative waiver on violent juvenile crime. *Crime & Delinquency, 40*(1), 96–104.

Jensen, G.F., Erickson, M.L., & Gibbs, J.P. (1978). Perceived risk of punishment and self–reported delinquency. *Social Forces, 57,* 57–78.

Jones, M.A., & Krisberg, B. (1990). *Images and reality: Juvenile crime, youth violence and public policy.* San Francisco: National Council on Crime and Delinquency.

Juvenile Delinquents Act, R.S.C. 1970, c. J-3.

Kaufman, P., Chen, X., Choy, S.P., Chandler, K.A., Chapman, C.D., Rand, M.R. & Ringel, C. (1998). *Indicators of school crime and safety, 1998.* Washington, DC: U.S. National Centre for Educational Statistics, U.S. Bureau of Justice Statistics.

Kazdin, A.E. (2000). Adolescent development, mental disorders, and decision making of delinquent youths. In T. Grisso & R.G. Schwartz (Eds.), *Youth on trial: A developmental perspective on juvenile justice* (pp. 33–65). Chicago: University of Chicago Press.

Keane, C., Gillis, A. R., & Hagan, J. (1989). Deterrence and amplification of juvenile delinquency by police contact. *British Journal of Criminology, 29*(4), 336–52.

Kijewski, K. (1983). The effect of the decision to charge upon subsequent delinquent behaviour. *Canadian Journal of Criminology, 25*(2), 201–7.

Kilgour, D. (1994). Effective crime prevention in the 1990s. On-line. Available: http://www.david-kilgour.com/speeches/crime.htm

Killias, M., Aebi, M., & Ribeaud, D. (2000). Does community service rehabilitate better than short-term imprisonment? Results of a controlled experiment. *Howard Journal of Criminal Justice, 39*(1), 40–57.

Klein, E.K. (1998). Dennis the Menace or Billy the Kid? An analysis of the role of transfer to criminal court in juvenile justice. *American Criminal Law Review, 35*(2), 371–410.

Klein, M.W. (1974). Labelling, deterrence, and recidivism: A study of police dispositions of juvenile offenders. *Social Problems, 22*(2), 292–303.

Klemke, L.W. (1978). Does apprehension for shoplifting amplify or terminate shoplifting activity? *Law & Society Review, 12*(3), 391–403.

Kowalski, M. (1999). Alternative measures for youth in Canada. *Juristat, 19*(8). Cat. no. 85-002-XPE. Ottawa: Canadian Centre for Justice Statistics, Statistics Canada.

Kowalski, M., & Caputo, T. (1999). Recidivism in youth court: An examination of the impact of age, gender, and prior record. *Canadian Journal of Criminology, 41*(1), 57–84.

Kraus, J. (1978). Remand in custody as a deterrent in juveniles. *British Journal of Criminology, 18*(3), 285–9.

Krivel, P. (1996, 12 Sept.). 'Helpers' convicted in assault on girl, 13. *Toronto Star*, p. A3.

Kyvsgaard, B. (2003). Youth justice: The case of Denmark. In M. Tonry & A.N. Doob (Eds.), *Comparative youth justice*. Chicago: University of Chicago Press.

Ladouceur, C., & Biron, L. (1993). Écouler la marchandise volée, une approche rationnelle? *Canadian Journal of Criminology, 35*(2), 169–82.

Law Commission of Canada. (2000). *Restoring dignity: Responding to child abuse in Canadian institutions*. Ottawa: Law Commission of Canada.

Law Reform Commission of Canada. (1976). *Our criminal law*. Ottawa: Law Reform Commission of Canada.

LeBlanc, M., & Fréchette, M. (1989). *Male criminal activity from childhood through youth: Multilevel and development perspectives*. New York: Springer-Verlag.

Lee, N. (2000). *Recidivism in youth court histories*, Part 1: *The likelihood and rates of recidivism 2000-2*. Ottawa: Department of Justice Canada, Research and Statistics Division.

Leon, J.S. (1977). The development of Canadian juvenile justice: A background for reform. *Osgoode Hall Law Journal, 15*(1), 71–106.

Leschied, A.W., Cunningham, A., & Mazaheri, N. (1997). *Safe and secure: Eliminating peer-to-peer violence in Ontario's phase II secure detention centres*. North Bay, ON: Ministry of Solicitor General and Correctional Services.

Levitt, S.D. (1999). The limited role of changing age structure in explaining aggregate crime rates. *Criminology, 37*(3), 581–97.

Liebling, A. (1999). Prison suicide and prisoner coping. In M. Tonry & J. Petersilia (Eds.), *Prisons* (pp. 283–360). Chicago: University of Chicago Press.

Loeber, R., & Farrington, D.P. (1998). Never too early, never too late: Risk factors and successful intervention for serious and violent juvenile offenders. *Studies on Crime Prevention, 7*(1), 7–30.

Macdonald, J. (2001). Quebec is exceptional in dealing with its wayward youth. Unpublished manuscript, University of Toronto.

MacKenzie, D.L., & Souryal, C. (1994). *Multisite evaluation of shock incarceration*. National Institute of Justice Research Report. Washington, DC: National Institute of Justice.

Marinos, V. (1998). What's intermediate about 'intermediate' sanctions? The case of young offender dispositions in Canada. *Canadian Journal of Criminology, 40*(4), 355–75.

Markwart, A., & Corrado, R.R. (1989). Is the *Young Offenders Act* more punitive? In L.A. Beaulieu (Ed.), *Young offender dispositions: Perspectives on principles and practice* (pp. 7–26). Toronto: Wall and Thompson.

Matarazzo, A., Carrington, P.J., & Hiscott, R.D. (2001). The effect of prior youth court dispositions on current disposition: An application of societal-reaction theory. *Journal of Quantitative Criminology, 17*(2), 169–200.

Matthews, R., & Pitts, J. (1998). Rehabilitation, recidivism and realism: Evaluating violence reduction programs in prison. *Prison Journal, 78*(4), 390–405.

McCord, J. (1978). A thirty-year follow-up of treatment effects. *American Psychologist, 33,* 284–9.

– (2002). Counterproductive juvenile justice. *Australian & New Zealand Journal of Criminology, 35,* 230–7.

McCorkle, R.C. (1993). Fear of victimization and symptoms of psychopathology among prison inmates. *Journal of Offender Rehabilitation, 19*(1), 27–41.

McCorkle, R.C., & Miethe, T.D. (1998). The political and organizational response to gangs: An examination of a 'moral panic' in Nevada. *Justice Quarterly, 15*(1), 41–64.

McDowell, D., Loftin, C., & Wiersema, B. (2000). The impact of youth curfew laws on juvenile crime rates. *Crime & Delinquency, 46*(1), 76–91.

Moffitt, T.E. (1993). Adolescence-limited and life-course-persistent antisocial behavior: A developmental taxonomy. *Psychological Review, 100*(4), 674–701.

– (1997). Adolescence-limited and life-course-persistent offending: A complementary pair of developmental theories. In T.P. Thornberry (Ed.), *Developmental theories of crime and delinquency* (pp. 11–54). New Brunswick, NJ: Transaction Publishers.

Moldon, M.B., & Kukec, D. (2000). Youth custody and community services in Canada, 1998–99. *Juristat, 20*(8). Cat. no. 85-002-XPE. Ottawa: Canadian Centre for Justice Statistics, Statistics Canada.

Moore, D.B., & O'Connell, T.A. (undated). Family conferencing in Wagga Wagga: A communitarian model of justice. Unpublished manuscript.

Moyer, S. (1996). *A profile of the juvenile justice system in Canada.* (Available from Moyer & Associates, 344 Bloor St W, Suite 405, Toronto, M5S 1W9.)

Mutchnik, R.J., & Fawcett, M. (1991). Group home environments and victimization of resident juveniles. *International Journal of Offender Therapy & Comparative Criminology, 35*(2), 126–42.

National Post. (2001, 31 May). 'Grade 2 boy suspended for poultry prank,' pp. A1, A10.

O'Donnell, I., & Edgar, K. (1999). Fear in prison. *Prison Journal, 79*(1), 90–9.

Office of Juvenile Justice and Delinquency Prevention. (1999). *1999 National Report Series: Juvenile Justice Bulletin.* NCJ 178992. Rockville, MD: Juvenile Justice Clearinghouse.

Olds, D., Henderson, Jr, C.R., Cole, R., Eckenrode, J., Kitzman, H., Luckey, D., Pettitt, L., Sidora, K., Morris, P., & Powers, J. (1998). Long-term effects of nurse home visitation on children's criminal and antisocial behaviour. *Journal of American Medical Association, 280*, 1238–44.

O'Malley, P., Coventry, G., & Walters, R. (1993). Victoria's 'Day in Prison Program': An evaluation and critique. *Australian & New Zealand Journal of Criminology, 26*, 171–83.

Ombudsman, Province of British Columbia. (1994, June). *Building respect: A review of youth custody centres in British Columbia.* Public Reports no. 34 (June).

Ontario, Ministry of Attorney General. (2001). Protecting the public and holding young offenders accountable. On-line. Available: http://www.attorneygeneral.jus.gov.on.ca/html/YO/FACTSHEET.htm. 14 June.

Ontario Office of the Child and Family Services Advocacy. (1998). *Youth care in Ontario: Voices from within youth speak out.* Toronto: Queen's Printer for Ontario.

Paiement, R. (1996). *Technical report: An exploratory study of youth justice committees.* TR1996-8e. Ottawa: Department of Justice Canada.

Parent, D.G., Lieter, V., Kennedy, S., Livens, L., Wentworth, D., & Wilcox, S. (1994). *Conditions of confinement: Juvenile detention and corrections facilities, research report.* Rockville, MD: U.S. Department of Justice, Office of Juvenile Justice and Delinquency Prevention.

Pate, K. (1990). Victim–young offender reconciliation as alternative measures program in Canada. In B. Galaway & J. Hudson (Eds.), *Criminal justice, restitution, and reconciliation* (pp. 135–44). Monsey, NY: Criminal Justice Press.

Paternoster, R. (1989). Decisions to participate in and desist from four types of common delinquency: Deterrence and rational choice perspective. *Law & Society Review, 23*(1), 7–40.

Paternoster, R., Saltzman, L.E., Waldo, G.P., & Chiricos, T.G. (1983). Estimating perceptual stability and deterrent effects: The role of perceived legal punishment in the inhibition of criminal involvement. *Journal of Criminal Law & Criminology, 74*(1), 270–97.

Perrone, P.A., & Chesney-Lind, M. (1998). Representations of gangs and delinquency: Wild in the streets? *Social Justice, 24*(4), 96–116.

Peterson-Badali, M., & Abramovitch, R. (1992). Children's knowledge of the legal system: Are they competent to instruct legal counsel? *Canadian Journal of Criminology, 34*(2), 139–60.

– (1993). Grade related changes in young people's reasoning about plea decisions. *Law & Human Behaviour, 17*(5), 537–52.

Peterson-Badali, M., & Koegl, C.J. (2001). Juveniles' experiences of incarceration: The role of correctional staff in peer violence. *Journal of Criminal Justice, 29*(1), 1–9.

Peterson-Badali, M., Ruck, M.D., & Koegl, C.J. (2001). Youth court dispositions:

Perceptions of Canadian juvenile offenders. *International Journal of Offender Therapy & Comparative Criminology, 45*(5), 593–605.

Petrosino, A., Turpin-Petrosino, C., & Finckenaur, J.O. (2000). Well-meaning programs can be harmful! Lessons from experiments of programs such as Scared Straight. *Crime & Delinquency, 46*(3), 354–79.

Pfeiffer, C. (1998). Juvenile justice in Europe. In M. Tonry (Ed.), *Crime and justice: A review of research,* vol. 23 (pp. 255–328). Chicago: University of Chicago Press.

Platt, A.M. (1977). *The child savers: The invention of delinquency.* Chicago: University of Chicago Press.

Power, K.G., & Beveridge, L. (1990). The effects of custody in a Scottish detention center on inmate self-esteem. *International Journal of Offender Therapy & Comparative Criminology, 34*(3), 177–186.

R. v. McGinn, [1989], 49 C.C.C. (3d) 137.

R. v. M. (J.J.), [1993], 2 S.C.R. 421.

R. v. S. (S.), [1990], 2 S.C.R. 254.

Reiss, A.J., Jr. (1988). Co-offending and criminal careers. In M. Tonry & N. Morris (Eds.), *Crime and justice: A review of research,* vol. 10 (pp. 117–70). Chicago: University of Chicago Press.

Reynolds, K.M., Seydlitz, R., & Jenkins, P. (2000). Do juvenile curfew laws work? A time-series analysis of the New Orleans law. *Justice Quarterly, 17*(1), 205–30.

Roberts, J.V. (1992). Public opinion, crime, and criminal justice. In M. Tonry (Ed.), *Crime and justice: A review of research,* vol. 16 (pp. 99–180). Chicago: University of Chicago Press.

– (1999). *Police training and young persons in conflict with the law: Report of a national survey.* Ottawa: Department of Justice Canada.

Roberts, J.V., & von Hirsch, A. (1999). Legislating the purpose and principles of sentencing. In J.V. Roberts & D.P. Cole (Eds.), *Making sense of sentencing* (pp. 48–62). Toronto: University of Toronto Press.

Sampson, R.J., & Laub, J.H. (1997). A life-course theory of cumulative disadvantage and the stability of delinquency. In T.P. Thornberry (Ed.), *Developmental theories of crime and delinquency* (pp. 133–62). New Brunswick, NJ: Transaction Publishers.

Schiraldi, V., & Ziedenberg, J. (2001). Schools and suspensions: Self-reported crime and the growing use of suspensions. Justice Policy Institute Policy Brief. On-line. Available: http://www.cjcj.org/sss/sss.html

Schissel, B. (1997). *Blaming children: Youth crime, moral panic and the politics of hate.* Halifax: Fernwood Publishing.

Scott, E.S. (2000). Criminal responsibility in adolescence: Lessons from developmental psychology. In T. Grisso & R.G. Schwartz (Eds.), *Youth on trial: A developmental perspective on juvenile justice* (pp. 291–324). Chicago: University of Chicago Press.

Scott, E., Reppucci, N.D., & Woolard, J. (1995). Evaluating adolescent decision making in legal contexts. *Law & Human Behaviour, 19*, 221–44.

Sherman, L.W. (2000). Recidivism patterns in the Canberra reintegrative shaming experiments (RISE). On-line. Available: http://aic.gov.au/rjustice/rise/recidivism/

Shields, I., & Simourd, D.J. (1991). Predicting predatory behaviour in a population of incarcerated young offenders. *Criminal Justice & Behaviour, 18*(2), 180–94.

Sidgmore, J. (2002, 14 Aug.). Letter from John Sidgmore. On-line. Available: http://www1.worldcom.com/infodesk/statements/081402/

Simon, J. (1995). They died with their boots on: The boot camp and the limits of modern penality. *Social Justice, 22*(2), 25–48.

Singer, S.I., & McDowell, D. (1998). Criminalizing delinquency: The deterrent effects of the New York Juvenile Offender Law. *Law & Society Review, 22*(3), 521–36.

Snyder, H.N. (1999). The overrepresentation of juvenile crime proportions in robbery clearance statistics. *Journal of Qualitative Criminology, 15*(2), 151–61.

Snyder, H.N., & Sickmund, M. (1999). *Juvenile offenders and victims: 1999 national report.* NCJ 178257. Washington, DC: U.S. Department of Justice, Office of Justice Programs, Office of Juvenile Justice and Delinquency Prevention.

Snyder, H.N., Sickmund, M., & Poe-Yamagata, E. (2000). *Juvenile transfers to criminal court in the 1990's: Lessons learned from four studies.* Washington, DC: U.S. Department of Justice, Officer of Justice Programs, Office of Juvenile Justice and Delinquency Prevention.

Spergel, I.A. (1990). Youth gangs: Continuity and change. In M. Tonry & N. Morris (Eds.), *Crime and justice: A review of research,* vol. 12 (pp. 171–276). Chicago: University of Chicago Press, 1990.

Sprott, J.B. (1998). Understanding public opposition to a separate youth justice system. *Crime & Delinquency, 44*(3), 399–411.

Sprott, J.B., & Cesaroni, C. (2002) Similarities in homicide trends in the U.S. and Canada: Guns, crack or simple demographics? *Homicide Studies 6*, 348–59.

Sprott, J.B., & Doob, A.N. (2000). Bad, sad, and rejected: The lives of aggressive children. *Canadian Journal of Criminology, 42*(2), 123–33.

– (2003). It's all in the denominator: Trends in the processing of girls in Canada's youth courts. *Canadian Journal of Criminology & Criminal Justice, 45*(1), 73–80.

Sprott, J.B., Doob, A.N., & Jenkins, J.M. (2001). Problem behaviour and delinquency in children and youth. *Juristat, 21*(4). Cat. no. 85-002-XPE. Ottawa: Canadian Centre for Justice Statistics, Statistics Canada.

Sprott, J.B., & Snyder, H.N. (1999). Youth crime in the U.S. and Canada, 1991 to 1996. *Overcrowded Times, 10*(5), 1 & 12–19.

Standing Committee on Justice and Legal Affairs. (1997). *Renewing youth justice: Thirteenth report of the Standing Committee on Justice and Legal Affairs.* Ottawa: Canada Communication Group – Publishing, Public Works and Government Services Canada.

Steinberg, L. (2000, April). Youth violence: Do parents and families make a difference? *National Institute of Justice Journal*, 31–8.

Steinberg, L., & Schwartz, R.G. (2000). Developmental psychology goes to court. In T. Grisso & R.G. Schwartz (Eds.), *Youth on trial: A developmental perspective on juvenile justice* (pp. 9–31). Chicago: University of Chicago Press.

Stevenson, K., Tufts, J., Hendrick, D., & Kowalski, M. (1998). *A profile of youth justice in Canada.* Cat. no. 85-544-XPE. Ottawa: Statistics Canada, Canadian Centre for Justice Statistics.

Stewart, E.A., Simons, R.L., Conger, R.D., & Scaramella, L.V. (2002). Beyond the interactional relationship between delinquency and parenting practices: The contribution of legal sanctions. *Journal of Research in Crime & Delinquency, 39*(1), 36–59.

Styve, G.J., MacKenzie, D.L., Gover, A.R., & Mitchell, O. (2000). Perceived conditions of confinement: A national evaluation of juvenile boot camps and traditional facilities. *Law & Human Behaviour, 24*(3), 297–308.

Szymanski, L.A. (1998, April). Direct file, prosecutor discretion, prosecutorial waiver. *NCJJ Snapshot, 3*(4). Pittsburgh: National Center for Juvenile Justice.

– (1998, May). Statutory exclusion, offense exclusion, legislative waiver, statutory waiver. *NCJJ Snapshot, 3*(5). Pittsburgh: National Center for Juvenile Justice.

– (1998, June). Judicial waiver to criminal court. *NCJJ Snapshot, 3*(6). Pittsburgh: National Center for Juvenile Justice.

– (1998, July). Once an adult/always an adult. *NCJJ Snapshot, 3*(7). Pittsburgh: National Center for Juvenile Justice.

– (2002, April). Direct file, prosecutor discretion, prosecutorial waiver (2001 update). *NCJJ Snapshot, 7*(4). Pittsburgh: National Center for Juvenile Justice.

T3 Associates Training and Consulting. (2001). *Project Turnaround Outcome Evaluation – final report.* Toronto: Ontario Ministry of Correctional Services.

Tanner, J. (1996). *Teenage troubles: Youth and deviance in Canada.* Toronto: Nelson.

Tanner, J., & Wortley, S. (2002). *The Toronto Youth Crime and Victimization Survey: Overview report.* Toronto: Centre of Criminology, University of Toronto.

Task Force on Vandalism. (1981). *Vandalism: Responses and responsibilities.* Toronto: Queen's Printer for Ontario.

Thomas, C.W., & Bishop, D.M. (1984). The effect of formal and informal sanctions on delinquency: A longitudinal comparison of labelling and deterrence theories. *Journal of Criminal Law & Criminology, 75*(4), 1222–45.

Tibbetts, S.G., & Piquero, A.R. (1999). The influence of gender, low birth weight, and disadvantaged environment in predicting early onset of offending: A test of Moffitt's interactional hypothesis. *Criminology, 37*(4), 843–77.

Tonry, M., & Doob, A.N. (2003). *Comparative youth justice.* Chicago: University of Chicago Press.

Toronto *Sun.* (1996, 27 May). Editorial cartoon, p. 10.

Tremblay, R.E., Boulerice, B., Harden, P.W., McDuff, P., Pérusse, D., Pihl, R.O., & Zoccolillo, M. (1996). Do children in Canada become more aggressive as they approach adolescence? In *Growing up in Canada: National longitudinal survey of children and youth* (pp. 127–37). Cat. no. 89-550-MPE, no. 1. Ottawa: Human Resources Development Canada, Statistics Canada.

Trépanier, J. (1989). Principles and goals guiding the choice of dispositions under the *Young Offenders Act.* In L.A. Beaulieu (Ed.), *Young offender dispositions: Perspectives on principles and practice* (pp. 27–66). Toronto: Wall and Thompson.

– (1999). Juvenile courts after 100 years: Past and present orientations. *European Journal on Criminal Policy & Research, 7*(3), 303–27.

Tunnell, K.D. (1996). Choosing crime: Close your eyes and take your chances. In B.W. Hancock & P.M. Sharp (Eds.), *Criminal justice in America: Theory, practice, and policy* (pp. 38–50). Englewood Cliffs, NJ: Prentice-Hall.

Ulzen, T., & Hamilton, H. (1998). Psychiatric disorders in incarcerated youth. *Youth Update, 16*(1), 4–5.

United Nations standard minimum rules for the administration of juvenile justice ('The Beijing Rules'). G.A. Res. 40/33, Annex, 40 U.N. GAOR Supp. (No. 53) at 207, U.N. Doc. A/40/53 (1985).

United States Department of Education and the Department of Justice. (1998). *1998 Annual report on school safety.* NCJ-172215. Washington, DC: Bureau of Justice Statistics Clearinghouse.

Unland, K. (1996, 12 Sept.). Two boys guilty in assault. *Globe and Mail,* p. A3.

Varma, K.N. (2000). *Exploring age and maturity in youth justice.* Unpublished doctoral dissertation, Centre of Criminology, University of Toronto.

– (2002). Exploring 'youth' in court: An analysis of decision-making in youth court bail hearings. *Canadian Journal of Criminology, 44* (2), 143–64.

von Hirsch, A. (1976). *Doing justice: The choice of punishments.* New York: Hill and Wang.

von Hirsch, A., Bottoms, A., Burney, E., & Wikström, P.O. (1999). *Criminal deterrence and sentence severity: An analysis of recent research.* Oxford: Hart Publishing.

Walgrave, L. (2003). Assessing the role of restorative justice in the future of juvenile justice. In M. Tonry & A.N. Doob (Eds.), *Comparative youth justice.* Chicago: University of Chicago Press.

Walgrave, L., & Mehlbye, J. (1998). An overview: Comparative comments on juvenile offending and its treatment in Europe. In J. Mehlbye & L. Walgrave (Eds.), *Confronting youth in Europe: Juvenile crime and juvenile justice* (pp. 21–53). Copenhagen: AKF Forlaget.

Walker, H.M., Kavanagh, K., Stiller, B., Golly, A., Severson, H.H., & Reil, E.G. (1998). First step to success: An early intervention approach for preventing school antisocial behaviour. *Journal of Emotional & Behavioural Disorders, 6*(2), 66–80.

Wright, D.T., & Mays, G.L. (1998). Correctional boot camps, attitudes, and recidivism: The Oklahoma experience. *Journal of Offender Rehabilitation, 28*(1/2), 71–87.

Yoshikawa, H. (1994). Prevention as cumulative protection: Effects of early family support and education on chronic delinquency and its risks. *Psychological Bulletin, 115,* 28–54.

Young, A. (1989). Appelate court sentencing principles for young offenders. In L.A. Beaulieu (Ed.), *Young offender dispositions: Perspectives on principles and practice* (pp. 67–106). Toronto: Wall and Thompson.

Young Offenders Act, R.S.C. 1985, c. Y-1.

Youth Criminal Justice Act, S.C.

Zaremba, B. (1994). *Juveniles understanding of Miranda rights statements.* Virginia: Newport News.

Zimring, F.E. (1981). Kids, groups and crime: Some implications of a well-known secret. *Journal of Criminal Law & Criminology, 72*(3), 867–85.

– (1998). *American youth violence.* New York and Oxford: Oxford University Press.

– (2000). Penal proportionality for the young offender: Notes on immaturity, capacity, and diminished responsibility. In T. Grisso & R.G. Schwartz (Eds.), *Youth on trial: A developmental perspective on juvenile justice* (pp. 271–89). Chicago: University of Chicago Press.

Zimring, F.E., & Fagan, J. (2000). Transfer policy and law reform. In J. Fagan & F.E. Zimring (Eds.), *The changing borders of juvenile justice: Transfer of adolescents to the criminal court* (pp. 407–424). Chicago: University of Chicago Press.

Index

Page references followed by an italic *f* indicate the presence of a figure; page references followed by an italic *t* indicate a table.